MIRACLE ON THE GRIDIRON

To Phyllis,
The toughest Little Lady
in Tennessee!

By Jim Black

Jim Black

Front cover photo courtesy of Wichita Falls Times Record News
Back cover photo courtesy of Archer City High School

First published by Dog Ear Publishing
4010 W. 86th Street, Ste H
Indianapolis, IN 46268
www.dogearpublishing.net

dog ear PUBLISHING

ISBN: 978-160844-169-3

This book is printed on acid-free paper.

Printed in the United States of America

In memory of my dad
Cloyd Irving Black (1914 - 1962)

TO THE READER:

The following is based upon newspaper accounts, radio broadcasts, and interviews with the players, coaches, trainers, cheerleaders, fans, and journalists who lived it. When choosing between conflicting viewpoints or remembrances, I selected those reflected by the majority. Although this began as a work of non-fiction, I found it impossible to accurately and satisfactorily depict complete conversations after the passage of nearly forty-five years. For continuity and characterization purposes, some of the dialogue is my own.

While the story of the 1964 Wildcats actually began in 1961 with the arrival of head coach Grady Graves in Archer City, this book focuses on their historic '64 season and the players and coaches on that year's roster. Some characters and occurrences from the preceding three years have been omitted for brevity, except those I deemed noteworthy.

I was eleven years old the year of their triumphant season and attended every game. A great many sights and sounds remain etched in my mind, but none more vivid than my memory of standing in the bleachers in Austin moments after the final gun, engulfed by a deafening wall of noise and the Archer fans cheering, hugging, laughing, crying; all of us awash in the moment, trying to soak it up and gather it all in, wishing that somehow the feeling would never end. And it hasn't.

1964 ARCHER CITY WILDCATS

No.	Name	Pos.	Class	Wt.
10	Barry Morrison	QB	Sr.	157
11	Mickey Horany	WB	Jr.	145
23	Bob Gaines	QB	Fr.	132
26	Billy Holder	WB	Soph.	143
30	Jim Harney	FB	Soph.	137
32	Larry Graham	E	Jr.	142
35	Mike Stewart	TB	Sr.	141
36	Andy Rogers	T	Soph.	163
52	Billy Pitts	G	Sr.	151
60	Gary Johnston	G	Jr.	156
61	Robert Tepfer	G	Jr.	160
62	Bobby Hammontree	G	Jr.	160
63	Jimmy Boone	G	Jr.	152
70	Buddy Knox	C	Soph.	165
72	Butch Hannah	T	Soph.	167
73	Charlie Goforth	T	Fr.	168
74	Gary Tepfer	FB	Sr.	157
75	Jimmy Reeves	T	Soph.	169
81	Ray Bussey	E	Sr.	152
82	Mike Atchley	TB	Fr.	137
84	Barney Oliver	E	Sr.	163
85	Steve Parsley	T	Sr.	152

Head Coach - Grady Graves

Assistant Coaches - Bobby Ray, Roy Williams

Trainers - Donald Dorris, Danny Hall, John O'Donohue, David Wright

Cheerleaders - Trecie Trigg, Judy Crowley, Sue Ann Brock, Jodie Wright, Pat Holder, Glenda “Wort” Lear

CONTENTS

PROLOGUE

Nelson Field Austin, Texas December 19, 1964
Class A State Football Championship
Archer City Wildcats versus Ingleside Mustangs

. . . and a huge play coming up now with fourth down and a yard to go for the Ingleside Mustangs hoping to keep their drive alive. Archer City, meanwhile, trying to hang on and finish off their remarkable Cinderella season. Keese with his strong side to the left this time, has Fregia flanked out far left with 33 seconds showing on the scoreboard clock. Here's the pitchout going to Jones; he cuts in at the 45, across the 40, finds running room down to the 36-yard line. He just would not be stopped as he picked up the first down. The crowd is on their feet, and the clock continues to run with 20, now 19, 18, 17 seconds remaining as the official spots the ball. Keese gathers his team together and quickly under center takes the snap, and here's another pitch going back to Jones who starts right, now looking to throw, HAS A MAN OPEN AND THROWS LONG DOWN THE FIELD . . .

High above the sparse grass and fading hash marks, the ball, a battered Spalding model J5-V, hangs in the cold night air momentarily frozen in time—a Maltese falcon of sorts, the stuff dreams are made of. Some fans can't bear to watch. They close their eyes or turn away while others stare intently, hoping to impose their will on the ball and influence the game's outcome. Breaths are held, wishes made, and prayers offered. For an eerie few seconds, the stadium becomes quiet. Then, as the ball begins its final decent, unnoticed along one sideline, a single soul is smiling. Gone are his clenched jaw and infamous glare of the past four years for he alone knows what the outcome will be. Luck will not intervene. Not here. Not now. People create their own destinies, decide their own fates. It is, of course, what he loves most about football—the simpleness of it. Sure, there's the occasional crazy bounce, fluke play, or bad call; but over the long haul, you get what you deserve. And these young men have earned this. They have worked too hard and sacrificed far too much to come up short now. They've done all he's asked of them, and nothing is going to take what rightfully belongs to his boys.

PART ONE

CALAMITY

CHAPTER 1

Changing of the Guard

It's been said that within a month of arriving in town, Grady Graves had all of Archer City saying *yes sir* and *no sir*. One thing was certain: The football program and the town were in for a change.

When asked by the school board why he should be hired as head coach, the thirty-two-year-old replied, "There are hundreds of towns, a thousand, just like Archer City scattered all across Texas. Many of them have successful football programs, and their kids are no different than the kids you have right here. They just need some direction and some discipline, that's all. And some want-to. Which I believe they have. Now, it won't happen overnight. It's gonna to take some time, but we *will* win here."

This was music to the board members' ears as the last successful Wildcat season was a faded memory at best. A 1955 graduate of Texas Tech, Grady Graves had coached two years at Electra High School and was finishing his second year at nearby Olney as head basketball coach and assistant football coach. Despite not having any football head-coaching experience, the tall, slender, crewcut Graves was selected to replace current head coach Alex Crowder, who was retiring to become principal of the Archer City elementary school.

The next week, Grady and his wife Gay packed up their three-month-old son and belongings and drove eighteen miles north to Archer City. He had a job to do and a promise to fulfill and was anxious to get started.

One of the first things the new coach did was to gather together the players who would comprise the 1961 team, including seven eighth-graders who would become freshmen.

Once everyone was in position standing against the wall in the gymnasium, he entered and stood at center court.

"Howdy, boys."

His greeting was met with muffled hi's and hello's.

Grady smiled and walked closer. "From now on, you'll answer with the same enthusiasm you were spoken to, *and* you'll call me sir. That understood?"

"Yes sir."

He moved closer. "Fine. My name is Grady Graves. I'm the new head football coach, and here's what you can expect when football season arrives. Times will be tough. The work will be extremely hard—harder than anything you've ever experienced or imagined. You're not gonna like me, I can guarantee you that. There will be times you'll wanna quit. And some of you will. A lot of you, in fact, and the sooner the better, so you don't waste my time and yours. What I'm lookin' for are players with the desire and the dedication to succeed. To be successful, you must possess a willingness to make contact, and above all, you must be willing to sacrifice. If you have those qualities, you can wear the Wildcat uniform. The next thing you need to know is there are some rules.

"Rule number one: You *will* cut your hair. If it's long enough for me to grab hold of, it's too long. Burrs and flattops are in order.

"Rule number two: You will conduct yourselves properly at all times. At school, at home, everywhere. This starts with addressing your parents, teachers, coaches, and town elders with *yes sir*, *no sir*, *yes ma'am*, and *no ma'am* and always being courteous. And I better not ever catch wind of you cussin'. By behaving in this manner, you'll be setting an example the whole town can look up to and learn from.

"Rule number three: I don't wanna hear any of this 'I or me' business. I see some jackets with patches on them—All-District Track, Basketball, even one or two for football. No more. There will be no patches of any kind until we win somethin' as a team. From now on, boys, it's *we* and *us*. Together. Oh, and speakin' of jackets, they don't belong on your girlfriends. You're gonna earn 'em; you wear 'em. Give 'em an old one.

"Rule number four: Curfew. Home and *in bed* by ten o'clock every night durin' football season, and no dates the night before a game. No exceptions. And trust me, this will be monitored. Any questions?"

With minds racing, there were plenty, but no one spoke.

"And believe me when I tell you it's in your best interest not to break any of these rules." He paused briefly, taking inventory, before continuing.

"Okay, one last thing. I'm not here to piece together a team and win a few games this year. I'm here to *build* a winner. So you should know up front that most, if not all, of the freshmen and sophomores will get the majority of playing time this year. You juniors and seniors, well, you're gonna have to be exceptional to beat any of 'em out. Now, if there's anyone here who doesn't like the rules or the plan, there's the door."

No takers.

"All right, then. We'll see you this August at the start of two-a-days. You're all free to go now, *except* for the eighth-graders. You stay."

As the others filed out, the youngest and smallest of the group remained behind. Wanting to share nervous glances but too afraid to take their eyes off Grady, all were thinking the same thing: *I just wanted to play some football. What the heck have I gotten myself into? Those upper classmen are gonna kill us. If this guy doesn't do it first.*

"Boys, I've seen you play some in junior high and remember some of your names but not all. So let's have 'em. Startin' with you."

"Barry Morrison."

"Billy Pitts."

"Steve Parsley."

"Gary Tepfer."

"Barney Oliver."

"Mike Stewart."

"Ray Bussey. Sir!"

Grady looked them over and said, "There's somethin' you boys need to know. As hard as it's gonna to be on those other guys, it's gonna to be even tougher on you. Now, I can't do anything with those juniors and seniors—they're too far along. And I can't make any promises, but I will tell you this: If you're up to the challenge and stick with me for four years, I *will* make football players out of you. And someday, we'll win somethin' worthwhile. Any questions?"

"No sir!"

Grady smiled. It would be one of the last smiles they would see from him over the next four years. "Okay, then. See you in August."

He watched them head out, and just as they reached the door he called out.

"And if you know what's good for you, you'd better be in shape!"

CHAPTER 2

Marked Men

Stepping into the bright sunlight, Steve Parsley spit into the grass and turned around. "What the hell?"

"You mean heck, don't you?" Ray Bussey replied with a grin. "You heard what Coach said about cussin'."

"No, I mean 'what the *hell.*' He just said we couldn't cuss around *him.*"

"That's not what I understood him to say."

"You gonna go tell him?"

"Cool it, guys," Mike Stewart intervened. "Sounds like we've got more to worry about than that. Whatta *you* think, Barry?"

Barry Morrison shrugged and scratched his head. "Man, I'm not sure. He sounded pretty serious to me. Barney?"

Lost in thought, Barney Oliver answered without looking up. "Yeah, I don't think he was funnin' with us."

"Well, if you ask me, he's just what we need." All eyes shifted to Gary Tepfer. "I mean, we did sign up to play football. Now we get to play. What's the big deal? You see a problem here, Billy?"

Billy Pitts, a boy of few words, answered in his usual way—without wasted effort or words. "No."

Gary turned toward Steve. "So what's the problem?"

Steve spit, looked up, and grinned. "Hey, I just said, 'what the hell.' I didn't say there was a problem. Least not yet there ain't."

"You don't *have* to play," Ray suggested.

"*I* know that. But unlike *some*, I happen to like hittin' people. What's *your* excuse? Your daddy makin' you play?"

"No! Well, sort of. It was either this or be a dairy farmer."

"What?"

"Dad said if I didn't play he was gonna take me down and get me a job at one of those dairies over in Windthorst and that I'd have to work before school, after school, and all summer. I asked him when was I supposed to have time to go to the lake and hunt and fish, and he said them dairy farmers don't have time for that kinda stuff and neither will I. So here I am."

After the laughter died, Mike, with his faithful grin, announced, "Yeah, well, here we *all* are."

And with that, they headed back to class. With no clue of what was waiting for the seven of them farther down the road.

Grady Graves's next move was to fire approximately thirty "assistant coaches." He did so at his first meeting with the Quarterback Club, a group of football supporters comprised mostly of dads and staunch followers. There were no women present as membership in the Quarterback Club was limited to men only. The wives contributed in other ways—baking for the pancake suppers and spaghetti dinners to raise money to purchase things for the team the school couldn't afford and decorating the gymnasium each year for the annual football banquet.

As others would eventually learn, the new head coach didn't mince words.

"Gentlemen, as you know, I brought Bobby Rexrode with me from Olney to be our line coach. And we have a fine coach already here in Odell Harcrow. That gives me two assistants. That's plenty. If I want anyone else's advice, I'll ask for it."

Quarterback Club president Monroe Williams broke up the muffled groans and whispers. "Okay, Coach, anything else?"

"Yes, there is. Most of you have boys on the team. And I can't have 'em bein' pulled in different directions. For us to be successful, they have to do as I say. So I want you and your wives to turn 'em over to me completely. What I say goes."

More muffled groans and whispers.

Grady continued. "Turn them over to me and I will make fine young men out of them all. And football players. And I'll build a team the whole town can be proud of."

Resting in north central Texas less than an hour from the Red River and Oklahoma state line, Archer City, like countless other small towns without identities in the 1960s, was a town in search of itself. An onlooker might conclude the 1,753 hard-working, mostly church-going residents sharing their lives there did so more by happenstance than design, and he would be right. Precious few ever moved to town; most were born there or in nearby Wichita Falls.

And like so many, Archer—as it is commonly referred to by the locals—was a poor town in those days. Money and jobs were scarce. For the most part, wives stayed home caring for kids while husbands found work mostly in the oilfield or over in Wichita Falls if able to afford gasoline for the 45-mile round-trip drive.

Needless to say, there was little to do in the way of entertainment. Those owning televisions received only three channels. A small movie house called the Royal offered films on weekends, and the local hangout—Troy's Drive-In—provided burgers and shakes, a jukebox, and pinball. Everything else was either in Wichita Falls, or as they say, left to one's imagination—except for four months late in the year when football was king, just as it still is today in small towns throughout Texas and the nation.

Suddenly, one night each week, people had somewhere to go and something to do. As well as a chance to belong and be a part of something. The games offered something else: They offered hope—an opportunity for some, through the team's success, to gain some small measure of fulfillment in lieu of their own lost hopes and dreams.

In 1964, the local team hoisted the townspeople on its shoulders and took them on the journey of a lifetime. But that improbable, most unlikely of seasons and fulfiller of dreams, did not simply appear from nowhere. Rather, it began quietly, unnoticed, three years earlier on a scorching August day in 1961 with the sound of a shrill whistle signaling the start of football practice.

CHAPTER 3

Second Thoughts

The tiny, dingy Wildcat locker room, located in the gymnasium beneath the bleachers on the south wall across the gym floor from the coaches' office, was crowded and noisy with shouting, laughter, and an occasional towel popping. Most of the players were fully dressed and raring to go a full fifteen minutes early when Grady walked in carrying something. They watched as he hammered a nail in the wall at the west end of the room and hung a large, green chalkboard from it. At the top, he wrote the words "GOOF-OFF SQUAD." Then he turned and faced them.

"That's for anybody who screws up. If I catch you out past curfew, with a failing grade, or any other such nonsense, you'll find your name up there and there will be heck to pay in the form of extra work after practice. Also, and more importantly, if you screw up and don't see your name the next day, you'd better write it up there yourself. Cause if you don't, and I know about your indiscretion, the penalty will be doubled. Or tripled. That clear?"

"Yes sir."

"You loaf in practice, and you won't have to wait till the next day."

"Yes sir."

He surveyed the room. "Everybody ready?"

"Yes sir!"

"Men, let's go to work."

And out they went, hooping and hollering. *Let's go Cats! Let's go! Hustle up! All right, all right!* Grady motioned for them to gather around him. The morning temperature was 84 degrees.

"Boys, you'd better enjoy this cool weather while you can, cause it's gonna get a mite warm later on. Calisthenics!"

Ten minutes later, he blew his whistle. "Well, since you clearly aren't interested in what you're doin', line up on the goal line."

Following a grueling assortment of 20, 50, and 100-yard strength-sucking sprints, he asked, "Now are you gonna get with the program?"

"Yes sir!"

"Then let's get back to it."

After twenty minutes of jumping jacks, twist and bends, and push-ups and set-ups, another whistle. "Backs and ends here with me. Linemen go with Coach Rexrode. Let's go!"

Ten minutes into the drop-and-rolls, another whistle.

"Men, if you can't even get through these agility drills, you're in for a tough road this afternoon. Now, I will not tolerate sloppiness. Line up on the goal line!"

More sprints.

Whistle. "Let's go! Back in your groups!"

After thirty more minutes of agility drills came a final whistle.

"Well, this mornin's turnin' out to be pretty much of a waste. Line up on the goal line!"

Following a cold shower and cafeteria lunch of a small salad, roast beef, green beans, and iced tea, the team was sent to the gym floor to rest up for the afternoon practice with explicit instructions not to leave the premises. The freshmen had congregated on the west end beneath the basketball goal. After a few restless minutes, Mike sat up.

"Anybody wanna quit?" he asked, just above a whisper.

Barry looked over and smiled. "I'll quit if you quit."

Mike grinned back. "I'll quit if *you* quit."

Barry sat up. "*I'm* not quittin' first!"

"Me neither!"

The two looked over at Barney.

"Don't look at me! I ain't about to quit first!"

Then Billy.

"Nope."

"How 'bout you, Tepfer?"

"Heck no!"

Barry looked around, spotted Steve, and kicked him. "Parsley?"

Without opening his eyes, he answered, "Bussey's your man."

Ray bolted upright. "Not me! Dad always told me, 'Finish what you start. You don't have to go back,' he said, 'but don't quit in the middle. Don't matter if it's fightin' or windmill fixin'.' And that's what I plan on doin'!"

When he'd finished, Gary sat up. "Dadgum, guys. We've had one mornin' practice for cryin' out loud. Don't you think it's a little early for this?"

Mike shook his head. "It's not this mornin's practice I'm worried about."

With that, they all laughed and lay down. A minute later, Steve sat up.

"Why can't we go anywhere? That's what I wanna know. I've got stuff to do."

Mike let out a deep breath. "I'm too tired to go anywhere."

Barry concurred. "Me, too."

"Wimps." Miffed, Steve stretched back out with the others.

"I knew it was gonna be like this. Didn't y'all?"

Mike turned and looked at Ray. "Whatta you mean?"

"Dad told me when he got home from that first Quarterback Club meetin'. Said Coach Graves told 'em he's got a plan for us and wants us to be *his* boys for the next four years. All our folks are supposed to do is room and board us. That's it."

Mike thought for a minute, then nudged Barry. "I seem to remember Daddy sayin' somethin' about that."

"Me, too."

A short while later, it was quiet. All eyes closed. All asleep or deep in thought. Then it came.

"Anybody wanna quit?"

CHAPTER 4

Learning the Hard Way

Grady Graves's workout philosophy—which he credited Bear Bryant with—was simple. "My workouts are hard. If a boy's gonna quit, I don't want him quittin' during a game. I want him to quit in practice."

The afternoon portion began promptly at 3:00 with the thermometer reading 103 degrees. Any clouds had long since departed for Oklahoma, and things quickly picked up where they'd left off earlier in the day.

"Line up on the goal line!"

These had become the six most feared and hated words in the English language.

After forty-five minutes of running, the players were sick and exhausted. Many were light-headed and dizzy. And practice was just getting started.

"Everybody loosened up now?"

"Yes sir!"

"Well, catch you breath for a minute, then we'll go to work."

Mike was bent over, hands on knees, staring at his roast beef and green beans on the ground at his feet. "Barry, how the heck are we gonna last another two hours?"

"Quit talkin'. You're wastin' energy."

Ray wandered over. "I sure could go for a cold Popsicle from Ruby's Grocery right about now."

The two glared at him but were cut off by Grady's whistle before they could reply.

"BUSSEY! Get over here!"

The rangy freshman jogged over, helmet in hand. "Yes sir?"

"Son, why aren't you wearin' your helmet?"

"You told us to take a break, Coach."

"Put that head gear back on this instant! Once you step on the field, *do not*, for *any* reason, take it off. I don't care if it's practice or a game. *You hear me?"*

"Yes sir!"

"Everybody got that?"

"Yes sir!"

"Doin' so is a sign that you're tired and feel the need to rest. You tired, son?"

"Yes sir. A little."

Wrong answer.

"Line up on the goal line! All of you!"

When they dragged to a finish thirty minutes later, Grady continued. "And just so you know—there'll be no sittin' or kneelin', either. *Unless* I tell you. That understood?"

"Yes sir!"

He paused, taking stock of his listeners.

"Okay, let's go. Backs and ends over here. Linemen over there."

Finesse was okay for all those other head coaches, but not for Grady. Blocking and tackling won football games. Pure and simple. Put your helmet in the runner's chest, wrap your arms around him, and drive him to the ground. Hard. That's all there is to it. To be a good tackler, all you needed was want-to and toughness. So the drill was simple. He pitched the ball to a runner, blew his whistle, and the two collided. If he felt the ball carrier hadn't run hard enough or the hit was insufficient, they went again. And again. And again.

Across the field, under Coach Rexrode's direction, opposing players lined up head-on straddling a 6-foot length of 1"x12" board. When the whistle blew, each tried to drive the other off the other end of the board. "The key to being a good blocker," he told them, "is simple. Stay low and drive with your legs." Over and over and over.

Whistle.

"Listen up! In order for us to be successful you *have* to have perfect form and technique in both blocking and tackling. Two reasons. First, you lack size. And second, as Coach Rexrode's fond of sayin', you've all got that Archer County disease—you're slow. Now, we're gonna stay out here till you get it right. I don't care *how* long it takes. Let's start again!"

Half an hour later, Mike Stewart's head was pounding. Finally, he couldn't take it any more. While waiting his turn in the tackling line, he trotted over to the head trainer, Donald Dorris.

"What are you doin'?"

"I've got a fierce headache. My helmet don't fit my head."

"You ain't got no head. That's the problem."

Mike laughed. "Yeah, I know. Chester Crowley says it looks like my neck just haired over."

Donald smiled and dug two aspirin from the medicine kit and handed them to him. "You best get back over there."

Mike reached down and turned on the hose.

"I wouldn't do that if I's you."

"How come?"

"STEWART! GET OVER HERE!"

Mike downed the pills with a gulp of water and ran over as told.

CHAPTER 5

Running On Empty

Had the face mask not yet been invented, Grady Graves would have invented it. Most agreed it was his most valuable teaching aid.

He promptly grabbed Mike's, spun him around and jerked him to attention.

"What in tarnation do you think you're doin'?"

"Takin' some aspirin for my headache. My helmet don't fit right. It's too big for my head."

"Son, this is the smallest helmet we got. Besides, you don't *have* a head."

"I know. Chester Crowley says it looks like my neck just haired over."

Mike was smiling, but Grady wasn't.

Then, loud enough for everyone to hear, "In case you boys haven't figured it out by now, water is off limits. Got that?"

"Yes sir!"

"That clear, Stewart?"

"Yes sir!"

"Men, you cannot be strong and drink water. Or eat candy. Remember that. Now, I can't do much about the second part, but I can the first." He jerked Mike closer. "Next time, you swallow those aspirin dry. You hear me?"

"Yes sir."

WHAM! The sudden slap to his helmet could be heard for blocks. *"You hear me?"*

"Yes sir!"

Still holding his face mask, he jerked Mike's head this way and that. "Your helmet *is* a tad loose. I believe I'd see about wrappin' somethin' around my head so it'd fit a little better if I were you."

"Yes sir!"

"Now, get your butt back in line and see me after practice."

"In your office?"

"No! On the goal line!"

Oh Lord.

For the remainder of the season, Mike Stewart swallowed two aspirin at each and every practice. Dry. And wrapped an Ace bandage around his forehead so his helmet would fit better. It helped. A little.

At 7:00 P.M., following another two hours of drills and wind sprints, the whistle blew. *The* whistle belonged to Grady and had it's own distinct sound—there was no mistaking it.

Thirty-five boys had suited up that morning. Eight had vacated the premises. Those remaining, barely standing, couldn't believe they had survived the first practice.

"All right, you cry babies. Get your butts over there to the sideline, take a knee, take off your helmets, and I'll give you some durn water." All hurried that way careful not to run any faster than they had in their wind sprints.

Grady turned on the hose, and in record time whisked it past the line of kneeling players. Each received one gulp and, if he thought you'd been hustling, a splash on the head. A few keen observers farther down the line had the foresight to plug the holes in the tops of their helmets with their fingers and hold them underneath them to catch any stray water. Then, once Coach was gone, they lifted their helmets and drank from them. Some had caught a swig. Others, two. The mixture of water, sweat, and Butch wax tasted like a million dollars.

This ploy soon became commonplace as a means of survival.

Grady's shrill whistle blew, and the players climbed to their feet hoping they had the strength to make it to the locker room where abundant water awaited.

"Okay, now that we have determined none of you are in shape and no one cares about learnin' how to block or tackle, we best find out if anyone here's tough enough to play. Line up on the goal line!"

The practice field had no lights, so at precisely 9:00 P.M., with sunlight fading, Grady finally signaled an end to practice. The lone water break had not been repeated, and the players' bodies, furious with them, let them know. Wobbly, cramping, and dry heaving, they stumbled toward the locker room, the past two hours a blur of pain and suffering. Meanwhile Mike, the water thief, and three more unfortunate souls willed their bodies toward the goal line one last time. Once intact, the first official Goof-Off Squad ran some more, although half an hour later, in darkness, they could not remember doing so.

When he finally finished showering and dressing, Mike sleepwalked out to his car where he found Gary lying across the front seat.

"Thought I'd spend the night with you tonight, if that's okay."

"Sure," Mike replied. "Anybody else?"

"Naw, Coach Rexrode took Bussey home, and Barney left with Barry."

Gary, Ray, and Barney all lived several miles east of Archer in the country.

The two climbed in, and mustering his last available strength, Mike turned the key.

Gary punched him in the arm. "What the heck are you smilin' about?"

Mike glanced in his rear view mirror. "I didn't know I was."

"You're always smilin'."

"Habit, I guess."

"Well, you might wanna watch that. Coach might take it the wrong way."

"Gotcha."

As the car sped away, Gary looked over. "There you go again. What's so durn funny?"

"Goof-Off Squad," Mike said, laughing.

"You're nuts."

Minutes later they parked beside the Stewart's home and found Mike's dad Gene waiting for them on the front porch.

"So how'd it go?" he asked with a big grin.

"You were there. You should know."

Like many of the men about town, Gene religiously watched football practices from the street, leaning against his car. The group was commonly referred to as "The Sweaters."

"Looks like he's kinda fond of runnin' you boys."

CHAPTER 6

Taking Stock

Early in the morning practice the next day, Grady still wasn't liking what he was seeing. He blew his whistle.

"Sure are a lot of guys limpin' around out here this mornin'. I don't know why. None of you practiced hard enough yesterday to be sore." He paused, glaring at the group. "Let's get one thing straight right now. You *will* play hurt. With what few players we'll have after the quitters are all gone, most of you will have to play both ways—offense and defense. *And* special teams. So unless they have to carry you off the field, I'd better not see you headed my way. That's just the way it has to be in order for us to be successful, and you'd better start gettin' used to it right now. If your leg ain't broke, I don't wanna see you hoppin' around out here. So SUCK IT UP!"

Everyone knew what was coming next.

"Line up on the goal line."

Once drills resumed, Coach Bobby Rexrode walked over to Grady who was intently focused on the lackluster performance of his running backs and ends.

"Coach, here's one you haven't seen before, I bet. We got a guy over there practicin' barefoot."

"Barefoot?"

"Yes sir. Jerked his shoes and socks off right after wind sprints. Got blisters. Bad ones at that."

"Who is it?"

"Pitts. He's one of the freshmen."

Grady walked over and watched the young lineman battling a larger, stronger opponent unable to get good footing—his feet a bloody mess. After studying him a few plays, Grady turned to his assistant coach and smiled.

"Bobby, I believe we got ourselves a keeper."

"I'd say so."

"How 'bout the rest of the freshmen?"

"Well, the only other one I have is Parsley. He's not big but he looks to be quick as a bug, and he ain't afraid to hit somebody. Heck, I think he likes it. How 'bout you?"

"Tepfer seems pretty tough. Oliver, too. That Stewart kid's definitely got some talent. Morrison I'm not sure about, but I think there's somethin' inside him if we can get it out."

"What about the Bussey kid?"

"He likes to talk but looks pretty fast. The jury's still out on him."

"There's not a one that's got any size or meat on 'em. Might be a long season for them boys up against experienced teams with big, strong kids."

Grady reached down, pulled a stem of Bermuda grass, and chewed it. "Well, then, we'd best get 'em ready."

With a wink, he blew his whistle. "Okay, boys, line up on the goal line!"

At week's end, only twenty-three remained. They looked like walking dead. Felt like it, too. Their practice uniforms smelled like skunk's work, but none of them noticed. They were too concerned with getting their next breath in, and then out. And staying upright, without limping. It wasn't easy.

That evening at the Stewart house, Mike and Gary stood in the bathroom going through the motions of brushing their teeth when they heard the front door open and close followed by a familiar voice. They looked at each other, then silently inched their way down the hall to take a look. There, seated with his back to them only a few feet away, was Grady.

"So Gene, I understand Gary's stayin' the night with Mike again tonight."

"That's right," Gene smiled, careful not to look up at the startled boys in the hallway.

"It's five after ten. They here?"

"Sure are."

"In bed?"

Another smile. "Of course. You wanna see 'em?"

The boys exchanged nervous looks, took deep breaths, tiptoed past the entryway into the bedroom, and jumped into bed.

In the next room, Grady passed on the bed check.

"Naw, that won't be necessary," he said. "Well, I best be goin'." And he walked to the door.

"Come back any time, Coach," Gene said.

"Thanks, I'll do that."

And he would.

CHAPTER 7

Fiasco

A good crowd was on hand for the Wildcats' first scrimmage under Grady Graves. The opponent: the Throckmorton Greyhounds, a smaller Class B school some fifty miles southeast of Archer City. Upon arriving, Grady and Throckmorton head coach Tommy Boyd went over the ground rules. One team would control the football until they were stopped on downs or had a turnover. If they scored, they would keep it and go on offense again.

The Greyhounds took the ball first, and the Wildcat defense took their positions. True to his word, seven of the eleven were the freshmen Pitts, Stewart, Parsley, Tepfer, Morrison, Bussey, and Oliver. Three plays into it, the Greyhounds were in the end zone, and the next hour became an exercise of being drug into position by the face mask, kicked, shoved, slapped upside the head, and screamed at—all the while trying to concentrate on the task at hand: stopping Throckmorton. After ten straight touchdown drives, Coach Boyd trotted over to Grady.

"Coach, you want the ball? We're happy to play defense."

Grady shook his head.

"Well, how about a break? It's pretty hot out here."

Grady again shook his head. "You go ahead. We're good."

As the teams lined up once more, Gary Tepfer was silently offering thanks.

"Thank you, Lord. Thank you."

The reason? The big brute blocking back that had been running him over was gone. In his place, a little bitty guy. Gary's prayers had apparently not gone unnoticed.

Then, as soon as the ball was snapped, the squirt shot across the line in the blink of an eye and landed a forearm inside his face mask directly to the bridge of his nose. Out cold on his feet, he remained upright and unmoving as action flashed all around him. When his eyes finally began to regain their focus, he noticed the Greyhounds had lined up for the next play—the little bitty fella grinning at him. Then, in his ear came a chuckle.

"You all right?"

It was Grady.

Gary managed to nod.

At the snap, it appeared his next prayer was being answered as well. He just hoped God was through kidding around. The ball carrier was headed to the other side away from him. It got even better.

Fumble! Ray Bussey came out of the pile with it like he'd just recovered the Hope diamond.

Whistle.

"BUSSEY! Get over here! All of you!" They quickly gathered round.

"I don't know what that little dance was, but that crap's gonna stop. I will not tolerate showboatin' or any such nonsense. Not now. Not *ever!* And in case you haven't noticed, we're bein' taken to the woodshed. You've got nothin' to celebrate. Now, huddle up on offense, and let's see if we can get a first down before nightfall."

Barry Morrison looked to Grady for instructions, got none, and so nervously called a play.

"30 Dive. On hut. Ready, break."

As instructed, the freshmen took their places: Billy at center, Steve at guard, Ray and Barney at ends, Mike and Gary in the backfield, with Barry at quarterback.

As Gary took his position at fullback, he looked around. The tiny holy terror was nowhere to be found. *Thank goodness.* The rest of the Greyhounds were *all* smiling, though.

Determined, the tall, skinny 130-pound Barry barked the signals, took the snap—almost dropping it—and turned to hand it to his 135-pound fullback. The two collided, the ball bounding away and into the hands of a Throckmorton player. Thankfully, Stewart drug him down from behind just short of their goal line. Then Gary heard what sounded like a gunshot. Felt it, too. At his feet, the splintered remains of a clipboard lay scattered in the grass. Suddenly, Grady had his face mask in one hand and Barry's in his other. He jerked the two together, their faces just inches apart.

"You two know each other? Cause it sure don't look like it. Morrison, this is Tepfer. He's the fullback. Tepfer, this is Morrison. He's the quarterback. On 30 Dive, the quarterback hands the ball to the fullback who then runs forward with it. That too hard to remember?"

"No sir."

"Think you can get it right, this time?"

"Yes sir."

"You sure?"

"Yes sir!"

"You'd better! *Now, run it again!*"

In what felt like slow motion, Barry called the same play, lined up, took the snap, and handed off cleanly to his buddy who was immediately met by two blitzing Greyhounds before he could take a step. As a result of their jarring hits, the ball bounded away. In frantic pursuit, Barry managed to grab it near the sideline and tried to pass—he wasn't sure to whom—and was hit just as he let the ball go. In horror, he watched it flutter into a defender's hands. This time Mike didn't catch him. Touchdown Throckmorton.

The scrimmage quickly went downhill from there.

On the bus before heading home, Grady exploded.

"Some of you upper classmen seem amused at what went on here today. Think it's funny. Think *you* belong out there instead of these newcomers. Well, get used to the view.

We may not win a game, but we're gonna play hard." He then glared at Barry, Gary, and the others. "That *right?!*"

"Yes sir!"

The line of demarcation had been drawn. And there were a lot of unhappy campers.

CHAPTER 8

The Color Gold

It didn't take long for the divisiveness to erupt into all-out war. In the parking lot of Troy's Drive-In on a Saturday afternoon, all hell broke loose: an ugly, knock-down-drag-out brawl between a group of juniors and seniors and the chosen ones—the freshmen. It would have been a massacre had it not been for Tommy Eustace. To the dismay of the older boys, the toughest and most talented player ever to don a Wildcat uniform crossed the picket line, joined the ranks of the enemy, and evened up the odds. Not because he had the best interest of the underdogs in mind, but rather, because he respected Grady Graves and his decisions as head coach.

As shocked passersby stopped and looked on in horror, the two groups punched, kicked, bit, and gouged each other until a handful of onlookers, mostly women, intervened and broke it up. As the players dispersed, there were no handshakes or smiles. Hard feelings were not forgiven. Nothing had been resolved.

Prior to Monday's practice, Grady surveyed the participants with their black eyes, bruises, and split lips and said nothing. These things had a way of working themselves out. One way or another.

An impasse was never reached, and the split in the team soon migrated to the townspeople. While most of the Quarterback Club members remained determined to give Grady the benefit of the doubt, many about town didn't. They didn't like the benching of several of the older, more talented players, nor did they like watching the inexperienced ones clearly being overmatched week after week. Another group opposed the coach for another reason: They felt he was too controlling and far too hard on the boys.

In short, the town's excitement over having a new coach and a new beginning was dwindling fast, and the 1961 football season itself did nothing to change that.

In ten games that year, the Wildcats scored 50 points and allowed 293. Their record was 1-9, their lone victory coming in week six with a 14-12 win over Knox City. In the locker room following that game, several freshmen cried. As did Coach Rexrode.

When the season was done, an exhausted, hurting group of boys hung up their cleats and uniforms, thankful it was finished. Especially the workouts. The practices had never let up in intensity from day one. In eight short months they would begin again. *If* their bodies could recover in that amount of time.

Grady, on the other hand, was eager. The season hadn't been successful in the win column, but he hadn't expected it to be. Nor, most likely, would the next one. But this one had told him a lot about his young players. They were determined, played hard, and never quit hustling. They did have gumption. Next year couldn't get here quick enough. But first, there was something that needed tending to.

Two months later, on a chilly February morning, the wives of the Quarterback Club members were hard at work decorating the gymnasium for the annual football banquet that evening. The tables and chairs had all been set and decorated, and streamers hung from the rafters, the entire expanse a dazzling display of black and gold, the school colors. While others swept and picked up, Linnie Mae Hudson was busy putting stuff away when, behind her, the gym doors flew open and Grady walked in headed for his office. He stopped next to where she was working.

"How does it look?" she asked proudly.

"Black and Gold. Hmmmmf."

She thought she detected a note of sarcasm in his reply but wasn't sure.

"Yeah. Isn't it pretty?"

Without answering, he entered his office and shut the door.

That night, when she and her husband Pete arrived for the festivities, she couldn't believe her eyes.

The gold was gone. The gold streamers. The gold napkins. Even the gold plastic dinnerware. Each had been replaced with white.

The next day, Grady called the team together, minus the seniors.

"Anybody satisfied with how the season went?"

No one answered.

"Neither am I. We've got a long ways to go, and we're gonna be changin' a lot of things around here. Startin' with the school colors. As you saw last night, we now have new ones. Next year, those of you who show back up will have new uniforms. Black and white. With black helmets. And maybe, if they make one that small, we'll get one that fits you, Stewart."

Mike grinned.

"I said maybe. I don't know if you've earned it."

"Yes sir."

"Football jackets will change, too. From now on, they'll be black with a single block 'A'. No more of that fancy *A.C.* business."

The players snuck glances at each other.

"We're gettin' back to basics, boys. No need for frilly emblems and fancy colors."

Most were picturing the changes in their mind and thinking the same thing: black and white wouldn't be that bad. In fact, it sounded pretty good, but I wonder why . . . ?

"The reason? Gold looks too much like yellow," Grady informed them. "And men, yellow isn't a color. It's an action. Don't ever forget that."

PART TWO

HARD TIMES

CHAPTER 9

The Rebel

Bobby "Fuzzy" Ray was coaching basketball at nearby, tiny Antelope High School when Grady came calling. The crew-cut, likeable Ray wasn't all that interested in coaching football (Antelope didn't even have a football team) but was willing in order to become the new head basketball coach at Archer City. Grady introduced him on the first day of two-a-days.

"Okay, guys. Listen up. This is our new assistant coach, Bobby Ray. He'll be takin' Coach Harcrow's place who, as you know, has moved on. Coach Ray will also be the new head basketball coach. So if you plan on playin', you might wanna start gettin' on his good side."

There were assorted looks in the group. Most had never seen a basketball coach that short. Their attention quickly re-focused on Grady.

"Those of you who were around last year already know, and those of you who are new will soon learn, that water is scarce around here. I don't think you need *any*, but you'll continue to get your customary swig, and that's it. This year we've got salt tablets to replenish what you sweat out. They're over there on the bench, and I expect to see every one of you takin' 'em and takin' 'em often. That clear?"

"Yes sir!"

"Any questions?"

Silence.

"Men, I hope you didn't spend your summer sittin' around drinkin' Cokes in the shade cause we've got a lot of work to do this year and not much time to do it. Are you ready?"

"Yes sir!"

"Good. Line up on the goal line!"

The 1962 season had officially begun.

Thirty minutes into the practice, displeased with everyone's apparent lack of effort, Grady proceeded to jerk sophomore Steve Parsley aside and "rattle his cage." After thirty seconds or so, Steve stopped him.

"Hang on, Coach," he said, unbuckling his chin strap, removing his helmet, and handing it to a befuddled Grady. "Here you go. If you're gonna go on shakin' it like that, I just as soon my head not be in it."

Goof-Off Squad. Big time.

In a little over a year, the Rebel had carved himself quite a reputation. With the popularity of the movie *The Great Escape,* it was difficult deciding who did more time—Steve McQueen in the prison camp cooler or Steve Parsley on the Goof-Off Squad. It was quickly becoming no contest. Steve Parsley liked girls, beer, and fightin'. *And* pushing the envelope.

Following practice, the coaches gathered in Grady's office. Disgusted, he slammed a file cabinet shut, sat down, and looked at the other two.

"His attitude is unacceptable."

Bobby Rexrode popped open a Coke and looked over at Grady.

"Kid hits hard."

"A lot of 'em do."

"Yeah, but he's the only one who appears to like it. He's a tough little dude. The more he's hurtin', the harder he hits."

"He's a loafer."

"He *is* that, but he listens."

"Not to me, he don't."

Being the newcomer, Fuzzy had debated about speaking up. Till now.

"I don't know that much about him, but I do know this—he's quicker on his feet than anybody we've got."

"Yeah. I just wish he had Stewart's head on his shoulders."

Coach Rexrode laughed. "Stewart ain't got no head."

"Then Morrison's! Tepfer's! Bussey's! Anybody's!"

"There's still time."

Grady got up, walked to his window, and peered out.

"Not that much time."

If the Rebel had a polar opposite, it was number 84, Barney Oliver. No nicknames. Just Barney. Quiet—not as quiet as Billy Pitts, but then, no one was—and hard working. The Olivers lived several miles east of Archer City out "in the sticks" near Antelope. He and Ray Bussey and the Tepfer brothers (Gary's younger brother Robert was now a freshman on the team) rode the bus to school and were usually driven home following practice by one of the coaches. However, Barney preferred spending the night with teammates and did so often, developing great affection for Barry's parents, Patsy and Claude Morrison—the Archer County Sheriff. Like Barney's dad Staton, Claude spoke softly and carried himself with dignity—traits Barney emulated and came by easily. Following his freshman year, Grady and the other coaches pretty much knew what they had in Barney and liked it. He was becoming a tough defensive end, a good receiver, and shared time at fullback with Gary. Preferring to remain in the background, he avoided attention like the plague.

During calisthenics the next day, Grady walked over.

"Son, what are those?"

"My cowboy boots, sir."

"I can see *that*. Where are your football cleats?"

"Home, sir. I took 'em home to polish 'em and forgot 'em."

"And you're gonna practice in those?"

"Yes sir."

"Sure you wouldn't rather go barefoot?"

"No sir. Ground's kinda hot. And I don't want Parsley steppin' on my feet."

Grady bit his lip. "Well, maybe next time you'll remember."

"Yes sir."

And so Barney practiced. And ran wind sprints. In his cowboy boots. And no one tried any funny stuff because the toes on his boots were pointed and plenty hard. *And* because Barney might have been quiet and shy, but all knew better than to mess with him.

Now, you'd think something like practicing in boots would earn one an instant lifelong nickname. But it didn't. That says a lot about the guy they just called Barney.

CHAPTER 10

The Reckoning

As the bus pulled up at the S.H. Rider High School practice field in Wichita Falls, Barry looked over at Barney seated next to him.

"You believe we're gonna scrimmage them? A 4-A school? Look at 'em!"

Barney did. There were a lot of 'em, and they were big. And it was hotter'n a firecracker. On top of that, every Wildcat player was exhausted and sore—or hurt. *This ain't gonna be pretty,* he thought.

And it wasn't.

Two and one-half hours later, the whistle finally blew. The Wildcats had taken a beating. Most were just hoping to make it to the bus. They watched Grady walk over to Rider coach Joe Bob Tyler to thank him. Or so they thought.

Grady wasn't holding out his hand.

"Coach, what say we go a little longer? There's still some daylight left."

The Rider coach smiled. He wasn't backing down from the little school twenty miles to the south. "We're game if y'all are. Although the boys might need a break."

"We don't. We're ready to go."

"Okay, Coach. You want the ball?"

"Yep. We've gotta find us some offense before we leave here."

An hour later, the players' apparent salvation arrived in the form of another whistle.

Coach Tyler walked over to Grady.

"Coach, I think we've done about all we can do today. The boys are all dead on their feet, and their minds aren't in it anymore. Besides, it's fixin' to get dark and maybe even storm. We appreciate y'all comin' over."

"All the same, Coach, we're needin' the work. That streetlamp there oughta be enough. Whatta you say?"

His counterpart smiled. "Dadgum, Coach. Are all your practices like this?"

"Aren't yours?"

The two smiled.

"Well, heck. It *would* look kinda bad for *us* to quit now, wouldn't it?"

Grady didn't answer.

"Okay, let's go!"

Grady walked over and gathered the team together. They were a sad, whipped group. Barely afoot.

"Men, we are gonna stay out here all night if we have to. So you'd better quit worryin' about how tired you are and start playin' some football. I mean it."

There was no need for a water break. It began to rain.

An hour later, with only enough light from the lone streetlight to make out shapes, the Wildcat offense lined up, quarterback Barry Morrison took the snap, dropped back in the slop, looked downfield for a receiver, could see none in the dark and driving rain, steadied himself for the hit he knew was coming, and threw. The pass traveled barely twenty yards before splashing in the mud, incomplete. Suddenly a familiar hand grabbed his face mask, jerked him to his feet, and dragged him away from the other players. He didn't feel it. He no longer felt anything. He was amazed he was able to stand. Grady stared into his eyes just inches away. The two were isolated. No one could see or hear them clearly, not that it mattered. The young signal-caller was too far gone to be embarrassed about being singled out.

"Son, are you listenin' to me?"

Barry nodded.

"This is as bad as it gets. I know. You're wishin' you were anywhere but here, and after the beatin' you've taken the past few hours, I don't blame you. You're probably not even thinkin' too clear right now. But you have *got* to get this." He paused. "You are the quarterback, son. You *run* this show. Your teammates are lookin' to *you*. If you can't do this, they can't. *We* can't. Now, I know you have it in you. Somewhere. So you find it. Right now! You hear me? *You find it!* And when you do, we'll be waitin'."

He turned and walked away.

Time stood still. Standing alone in the dark and rain, Barry wasn't aware of its passing. His mind was numb, his knees shaking, his body aching. The weight of the world was on his shoulders. Some twenty or thirty feet away were his teammates; he couldn't see them, only a few vague shapes. He choked back his tears.

In the distance, the lone streetlight shown dimly—a single, flickering bulb battling the night and rain, refusing to succumb, leaving them all in darkness. He stared at it, squinting, the rain pelting his eyes and face. Then, for the briefest of moments, he understood. He and the light were one.

The quarterback reached up, his fingers trembling, and managed to buckle his chin strap. He then took a deep breath and walked toward the light.

In the huddle, he looked his teammates in the eyes, and spoke.

"186 Pass. On hut. And Ray, Barney. One of you get open! You hear me?"

Each nodded.

"Ready, break." And they headed to the line of scrimmage.

Behind center, Barry looked across at the Rider linebackers, knowing they'd be coming hard again. "Down! Set! Hut!"

He managed to hang onto the soaked, slippery ball and turned and sloshed back several yards trying not to slip in the mud. Then he planted his feet the best he could and looked downfield. To his left, Ray had disappeared into the night. To his right, the side nearest the streetlight, he thought he could make out a player or two far down the sideline. One of them had to be Barney. The linebackers were closing fast, Mike and Gary doing their best to block without traction. He was going to get creamed. Again. He stepped up and threw long down the field, the ball disappearing into the night just as he was pummeled and driven facedown into the slop. Buried beneath the two tacklers, he couldn't see or hear anything and, for a moment, feared he might drown in the muddy water. Then, suddenly, someone was tugging at his jersey, pulling him to his feet. It was Mike.

"You okay, pardner?"

Barry nodded, wiped the mud from his eyes, and stared into the distance. Barney was trotting back. *With the ball.*

"Barney made a heck of a catch," Mike said, grinning. "And that was one hell of a throw."

The scene was interrupted by Grady's whistle.

"Coach," he shouted in the direction of the Rider mentor. "Let's call it a night."

Once the last player collapsed into his seat on the bus, Grady stood and addressed them. He knew they were completely spent and in bad need of a shower, home, a comfy bed, and a weekend of sleep.

"Practice at nine tomorrow morning. Full pads."

He then turned, sat, replayed the scrimmage's final play in his head. And smiled.

CHAPTER 11

Split Decision

The next morning as Barney Oliver trudged into the locker room, several eyes shifted his direction. Finally, Steve motioned toward the wall. There on the Goof-Off Squad board were four names: Oliver, Parsley, and two others.

Barney wasn't surprised. Except for the lone pass reception at the end, he'd been whipped up one end of the field and down the other the entire scrimmage and knew it. He was surprised more names weren't up there.

As was the case with most practices, the toughest part that morning was the mental war raging in the players' heads. Grady always saw to it they hit the proverbial "wall" because somewhere beyond it, past exhaustion, came the real test. It was at that point, when basic needs of air and water weren't being met and no compromise had been reached, the body screamed in rebellion and the mind went to war: a raging, disparaging battle of thoughts and mindless chatter. No man's land.

Barney had been in just that state for much of the past hour. Now, as he and the other three lined up to run some more while the others went to shower, he became somewhat fearful. Could he die here? Was he close?

"We're doin' somethin' a little different today, boys. I want you to duck-walk the first fifty and bear-walk the second."

What?

"Ready." Whistle.

Not knowing what else to do, the four squatted down, hands on knees, and willed themselves forward. Upon finally reaching the goal line at the other end, Barney saw a possible avenue of escape: Two of the others had removed their helmets.

"This is nuts," one said. "He's gonna kill somebody. Let's get outta here."

Steve and Barney were doubled over, waiting for Grady's whistle at the other end of the field.

"Come on, guys. The hell with this."

"Whatta you think, Oliver?" Steve tried to spit but couldn't.

"I don't know."

Steve's right arm and hand were numb. Had been for some while. He turned toward Barney. "Well?"

In the distance, faintly, they could hear it. A whistle.

Barney dropped into a sitting position, his back, knees, and thighs on fire.

"What're you doin'?"

Another whistle. And off Barney went. Alone.

Steve stood, watching him for a moment. Then joined the other two.

Enough was enough.

As he inched toward the goal line, number 84 made up his mind that he would never again be beaten by his opponent no matter how big or fast. Period. He was done with the Goof-Off Squad.

Later that evening, Grady locked the gym door and headed home content. The past two days had been long and tough ones, but they'd paid three big dividends.

He had his quarterback.

He still had Barney.

And the Rebel was gone.

Throughout the season, the team displayed some improvement and when it was over, had three victories to show for it. In addition, they'd put 82 points on the scoreboard compared to 50 the year before and allowed 229 points against them, down from 293. More importantly, in Grady's mind, Morrison was developing nicely at quarterback, Stewart was proving to be an elusive runner, Tepfer was not only hard-nosed at fullback but getting faster all the time, and Pitts showed promise on both sides of the ball, as did Oliver and Bussey. The team still had a long way to go but would eventually get there, he felt. Doing it *his* way.

Aloof and controlling, Grady Graves was a hard person to like. He had his thumb on every aspect of the boys' lives, not even allowing pictures to be taken of them at practices unless it was prearranged and approved by him. In his history class, players had to stand to answer questions while the rest of the class didn't. And to the dismay of the men about town, he would not participate in coffee shop discussions about the team. His domineering nature had worn thin with many of the townspeople, especially with some of the players' parents. By season's end, they'd had all they could take, and a special meeting of the school board was called. In a packed meeting room, Superintendent Tim McPherson called the session to order, and one by one, parents and supporters spoke their mind.

"He's not a football coach, he's a tyrant."

"Two years here and what have we got to show for it? Four lousy wins and a team on the verge of quitting."

"He's run off some of the best players we've ever had."

"I don't like him tellin' me how to raise my boy."

"Me neither!"

"I can't even take mine to the doctor without his permission."

"Hell, my boy can't take a crap without his knowin'."

Laughter.

"This is no laughing matter. He's gonna kill one of 'em someday. It's a wonder he hasn't already, he's so blasted hard on 'em. My gosh, these are just kids."

"They're all hurt. Think he cares? No sir. All he cares about is Grady."

"Football's supposed to be fun. These boys aren't having fun. They're scared to death of him. I would be, too."

"Hell, I was treated better'n them while I was in the Army durin' the war. This ain't right, I tell ya."

A pause.

"Anyone else?"

Claude Morrison walked forward. The tall, authoritative sheriff was well respected and liked by most. He agreed with much of what was being said. He'd had his own battles with Grady. Barry had hurt his knee his freshman year, and when Grady learned Claude was taking him to the doctor, he phoned. "You do that, and he's off the team." "You do that, and you won't have a team," he'd told the coach. He himself didn't have much use for Grady, but his boy did. Barry wanted him to stay.

"We promised him four years, and we should own up to it. Personally, I'd do things different, but I'm not the coach. He is. I say leave him be."

Travis Bussey was next.

"I agree with Claude. I've seen a change in Ray since Grady's been here. A change in lots of these kids. Hard work and the such has done 'em all some good. And I believe him when he says we'll have a good team once he's done. He just needs a little more time."

To the chagrin of many, the school board agreed. Grady wasn't going anywhere.

Least not right now.

PART THREE

LIGHT AT THE END OF THE TUNNEL

CHAPTER 12

Return of the Rebel

At 6:00 A.M. on the first morning of two-a-day workouts in August 1963, Quarterback Club President Monroe Williams stood knocking on the front door of the Parsley residence. Shortly, a disheveled Steve, still half-asleep, opened it and squinted into the morning light outside. It was a moment before he recognized his visitor.

"Monroe?" Steve looked past him into the street. "What the hell time is it?"

"Time for you to get dressed and get goin'."

"Where?"

"Practice. You're playin' ball this year."

"*What?*"

"You heard me."

"No, I ain't either."

"Will you give me one good reason?"

"Two. I don't like Grady, and he don't like me."

"That don't matter. You're a good player, and you oughta be playin'."

"And I don't like his rules and all that crap he dishes out. All I wanna do is play football."

"I can't believe you're lettin' him get the best of you."

"He ain't."

"He darn sure is. He's up there doin' what he wants to do, and you're standin' here in your underwear."

Steve paused for a moment thinking. "He wouldn't let me come back anyway since I quit."

"Can't stop you. *If* you wanna play."

"I don't have a physical, and practice starts this mornin'."

"Doc's meetin' us at the clinic at 6:30. I've already talked to him."

"You're kiddin'."

"Nope. So get dressed."

"Well, hell."

At seven o'clock, the two walked into the coaches' office where Grady was seated at his desk and Roy Williams, a new assistant, was leaning against a file cabinet. Grady looked up and frowned. "What can I do for you?"

"This boy wants to play ball."

"Can't."

"Why not?"

"He's not signed up."

"He's signin' up. He made a mistake last year and he's ownin' up to it."

Steve shot Monroe a hard look but kept quiet.

"The boy doesn't have a physical."

"Sure does." Monroe handed over the paper.

Grady studied it for a moment, looked at Monroe, then at Steve. "You gonna stick it out this time? Or quit again when the goin' gets tough?"

"I'll stick."

"You've got a lot of work you're gonna have to make up."

Steve knew what that meant. Sprints. Lots of 'em. "I don't care 'bout that. But I ain't comin' back to sit on the bench."

"You'll do whatever I tell you to do."

"He will."

Grady glared at Steve. "You do the extra work and play like you're capable; you'll get to play. But I can't guarantee how much."

Monroe chomped down on his cigar. "All right, then. Get this boy some gear."

Grady continued to stare at Steve. "Coach Williams, take care of Parsley here. And I don't wanna see him wearin' any of the new stuff."

Roy grinned, walked over, squeezed the back of Steve's neck and guided him out the door. "Come on, Trouble. Let's go see if there's any small jock straps left."

Monroe watched them leave. "He's a good player, Coach. A mite hard-headed, but tougher'n a twenty-five-cent steak. And he'll stick this time. You can bet on that."

"He better."

"Oh, he will," Monroe said, smiling. "He's too pissed off not to."

CHAPTER 13

Welcome Back

A short while later in the locker room, nothing much was said to Steve. Most were glad he was back, and some hard kidding was definitely in order, but right now everyone silently went about the business of getting dressed for practice with overwhelming dread. Finally, Mike couldn't stand it any more.

"Wonder if we'll have to run any today?"

Everyone stared at him.

"Hey, maybe Coach got soft in the off season."

"Yeah, right."

"Speakin' of runnin', Barry, there's somethin' I been meanin' to ask you for two years now."

"What's that, Ray?"

"How come is it that in games you punt the ball thirty-five yards. Every time. But in practice, durin' punt coverage drills, you kick the bloomin' thing fifty?"

Gary wadded up a towel and fired it Barry's direction. "Yeah, what's up with that, anyway?"

Mike was next. "You, uh, think you might can flip those around this year?"

All laughter immediately ceased at the sound of the door opening. Sure enough, it was Grady. Everyone watched as he walked to the chalkboard, and in big letters, wrote the following: *PARSLEY.*

Without looking at them or saying a word, he then left.

"Dadgum, Steve, what'd you do?"

"Showed back up in *this* godforsaken place. That's what."

"Well, we thank you." Mike said. "Bad as it's gonna be out there today, it could be worse. We *could* be *you*," he said, laughing.

"Yeah, well, that girlfriend of yours would like that."

And they all laughed hard, their nervousness and anxiety draining away. Until Coach Ray stuck his head in. "Five minutes, guys."

The new season's first practice went just about the way all expected it to. They beat on each other for a while, ran wind sprints, beat on each other, ran, beat on each other, ran, and just as they were about to die, ran some more before being turned loose to shower and head to the cafeteria. Following lunch and three hours of sleepless nap attempts on the hard gym floor, they suited up and did it all again, this time with the temperature well over a hundred.

As anticipated, Steve Parsley was singled out for "lack of effort" and other infractions but he wasn't alone. Everybody caught flack. When the final session of wind sprints arrived late in the day, all were dehydrated, hurting, and dazed. Then, out of nowhere, at the far end of the field opposite Grady, a curious thing happened. As players got back down into their stances and waited for Coach Ray's whistle sending them back the other way, it began to rain ice. Not a downpour, mind you. Not even an sprinkle. But, unknown to Grady, occasional fragmented pieces of ice were plopping into the grass. Those lucky enough to spot one and grab it before it melted, enjoyed an brief taste of heaven. Upon further investigation, the godsends appeared to be coming from the cup in Fuzzy's hand. They also seemed to be directed toward those who were running the hardest or at least appeared to be. Whether or not any lives were actually saved is doubtful, but some spirits were. Sadly, by the time wind sprints were over, and the Rebel began his Goof-Off Squad dues, all had melted—though it's unknown to this day whether he would have gotten any or not.

That night, Steve and some of his non-football-playing buddies sat in his car at the Texaco sipping beer. They'd talked him into quittin' once. It wasn't happenin' twice. He loved knockin' the crap outta guys who thought they were tough stuff, and football gave him plenty of opportunities to do just that. He'd made it clear he was stickin' it out this time, and all talk of it was over.

"So where'd this Coach Williams guy come from?"

"Grady hired him to take Coach Rexrode's place."

"Where'd *he* go?"

"Sherman, I think."

"Didn't all three of 'em used to coach together at Olney?"

"I think so."

"So how come he didn't come to Archer with Grady back then?"

"How the hell should *I* know?"

"I heard he was workin' in the oilfields out near Post when Grady hired him. What's up with *that?*"

"I don't know!" Steve was getting a little perturbed. He liked Roy.

"Well, I heard . . ."

"*Hey!* Why do *you* care? *You* ain't suitin' up. Least, last time I checked you weren't. None of you were."

Just then Claude Morrison drove up in his patrol car. They all looked at each other. They weren't bein' *that* loud.

"Evenin', men."

Steve leaned out his window. "Sheriff. What can we do for you?"

"I don't want you drinkin' here at the Texaco anymore. I know you fellas don't cause any trouble, but it just don't look right. Especially with you bein' a ball player." He paused. "I'm not gonna stop you from doin' it, but take it on out in the country. Off the road in a field somewhere. And when you're done, pick up your bottles and anyone else's you see so cows won't be steppin' on 'em. And if you see a fence down, put it up. Fair enough?"

"Yes sir."

"All right then. Have a good evenin'."

And he left.

Steve watched him drive away, then started the car. "Well, you heard the man. Let's go put up some fences."

CHAPTER 14

The Quiet One

Assistant coach Roy Williams was short, stocky, wore thick horn-rimmed glasses, chewed tobacco, and after some time away from football was back in his element. A man of few words, he mostly just grunted. His linemen quickly learned to distinguish between his angry one—grrrrrrrrrrrmph!—and his approving one—hmmmmph! A tough, fiery individual, he was not the least bit hesitant to jump down, take a stance, and go one-on-one with players—battles he always won. But he had a soft side, too. He was grateful to be back doing what he loved and was quick with a pat on the rump or nod of encouragement. Mess up, though, and he had you by the face mask jerking you this way and that, tobacco juice flying in all directions, grunting his displeasure, never failing to get his message across.

Even in the off-season. During basketball practices when Coach Ray wasn't looking, he was known to run out on the court and have Robert Tepfer practice turning out his foot like he was going to pull and block on a trap play. Robert would do so and ask, "Whatta you think?" And Roy would grunt and leave.

Right now, he had his eye on Steve Parsley. Grady had made it clear to him the kid was a quitter, but he was back and as far as Roy was concerned, deserved every chance the others got—even if he *was* ornery as all get out. He soon found himself liking the kid.

"Parsley! Get over here and brrrrrmmmmph!"

"Say what?"

"Grrrrrrrrrrrrrrph!"

Steve took his stance and Roy immediately jumped down across from him, blew his whistle, fired out, and knocked Steve on his keister. The others laughed.

The Rebel was not happy. He took his stance again. Pads or no pads, the old guy was fixin' to get hurt.

Whistle. Steve shot forward, hit him a good lick, lost his footing and proceeded to get blocked backwards.

After repeating the process a few more times, Coach Williams stood up, red faced, slightly out of breath, and smiling.

"Son, if you can't block *me,* we're in trouble."

"I couldn't get my footin'."

"Brrrrrrrmph."

"What?"

"I had it. Get back down there and I'll show ya."

The two lined up, and in slow motion, Roy pushed forward and grabbed Steve's right ankle.

"Like this, hmmmmmmmmph."

"Won't I get called for holdin'?"

"Not if you do it right. Following two successful tries, Roy smiled and looked around. All right, someone else. Pitts! Get down there. Brrrrrrrrrmph. Rogers, across from him, hmmmmmph."

It was common knowledge that center Billy Pitts was one of the quietest, gentlest souls in all of Archer County. *And* that putting a football uniform on him was like giving Al Capone another baseball bat. Once in it, he became Godzilla in cleats. Or worse.

Interestingly enough, all he wanted was to be the very best football player he could be, and the path there, as he saw it, was to work as hard as he possibly could on every single play of every practice. He also expected everyone else to do the same—especially the person directly across from him. If he felt that player wasn't doing his best to help him achieve his goal, it upset him. And as he and Andy took their stances, trouble was just around the corner.

Good-natured, jovial freshman Andy Rogers, newly transplanted from Kansas, unfortunately was not familiar with

Billy's work doctrine. At the whistle, Andy backpedaled so Billy couldn't get to his feet, stood up, and crossed his arms to protect himself. Billy lunged forward and fell. They took their places and went again with similar results. After three more attempts, the taller, stronger Pitts was more than a little perturbed. It was bad enough having to chase down the back pedaler, but now Andy's elbows were leaving sore spots in Billy's upper arms. Finally, it came.

"Andy, if you don't stop that business right now, I'm gonna hurt you."

The youngster from Kansas was also unfamiliar with the adage, "If Billy Pitts says he's gonna knock your block off, you best go to suckin' your head in."

Once again, Andy resorted to his self-defensive blocking mode. Sadly, he was also unaware that Billy warns you only once.

Pitts fired off the line throwing a vicious forearm into Andy's face mask, sending him reeling. When he awoke, everyone was standing over him. Billy helped him to his feet. "Doggonit, Andy. You shoulda listened to me."

Andy reached up and felt his nose, now lying sideways across his face, gushing blood. Coach Williams had him by the arm. "Son, that might be how y'all do things up in Kansas, but down here, that'll getcha killed. Now, get on over there and let Donald see what he can do for that."

Andy trudged away, leaving a trail of bright red blood, all the while making a mental note to steer plum clear of number 52 in the future whenever possible. Once he was gone, Roy turned and said, "All right, we need somebody in his place."

No one budged.

CHAPTER 15

Road Warriors

A week later, the players got a much needed reprieve from two-a-days in a scrimmage against Olney. Fearful of another marathon nightmare like the one at Rider High School the year before, the Wildcat players were surprised and relieved when Grady agreed to halt it after only three hours. Exhausted, they climbed inside the bus, which felt like an oven after sitting in the sun and 104 degree temperature, and were soon headed down the highway toward home, windows open, a cold shower only half an hour away. Each was envisioning standing naked under a cold spout, eyes closed, mouth wide-open. Then, suddenly, the bus pulled over, still a few miles from town.

Grady stood. "Knox, Reeves, Hannah—off."

They looked at each other.

"See you at the practice field. And I'd better not catch wind of you hitchhiking."

The bus pulled away leaving them on the shoulder. They watched it drive away through the heat rising up off the asphalt pavement.

Half a mile farther down, another stop.

"Bussey, Morrison, Hammontree."

And so on. Finally, at the edge of town, one last stop. Grady looked at the two remaining souls, Stewart and Parsley.

"You're not ridin' the whole way. You'll have to get out here."

They watched the bus disappear down South Street toward the school.

"You believe he let me ride this far?" Steve asked.

"Nope. I can't." Mike looked around. "Well, there's no use gettin' in a hurry. Those other guys will be a while."

Three hours later the last of the stragglers reached the field, and just as they fell to their knees, Grady's whistle sounded. They couldn't see him in the dark, but they heard him.

"Line up on the goal line!"

On his second trip to the far end, sophomore Larry Graham tripped over something and fell. It was Parsley.

"What the hell are you doin'?"

Steve was lying spread-eagled across the ground.

"Restin'. What the hell does it look like I'm doin'?"

"Are you nuts?"

"He can't see this far in the dark."

The whistle sounded, and Larry started back the other way.

Maybe Parsley wasn't so crazy after all.

Over the next half hour, another brave soul or two risked their lives as well. But most didn't. The thought of getting caught by Grady was too terrifying. So they ran.

Coach Ray was nowhere to be seen, so there was no ice to be found plopping in the grass this time around. And since Grady had loudly confronted him in his office following the last such episode, a recurrence was unlikely. Besides, it was too dang dark to see it anyway.

In the dressing room prior to practice the next day, the players got the surprise of their young lives when Grady walked in and made an announcement.

"We coaches feel you boys have been workin' hard and deserve some recreation. Saturday, we're all goin' to Lake Possum Kingdom down by Graham. Travis Bussey, Harvey Boone, and some of the other dads will be joinin' us. We'll do some swimmin' and fishin', and there'll be a boat or two available for you skiers. And of course, plenty of good food. You guys up to it?"

The loud chorus of cheers gave him his answer.

"All right, then. Let's get some good work in the rest of the week and then go have some fun."

Grady wasn't kidding about the work. The remainder of the week's practices were awful. In *his* view, no one still knew how to block or tackle, but they did know how to run. So, run they did. To their amazement, they all survived and, although worn out and sore as hell, showed up early on Saturday for their trip to the lake.

Upon arrival, despite their suspicions, things began surprisingly well. The fish were biting, the ski boats were fast, the water felt great, and Grady and the other coaches were actually quite a bit of fun away from the football field. And as good as all that was, lunch was even better. There's nothing like hamburgers and hot dogs cooked outside on a grill with all the Coca Cola and Dr. Pepper you can drink, topped off by homemade ice cream. An hour after eating, most were lying around enjoying the sun and the sandy shore. Many were asleep. All heard it.

Was that a whistle? Had he brought his friggin' whistle?

"All right, guys. What say we work off some of that ice cream? Let's go. In the water!"

What the heck?

Shortly, everyone was awake and waist deep in the lake.

"Let's do a little runnin' in place, guys. Build up our thighs and calves."

You gotta be kiddin'.

"Let's go! Get those legs pumpin' and those knees high."

After fifteen minutes, the unspoken consensus was that running in place in waist high water was a good way to ruin a day at the lake. *Could it get any worse?*

Yep.

"All right. Enough of that. Let's get movin' now. Run till I tell you to stop."

There *was* something worse than running in place in Possum Kingdom—running *through* Possum Kingdom.

Fun at the lake, indeed.

CHAPTER 16

Hoodlums

The old, faded pickup flew over Devil's Drop west of Archer, trailing a cloud of dust. Behind the wheel sat Mike Stewart, a shotgun at his side. In the back, Gary Tepfer, Barry Morrison, and Barney Oliver, each holding a shotgun in one hand and hanging onto the truck for dear life with the other. Finally, Gary pounded on the cab, and Mike pulled over atop a cattle guard at the entrance to a wheat field and climbed out.

"I haven't seen a bird one, have y'all?"

"We wouldn't know. You're drivin' too durn fast!"

The three climbed out of the bed, careful not to shoot each other.

"Well, I feel like shootin' *somethin'!*" Barney said, walking to the middle of the road.

Barry smiled at the others. "Good thing Coach ain't here."

Mike threw open the lid to the ice chest, fished out an Orange Crush, and held the cold pop bottle to his forehead. "After yesterday, he'd better *not* show."

Gary laughed. "I'm too *tired* to shoot anything."

"Not me!"

BOOM!

"Good shot, Barney. You killed the fencepost."

"Felt good."

Barney then put his gun in the bed, fetched a Coke, let the tailgate down, and plopped down. "I don't think I ever wanna go near Possum Kingdom again."

"Me neither," Mike answered, unzipping his jeans. As he stood peeing in the bar ditch, he looked over his shoulder. "Are y'all's legs as sore as mine?"

The other three nodded.

Gary joined him. "Next time he says we've earned some recreation, I say let's pass."

"Can we do that?"

"I doubt it."

Once they'd finished their business, Mike downed his drink and placed the bottle on the fence post next to Barney's. "Wonder if football at other schools is this much fun?" he asked, walking back.

They all laughed.

"Okay, guys, on the count of three."

"Wait!" Barry squinted into the distance. "Someone's comin'."

"Probably just an old farmer."

"Better hold off, just in case."

Half a minute later, the game warden pulled up.

They looked at each other.

"Hello, men."

"Warden." He was from Seymour, and none of the four could remember his name.

"You fellas wouldn't be huntin' from the back of this truck, would you?"

"No sir," Mike answered. "Just a little target practice." He pointed at the bottle.

The game warden looked across the road at the bottle and the splintered post beside it. "Your aim seems to be a little off. And those fence posts aren't cheap."

"Yes sir."

He walked over and peered in the truck bed.

"How 'bout a Coke?" Barry suggested.

"No, thanks. I gotta get going. But I *am* going to have to tell the sheriff about this."

They looked at each other again.

"You are?"

"Yep." He then took their names. "Well, so long, fellas."

Once he was gone, Gary hopped off the truck.

"You think he'll really tell Claude?"

Mike opened another Orange Crush. "I just hope he don't tell Coach. I believe I'd rather go to jail."

They all laughed, grabbed their guns, and together blew the bottle to smithereens. Then they jumped in the truck and sped away leaving a trail of dust in their wake.

A few days later, Gary spotted the sheriff at the diner. Claude walked over, smiled, winked, and said, "Hello, hoodlum."

"Hello, Sheriff," he replied, his nervousness fading. Until . . .

"I want you to round up Oliver and Stewart and be at my house Saturday evening at six. We've got somethin' to discuss."

"Yes sir. Will do," he answered, his nervousness returning.

Fifteen minutes early on Saturday, the three stood at the Morrison's front door and knocked, not knowing what to expect—Barry had been tight-lipped about the whole thing. The game warden's Jeep was nowhere in sight.

Patsy Morrison answered and ushered them into a house full of the best smell they'd ever smelled. Claude came around the corner.

"Fellas, if you're gonna hunt birds, you need to learn to do it right."

They then sat down to a dinner of all the fried quail, mashed potatoes, biscuits and gravy they could eat. And iced tea.

At Claude's request, they were done shooting fence posts.

On Monday morning, as was their habit, each player glanced up at the Goof-Off Squad blackboard upon entering the dressing room, hoping to find it blank. Today, a single name stared back. *Tepfer.*

Steve Parsley walked over. "Well, looky here. Which one of you two finally screwed up and got caught?"

Unsure, Gary looked over at his younger brother.

Throwing his shoes into his locker in disgust, Robert replied, "You're lookin' at him."

"Whose handwritin' is that?"

"Mine."

"You wrote your own name up there?" Steve laughed.

"Yep. He's gonna find out sooner or later, if Mrs. Crowley hasn't already told him."

"What'd you do?" his buddy, Gary Johnston, wanted to know.

"I never read that book she told us to."

"You didn't?"

"Nope. I told her I prefer fiction and don't *like* readin' non-fiction. If I did, I'd read the newspaper."

The room rocked with laughter.

Steve wasn't done. "Yeah, well, that blackboard up there's about as real as it gets. Trust me."

More laughter.

Three hours later, Robert's reading preference did indeed come back to bite him.

"All right, guys. Hit the showers. Tepfer! On the goal line!"

Half an hour later, he was hanging on Grady's every word.

"I talked to Mary Lee. She's agreed to let you read somethin' else, but when you're done you have to give an oral report in front of the class."

That wasn't good. He despised having to talk in class. Hated it.

"You listenin'?"

He stared at the goalpost at the far end of the field. It looked a mile away. Farther.

"We can do some more if needed."

"No sir. Thank you. That's great."
"All right. And don't let it happen again. You hear me?"
"Yes sir.
"Now get goin'!"

CHAPTER 17

Finding Their Way

Summer had been particularly dry that year and despite the coaches diligently dragging sprinklers up and down the field for weeks on end, the field at the stadium had not recovered from the county rodeo and grass was sparse. But the players weren't worried about the rock-hard ground as much as the leftover shards of glass from broken beer bottles. *Those* could hurt. On September 6, the Wildcats opened the season in Archer City before a large crowd, survived the less-than-ideal playing conditions, and defeated the Class B Valley View Warriors 19-0. The home team's defense was stellar, allowing the visitors to move pass the 50-yard line just once.

A week later, the Electra Tigers came to town and defeated the Wildcats 26-0. The game was close until the fourth quarter when Electra scored twice.

The Olney Cubs handed Archer City its second straight defeat 20-15 the next week. The loss was particularly heartbreaking since the Wildcats dominated the game and led all statistical categories but still lost.

Leading 8-7 at Knox City the following week, Grady knew they stood at an important juncture in the team's season and his four-year plan. With two consecutive losses and district play beginning the next week, the game's second half was paramount. At intermission, he explained all this to the players by saying it would definitely be in their best interest to win the game, *if* they valued their health and well-being. In what would prove to be a big stepping stone in the evolution of the Archer City Wildcats, they scored four times in the second half and won 33-14.

Then a curious thing happened. They continued winning.

Fans had been hoping for improvement from the team over last season. Grady had been demanding it. Suddenly, they got it.

Cross-county rival Holliday was their first district opponent. The Eagles had won nine of their last ten meetings, including a 33-6 walloping the year before. But not this time.

Archer City blasted the Eagles 48-8 with their only score coming against the Wildcat reserves late in the game. The victory was costly, however, as starting quarterback Barry Morrison went down with a knee injury and was lost for the season.

He was replaced the next week by senior Donnie Linscott, and under the direction of their new signal-caller, the team secured their fourth win of the season, eclipsing the previous year's total of three, by defeating Paducah 41-0 despite losing three starters shortly before halftime. Heading back to the huddle, senior John Rutherford and sophomore Robert Tepfer heard some shouting and turned to see junior end Ray Bussey entangled with a couple of Dragons. They immediately went to his aid, pulling the three apart, Robert throwing in a solid uppercut for good measure—one he thought was delivered out of sight of the officials but was mistaken. The three Wildcat players were promptly ejected from the game, along with the two adversaries.

Not surprisingly, on Monday they found themselves staring up at their names on the Goof-Off Squad blackboard. Then, following practice, as expected, "Gentlemen, line up on the goal line."

After twenty additional agonizing 100-yard sprints, the coach blew his whistle.

"Boys, I don't mind you settlin' your differences with other players, but do it blockin' and tacklin' next time."

"Yes sir."

"I don't *ever* wanna see you gettin' tossed out of another game. That clear?"

"Yes sir."

"Get a shower."

They turned and headed away before he could change his mind, thankful they only had to run and had been spared duck-walking or worse. Fighting, evidently, was one of the lesser evils.

"Thanks, Bussey."

"Yeah, Bussey. Thanks a *lot*."

"I didn't need your help."

"Yeah, right. What the heck were you guys fightin' about anyway?"

Ray thought for a moment.

"Beats me."

A few overly scrappy Wildcats were the least of Grady's worries. Already plagued by two painful calcium deposits on his shoulders, fullback Gary Tepfer awoke Saturday morning with an even more painful one in his thigh. By Monday it had worsened. Despite his determination and toughness, number 74 would be sharing playing time with Barney Oliver at fullback. On defense, Parsley would have to help out at linebacker.

With two important district wins under their belts, the Wildcats made it three against Crowell who also had not lost a district contest. Pitching their second straight shutout, Archer City prevailed 13-0.

Up next was a bye week—a time when most teams rested up and healed. Not the Wildcats. If anything, workouts picked up. So did the running, and when their game with Chillicothe finally arrived, they were thankful. They rolled over the Eagles who, the week before, had defeated Crowell by a score of 46-0. For the third game in a row, the Wildcats' fierce, hard-hitting defense did not allow a point. The offense was equally impressive, scoring over forty points for the third time.

Then, in one of their finest games of the year, they traveled to Munday and defeated the defending district champions

27-6 behind 306 yards rushing. Suddenly, with one game remaining, Archer City sat atop the district standings along with Henrietta with five wins and no losses. Next week, the two would meet for the championship. Grady's team, who'd won one game their first year and three the past year, was ahead of schedule.

CHAPTER 18

The Big Game

Halfway through the pep rally on Friday, Billy Pitts was hurting. The sunlight filtering through the gym windows and the band's loud numbers had nearly done him in. When the celebration was over, he barely managed to make it to the locker room before throwing up—his migraine in full tilt. Since it wasn't his first, Grady recognized his symptoms and phoned Billy's mother, asking her to take him to see Dr. Schlomach, which she did. Later, as the time neared to board the bus, Billy hadn't returned so Grady drove to the Pitts's home.

From his bed, in a stupor from the suppository he'd been prescribed, the ill teen faintly heard his mom and Grady talking at the front door.

"No sir. He's sick, and he's not going to play."

"But we need him in the game."

"No sir. Sorry."

For a moment there was silence, and Billy fully expected to see his bedroom door suddenly fly open and Grady grab him and drag him to his car. Instead, he heard the front door softly close.

It was the first time Billy could remember anyone standing up to Coach Graves the way she had. Surprisingly, the repercussions he feared never materialized.

Grady wasn't happy about the situation, but he knew Billy had mettle and would have been there if could. He left it at that.

Two hours later, in their biggest game in decades, the Archer City Wildcats took the field before a packed home stadium of some three thousand fans. Grady's game plan was simple: Get Gene Franklin.

Gene Franklin was a man among boys. Big. Fast. Strong. And tough. Real tough. Rumors had his actual age at twenty-five, but this had not been confirmed. One thing *was* certain: He was a handful, and most thought Archer had no chance against him much less the rest of the Bearcats. Something had to be done, and that job was given to Barney Oliver.

Per Grady's instructions, the Wildcats would run 27 Belly on their first play from scrimmage—halfback off tackle—and Barney, subbing at fullback for the injured Gary, was to disregard his usual blocking assignment, find Franklin, and put him on the ground. Hard. Less than a minute into the game, he set about his task only to discover Mr. Franklin was waiting for him.

The collision was felt and heard throughout Archer County, and is still talked about today. For the longest time, neither player got up. Finally, Gene struggled to his feet. Smiling. Barney remained down until being examined by Archer City's Dr. Schlomach who was summoned from the stands. Eventually, he was helped to the sideline.

A short while later, he returned to the field.

"You okay, big fella?" Mike asked.

"Yeah. What play are we runnin'?"

"We're not. We're on defense. You sure you're okay?"

Barney and the Wildcats managed to survive Gene Franklin and the Bearcats that day, but not where it counted most. On the scoreboard.

Henrietta led 8-0 at the beginning of the fourth quarter, and with 6:02 remaining they scored again, taking the district crown 16-0. The Wildcats' final season record, seven wins and three losses, was the best recorded by an Archer City team in years and had brought their followers great enjoyment. Three years after Grady's arrival, the Wildcats were winning. He still had his staunch detractors, but the others couldn't wait till next year. Neither could he.

On the last day of the school year, just moments before the final bell, he asked principal J. B. Adams to summon the seven young men who would be playing their final season the next year to the first floor Music Room. Laughing and joking, they jostled into the tiny classroom to find coaches Graves, Ray, and Williams awaiting. The laughing and joking halted.

"Take a seat, guys," Grady instructed.

They did as they were told.

"Men, the three of us coaches attended a slew of play-off games following the season, and here's what we came away with." He paused, looking at each. "There is not a reason in the world we can't win the state championship next year. Not one."

No one moved or spoke.

Had they heard him right?

"So we want you to go home and think about that this off-season. You hear?"

Still in shock, there were some muffled *yes sirs.*

"Okay. We'll see you men next school year. Enjoy your summer."

In total silence, the seven walked out without ever hearing the bell. Once outside, they stopped and looked at each other. Steve Parsley asked the all-important question.

"You, uh, think he knows what the hell he's talkin' about?"

No one had an answer.

PART FOUR

GLOOM

CHAPTER 19

High Hopes

'CATS BEGIN DRILLS FOR GRID SEASON
Thirty-one boys have signed up for the 1964 Wildcat football team. Two-a-day workouts are scheduled to begin next week.

Barry Morrison, one of the area's best passers, has fully recovered from last season's knee injury and will be directing the offense in his fourth year at that position. He is joined in the backfield by veteran runners Mike Stewart and Gary Tepfer. Morrison also has two top-notch veteran receivers at ends—Ray Bussey and Barney Oliver. Bussey, however, will likely miss the first few games due to recent surgery on one foot. Sophomore Billy Holder will start in the backfield as well and could see action as Morrison's backup at quarterback. Grady Graves is also blessed with a veteran offensive line in the likes of center Billy Pitts, guards Robert Tepfer and Bobby Hammontree, and tackles Buddy Knox and Butch Hannah and a tough defense that showed great improvement last year. When all's said and done, the Wildcats should give defending district champion Henrietta a run for their money this time around. The Bearcats, Wildcat fans will remember, beat Archer City in the last game of the 1963 season, 16-0 for the title.

Head coach Grady Graves stated, "Well, once again, we're not very big and we're not very fast, but I think the boys will play hard. If they do, and we can avoid any additional injuries, we should be respectable." (Archer County News)

1964 ARCHER CITY WILDCATS SCHEDULE

Date	Opponent	Location
Sept. 4	Nocona	Away
Sept. 11	Electra	Home
Sept. 18	Olney	Home
Sept. 25	Open Date	
Oct. 2	Henrietta*	Away
Oct. 9	Holliday*	Away
Oct. 16	Paducah*	Away
Oct. 23	Crowell*	Home
Oct. 30	Throckmorton	Away
Nov. 6	Knox City*	Home
Nov. 13	Munday*	Home

* District Game
All games begin @ 7:30 P.M.

CHAPTER 20

Swivel Hips

When halfback Mike Stewart carried the ball, he bent his body in fourteen different directions. Or so it seemed. In reality, by the start of his junior year, he had perfected the move used by NFL great Elroy "Crazy Legs" Hirsch of the Los Angeles Rams. The result: an astounding 7.3 yards per carry average, the attention of college scouts, and a letter to Grady from head coach Darrell Royal of the University of Texas Longhorns wanting to know if he thought Mike was suited to the college game given his size.

His teammates called him "Swivel Hips" Stewart—albeit not always affectionately. Opposing teams, it seems, weren't the only ones who couldn't get him down, and that made for some long tackling drills. During one such extended session, Mike was returning punts along the sideline. The tacklers were instructed to use the sideline, cut him off, and make the tackle. Unable to get the good, solid hits Grady was looking for, they continued until finally, exhausted on the bottom of the pile, Mike whispered, "Dadgum, guys. You're wearin' me out. Just remember, no matter what my hips do, I always go to the right."

With his senior year at hand, the talented youngster had the world by the tail and Wildcat fans harboring high hopes. This was, after all, the final season in Grady's four-year plan, and the team had improved every year, coming ever so close the year before. They could almost taste the victory of a district championship.

And then Mike slid into third base.

He, Barry, and Ray played Connie Mack League baseball for neighboring Windthorst during the summer (Archer

City didn't have a team), and late in the last game of the season at Spudder Park in Wichita Falls, Mike stood on second base with visions of stealing third. Midway through the pitcher's windup, he took off, raced down, slid hard beating the catcher's throw, hung a cleat on the bag, and heard something pop. He climbed to his feet, felt some soreness in his right knee, and continued the game. Over the next few weeks, his knee repeatedly swelled up, ached, and after a few days, eventually recovered. No way was he going to tell Grady about hurting it playing baseball. That would not be good. Rather, he'd just tough it out. And he did so until the afternoon of the first two-a-day practice of the season. On an end sweep, he got hit high and low and his right knee exploded.

He was helped from the field, and Dr. Schlomach was consulted. He recommended a specialist in Wichita Falls who gave them the bad news: a tremendous amount of torn cartilage requiring surgery. Knowing the Oil Bowl high school all-star game was coming up later that week in Wichita Falls and that esteemed head trainer Elmer Brown of Texas Christian University usually worked the game, Grady carried Mike to the Oil Bowl workouts for Brown's suggestion of a method for taping the knee so Mike could play. The two watched closely as six rolls of tape were carefully applied, stretching from his ankle to his hip. "This is only a temporary fix," they were told, "and it will have to be re-taped often."

"When?" Mike asked.

Elmer smiled. "You'll know. Trust me."

A steel brace was also recommended.

Returning home, it was a while before either spoke. Finally, Grady looked over.

"Whatta you think? Can you go?"

"Sure. Coach, after all we've been through the past three years, I'm not about to miss out on the party."

"Good," Grady answered. "That's real good."

And with that, he sped up.

It didn't take long to find that even with the tape job and brace, the knee would eventually work itself back out at which time Mike would go down in a flash of burning pain and have to be helped to the sideline where the brace and tape would have to be removed, the knee worked back into place, re-taped, and re-braced so he could go again.

The decision was made to limit him to offense for the most part. He and junior Mickey Horany would take turns shuttling plays in, and Mike would continue to hold on extra points and field goals. He would not play at all on defense—unless a critical situation were to arise. And finally, he would not be required much participation in workouts.

This bothered him the most because Grady, in four years, had not mellowed one iota, and workouts were what they had always been—pure hell. Grady hadn't backed off them even a little. And the running—so much running. Missing all that didn't hurt Mike's feelings the least little bit, but he felt bad for his teammates. If any were pissed at him, he would've understood. But they weren't. They knew he was hurt, and what he was sacrificing for the team.

Number 35's patented "dead leg" move for faking would-be tacklers out of their jocks was now, after all, exactly that.

CHAPTER 21

Triple Whammy

Mike Stewart wasn't the only player to fall victim to baseball that year. In the next-to-last game of the season, running out a grounder, Ray Bussey hit first base wrong and the top half of his foot went up—the bottom half down. Previously broken during basketball season, his cast had gotten wet and the foot had never healed properly. The subsequent break was even worse, requiring surgery in which a piece of bone taken from his hip was used to splice his foot back together. He would miss all of two-a-days and likely the first few games.

Grady Graves had never put much stock in old wives' tales and the such. Like, for instance, the adage that bad things always come in threes. But he was beginning to wonder.

Then, one week later in a preseason scrimmage against Decatur, Grady lost his third starter—junior guard Bobby Hammontree to a severe concussion. After discussions with doctors, his parents decided he would not return for the remainder of the year. The Wildcats hadn't played a game, and everything was going to hell in a handbasket.

On Monday of the following week, Grady sat preoccupied in the school lunchroom staring up. It took a moment to realize what it was he was staring at. *Wet, wadded-up napkins stuck on the ceiling.* He stood.

"Okay, who's responsible?" he asked, motioning.

All eyes turned upward. No one spoke.

"You've got five minutes, or you're *all* gonna pay." He walked outside.

All eyes turned toward sophomore Buddy Knox.

"Come on, Knox, tell him!"

"Yeah! We're all tired of runnin' cause of you!"

Grady returned. "Well?"

After several nervous seconds, Buddy slowly raised his hand.

"It was me, Coach."

Grady glared at him for a good ten seconds. Then, "Naw. It couldn't a been you, Knox." And out the door he went.

That afternoon, Grady moved Buddy Knox from his tackle position into Hammontree's vacated guard spot. Jimmy Reeves took Knox's place. Curiosities of sorts, Reeves, Knox, and starting tackle Butch Hannah had shown up at two-a-days as freshmen the previous year, and Grady hadn't given them a minute's notice. They were clearly fun-lovin' good ol' boys who didn't take anything seriously—not work, not school, and certainly not football. He figured they'd last a day. A week at the most. He was wrong. They were somethin' else, too—tough boogers. And while he was pretty sure beer drinking was one of their pastimes, he'd yet to catch them at it. In the meantime, they'd become pretty good ball players. Hannah could block like nobody's business when he wanted to, and the starting middle guard Reeves, could flat tear up a center. Like Stewart, he always had a smile on his face, but his was a bit more mischievous. It was not uncommon to see Jimmy's fist come up out of a big pileup on the field and then down on some poor unsuspecting soul. Every Friday, Coach Williams would ask Grady, "Coach, you gonna let Reeves outta his cage tonight?" And they'd laugh.

So his offensive line, although somewhat inexperienced, was set. Maybe things would work out after all. Now, if only nothing else came up.

No such luck. An hour into practice, trouble reared its ugly head still again. Gary Tepfer got up from a hard tackle limping. Grady called him over.

"You okay?"

"Yes sir."

"You don't look it."

"I'm good."

Grady nodded and sent him back in. Until now, it appeared the painful calcium deposit in Gary's thigh that plagued him last season had healed. Evidently it hadn't. He'd already outfitted the boy with special pads to better protect the two calcium deposits in his shoulders left over from the previous season—the large, oversized shoulder pads making him look bigger than he was. And now his leg problem was back. That meant Barney would again have to share time with him at fullback, and he needed Barney at end.

If it wasn't one thing it was another. Finally, he'd had all he could take.

Whistle. Loud.

"Holder! Whatta you think you're doin'?"

His gifted sophomore running back snapped to attention. "Sir?"

"Where is that play designed to go?"

"Up the middle, sir."

"Then would you mind tellin' me, and everybody else, why you're intent on goin' around end?" Grady was furious, and everyone knew it.

"The hole was plugged, sir."

"I don't give a rat's you-know-what if it was plugged. You hit it! *You hear me?!* I want you runnin' right up Pitts's crack!"

"Yes sir."

"You haven't run that play right yet. Probably heard somebody say 'Man, that Holder kid is fast' and think you can outrun everybody wide every time you touch the ball. Well, son, I've got news for you. You can't! And if you haven't figured this out by now, let me remind you that in three-down territory, we only have to make three and a half yards a play. In four-down territory, we only need two and a half. We don't need you tryin' to make sixty. You hear me?"

"Yes sir."

"Then quit pussy-footin' around and RUN IT RIGHT!"

"Yes sir!"

On the ensuing plays, Billy did as instructed: took the handoff and ran crashing into Billy Pitts's backside. Time after time. Finally, in the huddle, the quiet lineman spoke up.

"Billy, I think Coach means for you to run just off my butt to one side or the other."

"Nope. He told me to run up your crack, and that's what I'm gonna do."

The Pitts volcano was just about to blow when the whistle blew, saving the young running back added misery.

Everyone stopped what they were doing and gave Grady their undivided attention. He, too, was about to explode, and they knew it.

For a full minute, he stared at the ground, his jaw muscles working feverishly. When he finally spoke, it wasn't the tongue lashing they were expecting. It was worse.

"Line up on the goal line."

CHAPTER 22

The Houseguest

An hour and a half later, having showered and dressed, Gary Tepfer was having difficulty even tying his shoes. The thigh injury and the brutal workout together had nearly done him in. He looked up to see Grady staring at him.

"What's this I hear about you flying the coop?"

The story Grady had gotten was that Gary and Boyd McMahon were not seeing eye-to-eye. Gary was apparently intent on risking staying out past curfew with his cheerleader girlfriend Jodie Wright, and his stepdad was dead-set against it. When Boyd laid down the law, Gary left.

The fullback managed a nervous *yes sir* and prepared for the worst.

Grady studied him for a moment and then replied, "Well, if you need a place to stay, we have an extra bedroom." And with that, he left.

Surprising everyone, Gary accepted the offer, knowing his late nights would end, but feeling it beat going home. Upon arriving, he was immediately welcomed with open arms. This way, Grady could keep a close eye on his prize full-back.

"Come on in, Gary. You know my wife Gay, don't you?"

"Yes sir. How are you, Ma'am?"

"Fine, Gary. Glad to have you with us."

"Thank you, Ma'am. Thanks for havin' me."

"Honey, I'm going to give Gary a tour of the house."

"You two go right ahead." Gary followed Grady into the kitchen.

"Okay, son, here's where Gay will prepare our meals. You'll be expected to eat with the two us at the dinner table each morning and evening, and here's the sink where you'll be washing the dishes." Grady next entered the utility room.

"This is the laundry room where you'll be washing and ironing your own clothes as well as your bedspread, sheets, and towels." They continued down the hall.

"This will be your bathroom. As you can see, it's spotless and will be kept that way." A bedroom was next.

"And this is your room. Of course, you'll keep the bed made and the room orderly as it is now. You'll be allowed some time out after supper each evening but will be expected to return by eight for homework purposes. Lights out at ten sharp. Any questions?"

Gary didn't know where to start. So he didn't.

The new tenant lasted four days.

Following his return home, the Wildcats scrimmaged Valley View during which time the runaway was having a rough time carrying the ball—especially to the right side where his younger brother played guard. Robert was still upset with his older brother for leaving home and refused to block for him. As a result, number 74 was getting creamed. Finally Coach Williams walked over to the younger Tepfer.

"What's the matter with you? Don't you love your brother? You should."

Talk about hitting a tender spot. *Of course he loved his brother.*

On the next snap, with tears streaming down his face, Robert blocked the poor soul across from him thirty yards downfield following the whistle. On his way back to the huddle, Gary was waiting for him.

"It's about time. You were killin' me."

"You deserved it."

"Maybe. But I've paid my dues."

"How so?"

"Livin' with Coach Graves for four days. That's how!"

With Gary's situation resolved, the last week of two-a-days was fairly uneventful in Grady's eyes. In the players' eyes, however, the final ten workouts were anything but uneventful. With daytime temperatures well into the hundreds, the week felt like one long near-death experience. As practice was drawing to a close on Friday, John O'Donohue and the other freshmen were counting their blessings. They were only an hour or so away from surviving the ordeal, and could rest easy as Grady's attention and wrath were currently focused on Mr. Parsley.

"We're gonna be here all night if you don't start puttin' out. *You hear me?* Now get down there, shed those blockers, and make the dadgum tackle!"

Then it came.

"O'DONOHUE!!"

John looked up to find Grady glaring at him.

"Since you clearly aren't too interested in what's going on, get your butt over here and take Horany's place carryin' the ball."

Oh my gosh.

The tall freshman buckled his helmet and trotted over.

Grady wasn't done with Steve. He knelt down beside him and with his face only inches away, let him have it.

"Wanna quit? That's what you do, isn't it? Quit when the goin' gets tough? Walk away. Take the easy way out. Well, we're waitin', tough guy."

John studied the look on Steve's face and quickly determined this was exactly the wrong place to be, at exactly the wrong time.

Grady slapped Parsley's helmet, stood, pitched John the ball, and blew his whistle.

Just as he feared, Steve had had enough. He fired out low and hard, splitting the double-team block, planted his helmet in O'Donohue's chest, and drove him backwards, upwards, and down. Hard.

John struggled to his feet just as the whistle blew again.

"That's more like it. Okay, everybody line up on the goal line!"

For the next twenty minutes, the lanky freshman lagged farther and farther behind on each sprint, and Grady was getting madder and madder. Finally, at the opposite end of the field, where Coach Ray was standing, he hobbled over.

"Coach, I'm dying here. I think my leg's broken."

Fuzzy took one look, and the two headed for the locker room, then to see Dr. Schlomach. Afterwards, he took the youngster home, his leg in a cast. Upon returning to the gym, Grady and Roy were waiting.

"He's done," he told them, plopping down in his office chair. "But he wants to stay on as a trainer."

Grady nodded. "That's fine. Anybody who can run on a broken leg oughta be able to wash clothes."

CHAPTER 23

The Shakeup

WILDCATS FACE TOUGH INDIANS IN OPENER

The Archer City Wildcats will face a man-sized task Friday night when they open their 1964 gridiron season by tackling the highly rated Nocona Indians.

Class 2-A Nocona, loser of only one game last season, is blessed with many returning starters from last year's squad. On paper, the Wildcats are lacking in experience, depth, and size. However, the contest should prove interesting.

Unlike most coaches who pass the proverbial "crying towel," we've not heard a peep from head coach Grady Graves despite the fact at least three starters will not see action. These include end Ray Bussey, tailback Mike Stewart, and guard Bobby Hammontree, who has been lost for the season. Senior Fullback Gary Tepfer, still hampered by the thigh injury that sidelined him much of last year, will likely share time at fullback with Barney Oliver.

All in all, look for the Wildcats to play hard. (Archer County News)

At week's end, the bus pulled into the Nocona High School stadium parking lot and squeaked to a stop. Before the players could rise, Grady stood, turned, and faced them. There was something strangely different about their coach.

"You seniors have worked three years for this. Three hard years." Suddenly, his voice began to crack. The players snuck glances at each other. "I appreciate all your hard work. All of you. I've never seen anyone work as hard." The tough disciplinarian's eyes began to fill. "This is gonna be our year. I just know it. Your hard work is gonna pay off." He then abruptly turned and left the bus. Fuzzy and Roy exchanged glances and then followed. The players sat in silence, not believing what they'd just witnessed. After a moment, they rose and began filing off the bus. Usually this was accompanied by shouting and cheering. Tonight, not a word was spoken.

In the locker room, Grady remained quiet. A typical silent treatment meant he was especially mad. Infuriated. Not so this time. Still shaken by his show of emotion, the team took the field somewhat subdued.

Their play that night reflected it. The Indians amassed 257 total yards to their 130. The Wildcats turned the ball over three times and had only four first downs in the contest. Were it not for two turnovers, several penalties, and other miscues by the Indians, the score would have been much higher than the final 14-0.

Not the start they had intended. At Monday's practice, the Grady they all knew returned. With some surprises.

"Knox! You're movin' back to tackle. Get over here!" Grady hesitated before continuing. There was still time to change his mind. Then . . . "Parsley! Get in there at guard."

Steve looked over at Coach Williams and smiled. Since his return last year, he'd been asking him, "What do I have to do to start?" And Roy's answer was always the same. "Just keep playin' tough." Still, he was surprised at Grady's decision. Several players were.

Then came the real shocker.

"Morrison! End! Holder! Quarterback!"

For a moment, neither moved.

"You heard me!"

In a daze, Barry Morrison moved to the end position. He hadn't played well Friday, but no one had. One game into his senior year, he'd lost his starting quarterback position.

The young Holder took his place. Grady walked over to the huddle.

"Think you can run this offense?"

"Yes sir."

"Then do it."

For Barry, the next hour was a blur of getting over the shock of not being the quarterback. But practices following losses were notorious for being particularly long and brutal, and this one was no exception. Before it was over, his concern about playing end was gone. Survival mattered more.

When game time arrived on Friday, Grady still hadn't spoken a word to Barry about his losing his position. Strangely, he appeared to still be a team captain accompanying Gary and Barney to midfield for the coin toss at their say-so without any repercussions. He told himself there was no reason to be embarrassed about playing end, but he was. Right now, football just wasn't fun. Then again, it hadn't been much fun the past three and a half years.

In the dressing room, Grady handed out his normal butt-chewing—his one and only sentimental speech of the week before long forgotten. His message this time was clear.

"You get out there and beat these guys. Or else!"

With that, a fired up bunch hit the field and never looked back. After receiving the opening kickoff, under Holder's direction, they drove 54 yards to the Electra Tigers' five-yard line where, on fourth down, Holder lofted a pass too high for Morrison, who managed to tip it into the hands of Gary Tepfer. Touchdown. 7-0.

On the Wildcats' third possession, the home crowd stood and cheered as Mike Stewart took the field for the first time that season. Most questioned Grady's decision to use him this early, especially since this wasn't a district game. One wrong hit on his bad knee, and he could be lost for good. He checked into the huddle, smiling as always.

"Coach said I'm supposed to carry the ball."

Billy smiled. "Okay, then. How about 27 Belly?"

"Sounds good. Oh, and he said I better not get hit or you linemen are toast."

Buddy Knox looked up. "He really say that?"

"Naw. But block anyway, okay?"

Most were still laughing as they lined up and fired out at the snap.

Behind a tremendous block by Parsley, who personally dispensed with two defenders, the gimpy tailback shot through the huge hole, took off down the middle of the field, and went 68 yards for a touchdown. The Archer City crowd went crazy. A run by Holder for two points failed, and Archer led by 13. The score held until halftime.

The Tigers regrouped at intermission and came fighting back. After receiving the second-half kickoff, behind the running of their speedy quarterback Davy Baker, they drove down to the Archer City six. But the Wildcat defense stiffened and held on downs.

From there they drove 94 yards the other way with Stewart plunging over from the one. A halfback pass from Horany fell incomplete, and the score was 19-0. A scoreless fourth quarter followed, and the Wildcats had their first win of the year.

Steve Parsley turned in a good game on offense, blocking flawlessly in his first start. Coming off the bench on defense, he was even better—intercepting one pass, recovering a fumble, and clogging things up in the Electra backfield on almost every play. A one-man wrecking crew. In the papers, Grady credited the victory to a 100 percent team effort. No mention was made of the Rebel. None was expected.

CHAPTER 24

KA-BOOM!

"Whadda you think?"

L.J. Cathey shook his head. "It ain't loud enough."

Monroe Williams removed his cigar, spit, and replaced it. "You're right. If it's gonna look like a cannon, it oughta sound like one."

The piece of oilfield pipe mounted atop a pair of old wagon wheels looked like a cannon all right, and it was loud. But as far as they were concerned, they hadn't set out to build the thing half-ass. So they removed the twelve-gauge shotgun mounted inside the pipe, returned it to its owner, Johnny Lincscott, and hauled the contraption out to the Burns Petroleum yard. As they pulled in, Clyde Thomas came walking out.

"Monroe. L.J. What can I do for you?"

"This piss ant thing ain't loud enough."

Clyde looked it over. "How does it work?"

"Well, right now it don't. We were usin' a shotgun but took it out. Got any ideas?"

"How loud you want it?"

Monroe smiled and said, "Clyde, we want people to sit up and pay attention when the 'Cats take the field."

Clyde grinned, turned, and said, "Follow me."

They followed him into the welding shop where he drilled out a 5-foot length of 6-inch diameter solid steel. Near one end, he drilled a small hole through to the big one.

"There you go. Some black powder, newspaper, somethin' to pack it in with, a match to light it with, and you're all set."

The three of them smiled, removed the existing pipe and replaced it with their new barrel, then rolled it outside.

"Just don't shoot it off around here."

Monroe and L.J. laughed, shook Clyde's hand, and headed back to Monroe's house with their new toy. After rummaging through his shop, Monroe appeared with a can of gunpowder. Carefully, the two poured some into the small hole and then stuffed wadded up newspapers into the end using an oilfield sucker rod. After carefully aiming it away from any houses or vehicles, they lit it.

KA-BOOM!

Windows and loose metal rattled up and down the street for what seemed like minutes. Neighbors ran into their yards peering up at the sky. Occasionally the training jets from nearby Shepherd Air Force Base would fly low overhead causing a ruckus, but this was the loudest sonic boom yet. Through the dense smoke cloud, the culprits looked wide-eyed at each other and laughed.

"Now we're talkin'!"

Going into their contest Friday night, the Wildcats now had a new weapon in their arsenal. But the Olney Cubs had something even more powerful.

Pinky Palmer.

At the weekly Quarterback Club meeting, Grady told it like it was.

"Well, they're big. And Pinky Palmer is a load. Cub coach Don Williams says he's as good as anybody he's ever had, and he's had All-America Jim Grisham and Texas's Harold Phillip. He describes Palmer as 'unstoppable', and I can't argue with that.

"As far as us, Holder sprained his ankle against Electra and again in practice this week, but he'll still start at quarterback. Bussey might see some action, but he's nowhere near 100 percent. And, of course, neither is Stewart. And Tepfer's got a sprained ankle left over from Friday's game and a sore thigh. All in all, it doesn't look too good, but our kids will do their best, and at the final buzzer they'll still be giving their best effort."

That Friday night, sporting a freshly painted barrel and the likeness of a wildcat on each of its large wheels courtesy of Archer City artist Jimmy Powell, the Wildcat cannon—christened "Big Champ"—sat in a corner of the field just beyond the east end zone. Everyone entering the stadium noticed and commented on the 'Cats' new "mascot," but by the time the teams were preparing to run onto the field just prior to kickoff, most had completely forgotten about it. Then, just as the Wildcats took the field, L.J. lit the fuse.

The ensuing *KA-BOOM!* shook the stadium, setting off a frenzy of screams, dropped soft drinks, wide-eyed stares, and crying children. Once it was determined the stadium had not been rocked by a natural gas line explosion or plane crash, there was some nervous laughter and then cheers from the Archer City fans who also had just experienced the cannon for the first time.

It was the last time they would have anything to celebrate that evening.

Archer City took the opening kickoff and quickly moved to midfield. From there Gary Tepfer carried for four yards to the Cubs' 46-yard line where he was promptly hit by a truck allowed on the playing field. Groggily, he was helped to his feet by Palmer.

"You best stay on your own end of the field, you hear?"

The Wildcat fullback turned and, still dazed, headed toward the huddle. Once there, he let his feelings be known.

"There oughta be a law against freaks like him playin' safety and roamin' around free back there like that. He oughta be playin' someplace else. Like college."

"I heard he's goin' to Baylor," Mike offered.

"That don't help *us*, 'less he plans on goin' tonight."

"Why don't we pass the ball?" tackle Butch Hannah suggested.

Ends Barry Morrison and Barney Oliver looked at each other.

Barry gave the tackle a friendly shove. "Don't be givin' Billy any crazy ideas."

Billy shook his head. "Can't. It's fourth down."

"Great. Now we get to try and tackle *him*."

After punting the ball away, the Wildcats managed to hold Olney and force a punt themselves. Pinky Palmer uncorked a 66-yarder that sailed over the heads of the Wildcat return men and rolled to a stop at the Archer City five-yard line. After Stewart gained four yards, there was a mixup in the backfield, and the Wildcats elected to quick-kick on third down. The ploy backfired as Cub halfback Jeff Jackson raced back, retrieved the ball, and returned it 40 yards for a touchdown. The PAT failed.

Moving nearly at will, the Cubs scored the next three times they had the ball: Palmer on a two-yard plunge, quarterback Richard Tomlinson from three yards out, and Jackson again on a 20-yard pass reception. The halftime score was 27-0.

CHAPTER 25

Not Pretty

Following intermission and a dose of the silent treatment from Grady, a weary Wildcat team headed out for the second half. Most had rather have taken a tongue lashing than have the head coach not say a word. They knew that meant he was furious and likely already planning Monday's practice in his head. They had better do something and do it quick.

On Olney's first possession, Billy Holder picked off an errant pass and returned it to the Archer City 49-yard line. From there they drove all the way down to the Cub 20. However, the next four plays netted a minus four yards, and the Cubs took over on their 24. Seventeen plays and 76 yards later, halfback Joe Pearce hit pay dirt from five yards out, the kick was good, and Archer trailed 34-0.

Following the kickoff, the Wildcats took over deep in their own territory. On the sideline, Jimmy Reeves walked over to trainer David Wright.

"I cut my fingers."

"Whatta you mean you cut your fingers?"

He held his hand up. The web between the first two fingers was split open so deeply the forefinger was lying against his thumb.

"You darn sure did."

"Yeah. I got stepped on. I think it was Palmer."

David led him over to Coach Graves and said, "Coach, Jimmy's cut his fingers."

"Cut his fingers?"

"Yes sir. It's pretty bad. There's a deep split between 'em."

Grady glanced down at the gaping hole and said, "Well, stick some gauze in it and tape 'em together. We'll get him stitched up after the game."

"Yes sir."

"Bussey!"

At the far end of the bench, Ray was busy enjoying the cheerleaders and baton twirlers.

Freshman Mike Atchley nudged him. "I think Coach is callin' you."

"BUSSEY!"

The startled senior ran over three freshmen and a sophomore on his way to Grady.

"Yes sir?"

"How's your foot?"

"Well . . ."

"Get in there for Morrison."

Without hesitation, the nervous and still sore-footed end took off across the field to some cheers and hit the huddle energized.

"Barry, you're out. All right, guys! Let's go! Let's get a Cub! Let's go!"

"Bussey! Will you shut up? You haven't been out here all night like we have."

"Throw him a pass and see what he thinks then."

"Yeah. Over the middle."

"Why? He won't catch it."

"Butterfingers!"

"Come on, guys. Settle down." Like the rest, Gary Tepfer was tired, hurting, and pissed. "Cut the crap."

A couple of plays later the third quarter ended, and during the break, freshman quarterback Bob Gaines checked in.

"Billy, Coach said for you to go to tailback. Stewart, you're done for the night."

Like Ray, the young replacement was pumped.

"All right, guys! We can do this! Let's drive down and score! Whatta you say?"

Ten pairs of eyes glared back.

That's okay, he thought. *I'll do it.*

"36 Belly Keep. On hut. Ready, break."

At the line, the charged-up signal-caller got his first close-up look at the Olney Cubs, and his enthusiasm dropped a couple of points. Regardless . . .

"Down! Set! Hut!"

After a decent fake to Tepfer, the upstart secured the ball and headed around end. Seconds later *(Or was it hours? It felt like hours.)* three behemoths climbed off him leaving him imbedded in the Texas clay. A fourth reached down and jerked him to his feet.

"So you wanna play with the big boys, do ya?" Mr. Palmer asked, laughing.

A few plays later, the Olney reserves came in. Grady answered with what few subs he had, and the Cubs' second team scored a final touchdown making it 41-0.

Big Champ had not been heard from since its opening shot.

CHAPTER 26

The Proclamation

Barry Morrison stood on the sideline watching the clock tick off its final seconds, the weight of the night and the season bearing down on him. *This is not the way it was supposed to be,* he thought. For the past three years, football had dominated his life and his teammates' consuming them with hurt, fear, and anxiety. More than anything else, he hated the anxiousness of it. Particularly the first two years. He couldn't remember a single moment of not looking over his shoulder or walking on eggshells. Not one single second. Year three hadn't been much better, but he had finally begun to cope. To adapt. Then he got hurt. And now this: having to play end. *And* losing. It was hard to take.

The opening loss to Nocona was a killer. No doubt about that. Expectations had been so high. All their hard work and suffering was about to pay off this year, they were sure of it. Then they lost. It was heartbreaking to say the least, but it wasn't his doings. The team was riddled with injuries and had lost Bobby Hammontree for the season. Evidently, Grady saw it differently. And now the Wildcats were about to be 1 and 2. They had been through too much for it to end this way. The despair he was feeling was more than he could bear.

Something had to be done.

Minutes after the game, the boys sat in the bus in the dark parking lot amid the usual coughing, sniffling, and occasional curse word—risky as that was—as the soft light from the stadium drifted through the bus windows illuminating faces covered in perspiration and blood. Eventually, Fuzzy and Roy climbed in and plopped down in their customary seats on the front row behind Mr. Harville, the science teacher who drove the bus. After what seemed like an eternity, Grady appeared and stood facing them. Glaring.

Before he could speak, the entire team stood up.

"We want you coaches to know something," Barry began, his voice threatening to betray him. It was not the authoritative tone all were used to hearing when he called plays in the huddle or urged his teammates on in practices or games. Much as he tried, he could not muster it. The emotion was simply too much. He felt his eyes begin to water against his will and hoped it would go unnoticed in the dim light and shadows. Taking a deep breath, he spoke from his heart on behalf of the team.

"We will not lose another game."

Every pair of eyes Grady looked into returned his gaze. Not a single player bowed his head or looked away. Then, as if on cue, they all sat down.

Fuzzy turned back around and smiled at Mr. Harville as the lights around the field went out. Roy, too, turned and sat staring down at his hands folded in his lap. He swallowed hard, his heart racing with pride.

Grady didn't move. Didn't smile.

"You're right, Barry. We will not, I repeat, *not,* lose another game. Come to practice on Monday ready to clean up this mess you've made. Ready to go back to square one. And anybody not willin' to strap 'em on and get after it, best stay home. Cause it won't be pretty."

With that, he turned and sat as the bus pulled away, the deafening silence broken only momentarily by the sound of someone throwing up in the rear.

PART FIVE

TURNING POINT

CHAPTER 27

The Quarterback

Barry's mind was a hundred miles away from where it was supposed to be. A thousand. In the big scheme of things, *The Ancient Mariner*—or whatever it was called— was so far down the list he couldn't see it even though it was on his desk right there in front of him. Suddenly, he heard what he thought was his name and looked up. Mrs. Crowley was at the blackboard, her back to the class. He turned and gazed out the third floor window. Then, there it was again.

"Barry."

He turned and saw everyone staring at Mr. Adams, the principal, standing in the doorway. "This way, please."

Startled, he jumped from his chair, hurried across the noisy wooden floor, and joined the large man in the hall.

"Yes sir?"

"Coach Graves wants to see you in his office."

Barry swallowed hard. "Yes sir." He turned and hurried down the stairs. In a minute's time, he was across the yard and standing at Grady's office door in the gymnasium. He took a deep breath and knocked.

"Come in."

The shaken teen entered to find Grady behind his desk, and coaches Ray and Williams seated to each side, all facing a lone empty chair. He sat down, his heart on the borderline of stopping.

Leaning back, Grady stared and spoke. "How are the boys' spirits?"

"Good, sir."

"Anyone discouraged? Upset?"

"No sir. A little disappointed, but we're all good."

"Anything they'd like to see done differently?"

What kind of loaded question is that? Barry thought to himself. *Well, let's see, if you really wanna know . . .*

"Well, sir, I think we'd all like it if you stopped shuffling players around week after week."

The look on Grady's face told Barry that might not have been the right answer. *Dadgumit, he'd asked, hadn't he?* He swallowed hard again and continued.

"You've always taught us football is a game of instincts and instant reactions, but it's hard for players to develop them when they keep changing positions. Sir."

Grady's stare had evolved into his infamous glare. Seconds ticked by. They felt like minutes. Then . . .

"Okay. You're our quarterback. For the rest of the season. I can't guarantee the others will stay put, but you will. Win or lose."

Barry's mind was spinning at the speed of light. He hated it when it did that. Finally, he managed a response.

"Yes sir." It sounded weak and foreign. He hoped it wasn't heard that way.

"Now, get on back to class."

"Yes sir." Relying strictly on instinct, Barry rose from the chair, turned, walked six steps to the door, and grabbed the handle.

"Oh, and somethin' else."

Barry turned.

"You boys serious about what you said on the bus Friday night?"

"Yes sir. Dead serious."

Grady's stare bore right through Barry. He could almost feel the fluorescent ceiling light passing through the hole in him. He watched as the coach motioned for him to leave without saying another word.

He then turned the knob, crossed the gym floor, threw open the heavy double doors, and stepped out into a crisp fall breeze and the remainder of the season.

In final period study hall that afternoon, the newly reinstated QB sat surrounded by his three best friends. They were excited about the news, and he couldn't wait to tell his dad.

"What'd Claude think about you playin' end?" Mike asked, removing a stick of gum and offering the pack to the others.

"He was hot. But not as mad as Trecie."

Gary laughed. "Yeah. I bet she was."

"I was afraid she was gonna egg his house."

Barney laughed and reached for a piece of Mike's Doublemint. "She's braver'n me."

"Better lookin', too."

The four laughed and were quickly admonished by the librarian, Mrs. Fall. Eventually, the fun faded and was replaced with the same gnawing feeling of dread that had hovered over the four of them at this table for the past three years. Shortly, the bell would ring signaling an end to seventh period and the start of their trek to football practice. Today the cloud was particularly dark and thick, given they couldn't get Grady's foreboding words out of their heads, and they'd never known him to lie. *Anybody not ready to strap 'em on and get after it, best stay home. Cause it won't be pretty.* If that wasn't bad enough, the open date meant no game this week. Two uninterrupted weeks of tormented hell lay ahead. It was on all their minds. Finally, Mike couldn't take it anymore.

"Anybody wanna quit?"

The others turned, stared at him, and then burst out laughing.

"Quiet! Quiet over there, you boys!"

"Yes ma'am."

They were laughing hard now, trying their best to hold it in. No such luck. Soon they were crying, they were laughing so hard—their faces buried in their arms on the table.

"Boys! Boys! That's enough of that! You hear? That's enough!"

Just as they were gaining control, the bell rang. The four looked at each other and laughed even harder.

CHAPTER 28

Mr. Touchdown

They always call him Mr. Touchdown
They always call him Mr. Team
He can run and he can throw
Give him the ball and just look at him go
Hip Hip Hurrah for Mr. Touchdown
We're gonna beat 'em tonight
So give a great big cheer
For the hero of the year
Mr. Touchdown U.S.A.

As a youngster, pudgy Gary Tepfer didn't care that much for sports. When his buddies finally convinced him to try football—in junior high—a curious thing happened: He lost weight and the girls started noticing him. The rest, as they say, is history.

A lineman in junior high, Grady let him keep his jersey number but made him a ball carrier, and by his senior year, the convert had made quite a name for himself at fullback. No one ran the ball like number 74. He could bull ahead dragging a slew of tacklers for tough yards or shoot through an opening and be gone. And he loved playing defense. Especially linebacker. Mr. Touchdown loved playing linebacker.

"Okay, listen up. Tepfer, you're movin' to right defensive end. Morrison, you take his place at linebacker. Graham—safety. All right, let's line up."

Gary stared at Grady.

"Sir?"

"Sir, what?"

"End?"

"That's right. Now!"

Knowing better than to argue, Gary trotted over to his new position, but he was not happy.

"Barney, tell Mr. Tepfer here how one plays defensive end."

"Deliver a blow and find the ball."

"That's all there is to it. Okay, let's go."

Over the next ten minutes, Gary's performance at defensive end was mediocre at best. Coach would be forced to move him back to where he belonged. Or so he thought.

Whistle.

"Apparently you weren't listenin' too well. Or maybe you just need to work some on deliverin' a blow and findin' the ball. Robert! Get over here. Holder, you too! The rest of you can rest."

Junior guard Robert Tepfer was another of those quiet guys who let his play do his talking for him. He wasn't real big, but like many on the team he was chiseled from stone. And quick. And if he hit you, you felt it into next week. Being somewhat in his big brother's shadow suited him well. He didn't need nor want any light shined on him. Just respect. And he got it. His teammates would rather line up against anyone, with the exception of perhaps an irate Billy Pitts, than him. The reason? Someone was gonna get roughed up and it probably wasn't gonna be number 61. And if Grady had recently pushed his button, you'd better stand clear altogether. Grady knew how to rile him and did it often. Robert hated being called a loafer. Truth was, the younger Tepfer just didn't care much for playing offense, that's all. Defense, he loved. On occasion, Grady would tear into him and some poor Eagle, Owl, or the such would suffer the consequences. Right now, though, the time had come to collect from big brother. He was actin' like a spoiled kid whose toy had been taken away, and Robert wasn't big on it. Grady had picked the right guy to set him straight.

"Okay, now deliver a blow and find the ball—which should be easy since it's right there in Billy's hands. Robert! Don't you let him get to the ball carrier. And, Billy, I don't want you fakin' and dodgin'. I want you to run over him. That clear?"

"Yes sir."

"On my whistle."

After twenty minutes of fighting off the punishing blocks of his brother and getting run over by Billy, usually at the same time, Gary was hurting.

Finally, Grady stopped it. "That defensive end position doesn't look all that bad now, does it, son?"

"No sir," he answered, panting. "It doesn't."

"All right, then. Get back in there and play it like you mean it."

"Yes sir."

And for the next two weeks, he did. They all did. The hell they'd expected following the loss to Olney came in the form of relentless tackling drills, half-line scrimmages, punt and kickoff coverages and running. Oh, how they ran. Up and down the practice field. Across town to the football stadium. Double W's in the stands. And back to school. Endlessly.

Grady had gambled in taking that route. He'd actually thought of scaling back workouts and giving the wounded a chance to heal their aches and rest their legs. Doing so would also reduce the chance of additional injuries. But the easy road didn't pass through Archer. It went through other towns. Other teams. His boys took the hard road. Always had. Always would.

When it was done, he took stock. No new major injuries, just the players' usual nicks and hurts, but those would always be there. The time had come for Ray to step up to full-time duty, and Mike's knee was as good as it was going to get. He'd continue to alternate him and Mickey shuttling in the plays, but still no defense for Stewart. "Mighty Mite"—as the junior running back was known—was working out just fine. He was plenty quick and "tough as they come"; he just wasn't very big—barely 5'2" tall and 115 pounds—*with* a rock in his pocket. Carrying the ball, he would often get hit three or four times before hitting the ground. A human pinball. When he eventually did come to rest, number 11 would bounce back up, hand the ball to the ref, and run back to the huddle ready for more. Once, after a rare touchdown, opposing players could be heard arguing among themselves.

"Why didn't you tackle him?!"

"Hell, I couldn't see him! I thought somebody's helmet come off and was bouncin' across the goal line. I didn't know there was somebody under it."

In regard to the recent changes, all the coaches agreed Gary was becomin' a real force at defensive end, and that Morrison had settled in nicely at linebacker. Barry wasn't as fast as some of the other kids but wouldn't have to be to play the position. He just needed a nose for the ball, and he had that. And Graham, well, he was a bird of a different feather, but Grady liked the wiry junior's speed and aggressiveness at safety. While most of the boys seemed to live and breathe football, he didn't. Larry's thing was fast cars. To hear the others talk, he could build 'em *and* drive 'em, and evidently nobody around these parts could beat him. Football was just a pastime with him. That didn't sit well with the head coach, but the kid did play hard and didn't take crap off anybody. On more than one occasion, he'd been overheard in the locker room saying, "Well, let's just step outside and settle this." As far as Grady knew, there'd been no takers. Yeah, Graham would be just fine.

The whole team would play hard. No doubt. They were in shape. And tough. And determined. They were doggoned determined. That would have to do. There wasn't anything else he or the other coaches could do. They were out of time.

CHAPTER 29

The Concession

'CATS OPEN DISTRICT PLAY AT HENRIETTA
Friday night the Archer City Wildcats travel to Henrietta to take on the Bearcats in the first district encounter of the season. Henrietta returns seven starters from last year's team that defeated Archer City 16-0 for the championship in the last game of the season. Among them are all-district performers Jim Boddy at quarterback, halfback Jimmy Duewall, and 205-pound guard Phillip Wells. Probable starters for the Wildcats are Billy Pitts at center, Steve Parsley and Robert Tepfer at guards, Buddy Knox and Butch Hannah at tackles, Ray Bussey and Barney Oliver at ends, Barry Morrison at quarterback, Billy Holder at wingback, Mike Stewart at tailback, and Gary Tepfer at fullback.

A pep rally and victory parade are scheduled for Friday afternoon at 5:15 P.M. Game time is set for 7:30 P.M. (Archer County News)

Grady Graves had no use for the band, cheerleaders, or pep rallies. Especially pep rallies. For three years his rule had been firm—the players could attend, but they had to walk in as a team, eyes straight ahead, and upon taking their seats could in no way acknowledge the goings-on. No talking, no laughing, no nothing except concentrating on the game at hand that night. Now, after three years, he'd finally grown tired of all the complaining from the faculty and parents. The cheerleaders had complained the loudest, but they didn't matter to him. Reluctantly, he'd agreed this week to allow the boys to stand during the school song and maybe even smile occasionally. As far as any actual participation, he hadn't yet decided on that. The cheerleaders were always wanting one or more players to step out on the gym floor and accept some good luck token or some such nonsense, and he had always forbade it. Meanwhile, across town, that very topic was being discussed.

Jodie smiled, scooted over a little closer, and tried again.

"Come on. At least ask him. Everybody in school participated. It just so happened you won."

Gary had been the fiftieth person to say "Beat the Bearcats" to Vickie Purdue. The prize was a cake to be presented at Friday's pep rally.

"Naw, give it to somebody else."

"But *you* won it. Just ask him. All he can do is say no."

"That's what you think."

Jodie hesitated, then scooted even closer. Like every other boy in school, Gary loved the cheerleaders' uniforms. Particularly their black panties—or whatever they were—that sometimes showed when the girls did their jumps and high leg kicks. Right now, Jodie's knee-length skirt appeared even shorter than usual.

"Please."

Just as the fullback's judgment was waffling, his levelheadedness prevailed.

"No way."

"Dadgumit, Tepfer! I didn't know I's datin' a coward!"

"Forget it."

"You *still* afraid of him? After three and a half *years?*"

"Damn right I am."

Ticked, Jodie slid across next to the passenger door, tugged her skirt as far toward her knees as it would go, and folded her arms. If he wouldn't take matters into his own hands, they would. The cheerleaders weren't going to be denied any longer.

The next day, before practice, Grady called Gary into his office.

"Yes sir?"

"The cheerleaders are wantin' to give you some sorta cake or somethin' at the pep rally Friday. You know about it?"

"Yes sir."

"Well, to get 'em off my back, I'm gonna allow it. This one time. Just make darn sure you get it done and over with quick. You got that?"

"Yes sir. Will do."

"That cheerleader of yours—everything okay between you two?"

"Off and on." Gary couldn't help but smile.

"Well, anybody who can get you in church every Sunday has to be pretty strong-willed."

"Oh, she's spunky, all right."

Grady smiled back. "Yep. That whole bunch is."

Friday's pep rally went off without a hitch. With the band playing Mr. Touchdown, the team strode in before the entire student body and a host of townspeople and parents as they had countless times. Despite Grady saying they could at least give the appearance of enjoying the proceedings, not a lot of talk went on between them. Finally near the end, Jodie presented Gary his victory cake, and following a speech by Principal Adams, the boys filed out. On the 40-mile bus ride to Henrietta, the players wondered if talking might now be allowed on the bus. Not knowing for sure, no one risked it. It was a good thing they didn't.

CHAPTER 30

Bent On Revenge

Inside a jam-packed Bearcat Stadium on October 2, Henrietta kicked off at 7:30 P.M. as scheduled. At precisely 7:31, the Archer City Wildcats led 6-0.

Following the opening kick and a one-yard run by Mickey Horany, Gary Tepfer put his own new plan into action. Like Barry, he was sick of the way things were going. Sick of folks asking him what was wrong with the team. Sick of bein' hurt. Sick of everything. But mostly he was sick at the thought of havin' devoted three plus years of his life to a team that was goin' nowhere fast. So he'd made up his mind. First, if *any-body* dared try and run the ball his direction, he'd show 'em just how much he disliked playin' friggin' defensive end. And secondly, anybody with ideas of tacklin' him had better bring his sack lunch, brothers, and uncles. And *that* might not be enough.

"30 Dive. On hut. Ready, break."

"Down! Set! Hut!" Barry turned and handed him the ball.

Before Billy and Robert even could fully make their blocks, Gary tore through the slight opening right of center, ran over some poor unsuspecting soul, bounced outside shrugging off two wannabe tacklers, and sped 66 yards up the sideline to pay dirt. As his teammates arrived to congratulate him, he handed the ball to the referee, turned to them and said, "Piss ant Bearcats."

Morrison's pass for two was too long, but the tone had been set.

If the Archer City fans were expecting the "piss ant" Bearcats to lie down, though, they were mistaken. The Wild-cats expected them to come roaring back, and they did.

After returning the ensuing kickoff out to their 45, they needed just three plays to cover the remaining 55 yards, the last one, a 21-yard scamper by halfback Don Murphy. They, too, elected to go for two. Three times. (Archer City was flagged for being offside twice.) But the Wildcats were having no part of it, and the score remained tied at six.

On the Wildcats' next possession, Stewart took a hard hit and was helped to the sideline dragging his injured knee. Trainers frantically removed his brace, untaped him, pushed his knee back into place, re-taped him, and replaced the brace.

After an exchange of punts, Archer was forced to punt again, and Morrison hit a beauty which rolled dead at the Henrietta one-yard line.

Going nowhere on their first two tries, the Bearcats quick-kicked out to their 35-yard line. From there, behind the running of Tepfer and Horany, and a pass from Morrison to Oliver, the Wildcats pushed the ball to the Bearcat three-yard line where Billy Holder then punched it in. The kick failed, and Archer City led 12-6.

Following a Henrietta punt on the next series, Archer City fumbled on its own 22 and the Bearcats recovered. Six plays later, quarterback Jim Boddy climaxed the drive with a two-yard keeper. Henrietta elected to go for two, but Ray Bussey put an end to that by shooting through and dropping Murphy short of the goal. The first half ended with the score knotted at twelve each.

In the dressing room, the trainers once again went about the business of reworking Mike's knee. Once the brace and tape were removed, though, all they could do was stare. His knee was gone. In it's place, an ugly, purple melon.

His cousin, trainer David Wright, looked up at him.

"Good gosh, Mike, what are you doin' suitin' up?"

"You gonna tell Coach Graves any different?"

"No. But you shouldn't be out there." He looked up to see the head coach looking over his shoulder. If Grady had heard, he didn't let on. He put his hand on Mike's shoulder.

"I'm gonna let Mickey play most of the second half."

"Yes sir."

"Listen up, guys. One thing—we *own* the second half. You're in better shape than them, and you're tougher than them. The second half belongs to us. Period."

"Yes sir!"

Then, he turned back and glared at David.

"Get some ice on that thing for cryin' out loud."

The entire third quarter was a defensive slugfest with the Wildcats picking up only two first downs and the Bearcats just one. Then, early in the defining quarter, Archer City drove to the Henrietta 18-yard line. Attempting to pass, Morrison was hurried and his throw was intercepted and returned to the Bearcat 24. The Wildcat defense dug in, and three plays later Henrietta faced a fourth-and-one at their own 33. With less than six minutes showing on the clock, Bearcat coach Jerry McWilliams decided to gamble.

In the defensive huddle, the elder Tepfer told it like it was.

"They're not gettin' past me."

"Well, they sure ain't comin' through *me*," his younger brother shot back.

Barney was next. "Me neither."

And so on around the huddle.

The only one who didn't speak up was tackle Billy Pitts. In Billy's mind, words weren't going to get the job done. But exploding past the guy across from him like a mad bull, locating the ball, and dropping the runner like a sack of potatoes might.

Boy, did it. As Billy climbed to his feet, the Archer crowd went crazy.

The four-yard loss gave the Wildcats the ball on the Henrietta 29-yard line and one last chance to win the game.

But Henrietta wasn't going to lie down. Tepfer was stopped for no gain on first down. Then came an incomplete pass. Then another.

Suddenly it was fourth-and-10. They turned and looked to the sideline and stared as Mike Stewart came hobbling in with the play. Horany checked out.

Following Grady's instructions, Morrison kept Tepfer and Holder in to block, dropped back, looked for number 35, and threaded the ball between two defenders for ten yards. Mike dragged the two for another five and then struggled to his feet, pitched the ball to the ref, smiled at his teammates, and slowly limped off.

Grady then sent Graham in at end, moved Oliver to fullback, and Tepfer to tailback.

Barry waited for Larry to give him the play.

"All he said was to remind you guys we own the second half."

The entire line dug deep and blocked like there was no tomorrow. On first down from the 14, Barry handed to Oliver up the middle for four tough yards. Then Tepfer twice for seven. With first-and-goal from the three, Oliver bulled his way in for the score. Morrison kicked the PAT through, and with 3:32 remaining, Archer led 19-12.

Henrietta tried to come back and got as far as the Wildcat 45 before freshman Charlie Goforth, to the delight of the Archer City fans, slammed the door by dropping Jim Lemmons for a 10-yard loss.

The heroes were many for Archer, most notably a determined Gary Tepfer who, despite having only one score, rushed for 157 yards on 29 carries, mostly against a defense stacked to stop him. He also was a standout at defensive end.

Big Champ was fired a total of six times.

CHAPTER 31

Ditched

The win breathed much-needed life into the team.

So much so that the subs decided to organize a game of touch football on the courthouse lawn on Saturday. Getting into the Olney game the previous week had whetted their appetites despite getting clobbered. Still, it beat the heck out of getting clobbered day after day in practice with nothing to show for it but bumps, bruises, scratches, sprains, and worse. At least then, folks had realized they actually existed and even cheered for them. After an hour or so, they took a break.

Jimmy Boone hopped into the front seat of his black Studebaker sedan and motioned teammate Jim Harney over.

"Jump in, Jim. Let's go cut some harries."

Minutes later they were southeast of town on "Around the World" Road, fishtailing to beat all, when suddenly Jimmy zigged when he should have zagged. The car rolled over and came to a stop resting on its top. The two crawled out, made the determination they had survived basically unscathed, and burst out laughing. After a minute or so, the seriousness of the situation manifested itself, and Jimmy began pacing up and down on top of the drive shaft crying, "My dad's gonna kill me!" It was some time before a car finally approached. In it, teammate Mickey Horany and their friend Jack Kirkland. The two climbed out laughing. Eventually, the four of them sat down, unsure what to do next. Before long, in the distance, another car appeared.

It was Claude.

They watched him climb out of his cruiser. Jim's dad, Jack Harney—the deputy—was not with him.

"Everyone okay?"

"Yes sir. How'd you know we were here, Sheriff?" Jim asked. "'Cept for Jack and Mickey, there hasn't been a car one by here."

"Oh, I just had a feelin' that some of my boys were in trouble."

After surveying the situation, he ran a chain from his patrol car to the Studebaker and with the boys pushing, managed to pull it upright from the ditch. He then replaced the chain in his trunk, dusted his hands, smiled, winked, and left.

"Crap!"

"What's wrong?"

The front of Mickey's button-down shirt was drenched in motor oil.

"My mom's gonna kill me!"

"Whatta you think my dad's gonna do? Look at my car!"

After some discussion, it was decided both would postpone their misery by not heading home for a while.

"Whatta y'all wanna do now? Go back and finish the game?"

"I don't know," Mickey said, thinking. "What if Coach drives by and sees us?"

"What'll he care?"

"He might not think too highly of us playin' *touch* football."

"You wanna play *tackle?"*

"Are you *kiddin?"*

The courthouse lawn was strewn with stickers and goatheads.

"Well, how 'bout the practice field?"

The football practice field had no endearing qualities they could think of, but it *was* stickerless. Most were surprised Coach Graves hadn't transplanted some grass burrs there himself.

"I don't know. He sees us *there*, he might get the idea we don't get enough of that place durin' the week, and I don't wanna think what *that* might lead to."

"Yeah, you're right. Let's just call it a day and go to Troy's Drive-In and get somethin' to eat."

"Sounds good."

"I'm in."

"Me, too."

CHAPTER 32

Brief Encounters

Despite being held out of practices for the most part, Mike Stewart still suited up each day and participated in calisthenics and some light agility drills. After Monday's workout was finished, he undressed and was headed to the showers with the others when trainer Danny Hall stopped him short.

"Coach wants to see you."

"Now?"

"Right now. In his office."

Mike headed that way.

"Hey! Don't you think you should put somethin' on first?"

Embarrassed, he ran to his locker, threw on his jock strap, and skedaddled across the gym floor to Grady's office. As he knocked, he was besieged by catcalls and whistles. Turning, he realized that in his haste, he hadn't noticed the cheerleaders working late to take down banners from Friday's pep rally. Red-faced and somewhat embarrassed, Judy Crowley, his girlfriend, shouted, "Mike, where the devil are your clothes?"

Before he could answer, Grady called out, "Come in!"

He hurried inside.

Grady and the other coaches looked at him and smiled.

"You know there are women out there?"

"I do now."

They all laughed. Then things turned more serious.

"You gainin' weight?" Grady asked.

"Yes sir."

"How much?"

"'Bout fifteen pounds, Sir. Maybe twenty."

"How come?"

"Guess from not practicin'"

"We can fix that, you know."

"Yes sir."

"But right now that knee of yours is more important."

"Yes sir."

"So stop eatin'."

Yes sir."

"I mean it."

"Yes sir."

"And about that knee . . . if it gets *too* bad, we can get you a shot, if you're willin'."

"I'm willin'. And ready."

"Hurt that bad?"

"A fair amount. Durin' games."

"Okay, then. I'll arrange it."

"Thanks, Coach."

"You can go. But you might wanna wrap a towel around you first."

Before he could answer, one hit him in the chest courtesy of Coach Ray.

Then another from Coach Williams.

"Just in case."

"Oh, and send Parsley over."

"Yes sir."

A minute later he delivered the news.

"Coach wants to see you."

"He does?"

"Yep. And by the way, the cheerleaders are out there."

Steve smiled and started taking off his jeans.

"What are you doin'?"

"Might as well give 'em a thrill." And out the door he went in his briefs.

More catcalls and whistles.

"Ladies."

Roy was waiting at the door. "Come on in here, Romeo."

As he did, Grady shot him puzzled look. "Where are your pants?"

"I wasn't quite through dressin' and figured I'd better hurry."

The coach shook his head and took a deep breath. "You're movin' to tackle."

"Tackle?"

"Yes! I'm movin' Pitts to your guard position and Knox is gonna play center.

"You mean I don't get to pull on traps plays anymore and knock the crap outta Hannah in practice?"

Roy and Fuzzy tried hard not to chuckle.

Grady glared and said, "We'll let you pull from your tackle position since you keep tellin' us how quick you are."

"That'll work."

"I'm also startin' you at cornerback."

"Now we're talkin'."

"Go on. Get outta here."

He did as he was told, taking his own sweet time back across the court. Sadly, the girls had vacated the premises. Too bad. And his remarks had probably earned him some extra duty at the end of tomorrow's practice, but he didn't care. After spending his entire junior season and most of this one under Grady's thumb for quitting, he now had his chance to really show 'em.

Back inside, Grady turned to Roy. "What was it you said he told you?"

"Said he loves playin' cornerback cause he can get up a good head of steam before knockin' the crap outta people."

The kid had a mouth on him, that's for sure. And a stubborn streak to beat all. But he could flat play some ball.

CHAPTER 33

Eagle Soup

Against their better judgment, the night after their win over Henrietta, Jimmy Reeves and teammates Buddy Knox, Jim Harney, and Butch Hannah made an appearance at a dance at the Holliday Community Center. They weren't there looking to dance and weren't really looking for trouble. They were just lookin'. What they found was a group of cowboys, a few of which were Eagle players, out behind the Center. During a discussion over the Archer boys possibly being in the wrong town, a scuffle of sorts broke out and Jimmy's shirt developed a tear. After examining it, he looked up at the culprit responsible.

"You tore my mother's shirt!"

The Holliday boys looked at each other and laughed.

"What?"

What Jimmy meant was, the John Wayne wannabe had torn the shirt his mother had made for him. But he was evidently too stupid to figure that out, and Jimmy wasn't about to explain it.

"You tore my mother's shirt, asshole."

And the fight was on.

While the others sized each other up and decided a free-for-all brawl wasn't really necessary, Jimmy proceeded to teach the big cowboy a lesson about respectin' other people's property—especially their clothes. Shortly, he got his point across. As the four Wildcats turned and headed away, they were politely reminded of their game with Holliday on Friday.

"If you know what's good for you, you'll stay on the bus, Reeves. That goes for all of you!"

Six nights later, the four climbed off the bus together and looked at one another. Reeves scrunched up his face. "This town stinks."

"That's Knox," Harney said. "He's been doin' that all day."

Before Jimmy could reply, Grady walked past. He waited until the coach was out of earshot.

"Buddy. Save it for a pileup."

They all laughed and headed for the field house. Grady started in on the team before they could even get undressed. Usually he waited until they were in uniform.

"It's come to my attention some of you prefer spendin' your spare time playin' touch football, dancin', and fightin' instead of behavin' like you're supposed to. Evidently we aren't workin' you hard enough in practice, or you wouldn't have all that extra energy. But I 'spect we can fix that."

He looked around the room at the guilty parties. "In the meantime, we have a game to play tonight, and I suggest you go out there and take care of business and worry about Monday's practice later."

When tailback Jimmy Pautsky took a pitchout from Eagle quarterback Larry Slack on Holliday's first play from scrimmage, the entire Wildcat defense, led by middle guard Jimmy Reeves, converged on him with serious intent. At the last instant, he pulled up and lofted a pass to a wide-open Ronnie Maxwell. Fifty-five yards later, Holliday led 6-0. An unhappy group of Wildcats huddled up.

"Hey, Reeves. Isn't that the guy that tore your shirt?"

"That's him."

"I thought you said you straightened him out."

"I did."

"Don't look like it."

On the sideline, Grady Graves was livid. In *his* eyes, his new starting cornerback had cost them the touchdown, and his first inclination was to get Horany in there to replace Parsley and tear into him like never before, but he didn't. He knew the kid was already plenty upset with himself, so he decided to leave him be for the time being.

The referee blew the whistle ready for play, and the two teams lined up. The center across from Reeves hadn't torn anybody's shirt, but that didn't matter. The incensed nose tackle tore into him just the same. The result was a bad snap and missed PAT.

The Eagles then kicked off to the Wildcats and immediately threw up a brick wall forcing a punt. Taking over on their own 22, they moved to two quick first downs. Gary Tepfer called time out.

Ray Bussey was eyeing an incredulous Coach Graves on the sideline. "What'd you do that for? Coach'll kill you!"

"I don't care. We gotta get our heads on straight, or we'll never hear the end of it from these Holliday smart-asses. You hear me? Now, let's get the ball back and stuff it down their throats! Now!"

Number 74's pep talk did not go for naught. On the next play, they stopped the Eagles for no gain. Then on second down, at Holliday's 48-yard line, Barney Oliver crashed through and stole the ball from Slack as the quarterback was getting ready to pass. Archer City's ball. First-and-10.

Tepfer picked up three tough yards, and then Morrison kept around end for nine down to the 33. He repeated the play for eight more to the 25. Stewart then picked up five. Then, attempting to pass, Morrison was dropped for a 10-yard loss. Holder got it back with a 14-yard scamper, and on third down from the 16, Stewart darted for five and a first down at the 11. Tepfer went for seven, Stewart for three, and Morrison got the final yard for the score. The kick was good and Archer led 7-6.

In the second quarter, Stewart scored on a one-yard plunge, and Gary Tepfer later scored standing up from the six. Both kicks failed, and the halftime score was 19-6.

During intermission, Grady walked up and down the dressing room inspecting each of the starters. "Well, it appears you've got your heads outta your rears after that sorry start. So keep 'em there! *You hear?*"

"Yes sir!"

And that they did.

Early in the third quarter, Stewart scored on a six-yard sweep, and Ray Bussey caught a pass for the two-point conversion. Then, late in the period, Morrison and Stewart connected on a pass play covering 71 yards for a score. Mickey Horany carried over for two making it 35-6, and Grady then began relieving some of the starters, including Stewart who didn't play at all in the final period. It was a good thing. His shot had long since worn off.

Grady's hunch on Parsley was right. Following his miscue on Holliday's first touchdown, he played a whale of a game on both defense and offense.

Despite the lopsided victory, the celebration in the locker room was somewhat subdued with Grady's earlier threat of a horrific Monday practice looming over them.

And, of course, he wasn't kidding.

CHAPTER 34

No Rest For the Weary

The stifling heat of August's two-a-days had been replaced with the crisp, cool breezes of autumn. That helped a little, but after three hours of endless bone-crushing blocking and tackling drills and scrimmaging, the players were sucking wind as fast they could, barely able to get enough it seemed—the brisk air burning going down. They were nearing the state beyond being exhausted—a condition they knew well, exhibited by a ringing in their ears and difficulty in focusing their eyes and gathering their thoughts. Often players would shower, dress, and return home, never remembering having done so. Today would be one of those days. The feeling was coming on and wind sprints hadn't even begun.

The touch footballers and fighters were not singled out for the Goof-Off Squad. Neither was Parsley. Rather, the entire team shared in the punishment. While Grady was somewhat satisfied with the team's effort and win on Friday, he was not the least bit happy about, and had not forgotten, their mental lapse on Holliday's very first play—the halfback pass for their lone touchdown. If there was one thing he despised more than a less-than-total effort, it was not having one's head in the game. On that play, no one's was.

The best way to prevent such occurrences in the future, he'd found, was to plant a reminder in one's head, and having the players duck-walk, bear-walk, or somersault their way up and down the field following wind sprints worked particularly well. Only when he was satisfied they'd all gotten the message did he finally signal an end to it.

Shuffling toward the dressing room, the players looked and felt a hundred years old. Should they somehow manage to graduate high school and survive Grady, maybe someday they could look back on all this and laugh. But right now, getting to that point was not a given.

The dinner table at the Stewart residence that evening was a quiet one. Mike and his houseguest Barney had energy enough—barely—to lift their forks or speak, but not both at the same time. Finally, Mike set his fork down.

"Whatta you mean, I'm gettin' slow?"

His dad took a long drink of tea and grinned. "Cause I durn near beat you on that last touchdown the other night."

Like most fathers, Gene Stewart usually watched the games from against the fence surrounding the field. He also had a habit of taking off down the fence line trying to keep up whenever a Wildcat player broke into the open. He'd become pretty adept at dodging oncoming spectators and had yet to have a serious collision.

"I'da beat you if that lady and her stroller hadn't gotten in my way."

Barney laughed. "I believe you. You'da beat me at Crowell last year 'cept for havin' to jump those two cars at the end."

"You better be careful," Mike said, smiling. "One of these days you're gonna run over some big ol' boy who don't find it amusin'."

"Don't matter if he's big. Long as he ain't fast, too."

They all laughed. Gene loved Barney. And Gary Tepfer. All the boys Mike brought home to spend the night. In fact, he loved the whole team. And he was right in figuring lots of other folks did, too. He looked over at his guest.

"Barney, I swear, I don't know how you boys have the strength or energy to play on Fridays. And you're all bunged up. Seems to me a week off would go a long ways."

A week off. Barney had read about such a place. Called Shangri-La. Or somethin' like that. Far as he knew, it didn't exist.

"Sounds good to me. I know Mike's knee could sure use it."

"Don't you worry 'bout my knee. I'm not havin' to practice, remember?"

"No, but you play every Friday. I don't think I could."

"Sure you could, and you would, too; don't kid yourself. Idn't that right, Pop?"

"Hell, anybody who'll work out in cowboy boots is top shelf. I think Coach oughta make everybody do that at the start of two-a-days, or go barefoot like Billy. He'd weed 'em out a lot quicker."

When they'd finished laughing, Mike said, "Damn, Dad. You're as bad as Coach."

"No. I'm not. And speakin' of tough, what's this I hear about Billy's neck?"

"Hurt it a while back. Maybe even last year, they're not for sure. But it's startin' to bother him pretty good, so last week he started goin' to a chiropractor over in Wichita."

"A chiropractor? What's Grady think about that?"

"He idn't too big on it. Told Billy a witch doctor would do him as much good."

"What's he do, this doctor?"

"Well, to hear Billy tell it, he hooks a bunch of wires up to his neck, turns on a machine, and shocks the pee-wottle out of him. Says he flops around like a fish the whole time."

"And it helps?"

"He says it does."

"Bless his heart. All you boys are walkin' wounded. It's a wonder you win a game."

"Yeah, well, there's no turnin' back now. Least not for us seniors. We've come this far; we might as well finish it. Besides, we gave our word to Coach."

"How's that?"

"Told him we weren't gonna lose another game."

"Who did?"

"All of us. The whole team."

"When?"

"After the Olney game. Thought it might make practices easier the followin' week."

"Did it?"

"Not that I could tell. Were they, Barney?"

Barney shook his head and smiled. "Nope."

"You boys tell him you weren't gonna lose again all year or just durin' the regular season?"

"I don't know. Didn't get *that* specific." He turned and looked at Barney. "How'd you take it, pardner?"

"I took it to mean all year."

Mike looked back at his dad and grinned. "Well, there you have it."

CHAPTER 35

Two More Bite the Dust

While that conversation was taking place, coach Bobby Ray was telling members of the Quarterback Club, "Although they haven't won a lot of games, Paducah has lost several by close margins. We expect to have our hands full."

A nice way of saying the Dragons weren't very good and Archer City should be able to handle them. Which they did with the help of five turnovers. Paducah lost three fumbles and had two passes intercepted—one of which was returned 45 yards for a touchdown by Billy Holder, who also had a rushing touchdown. In total, the Wildcats finished with 244 yards on the ground, thanks mostly to Gary Tepfer's running amok. Number 74 had 174 yards on 28 carries. The real difference in the game, though, was the middle of the Wildcat defensive line—Jimmy Reeves, Billy Pitts, Butch Hannah—which completely ruled the roost, forcing the Dragons to take to the airways unsuccessfully.

With the victory, the Wildcats' record improved to 4-2 including three important district wins. Next up, the Crowell Wildcats, also undefeated in district play.

Crowell, a long-time pillar in the district, had tradition on its side and one of the best quarterbacks around—Dan Mike Bird—who could break a game wide-open anytime with his passing and running. Both teams knew a loss at this stage would hurt severely as there were still tough foes ahead—Munday and Knox City—both contenders.

To the delight of a drenched home-field crowd, Billy Holder wheeled around end for 31 yards in the rain on the Wildcats' first play from scrimmage all the way down to the Crowell 29-yard line. To their dismay, the Wildcats turned the ball over by fumbling on the next play. Crowell promptly marched to the Archer City 21 where the Wildcat defense stiffened and took over on downs. Behind the running of full-back Gary Tepfer, the home team promptly drove back into enemy territory, eventually reaching the three-yard line. On fourth down, foregoing a field goal attempt, the Wildcats were stopped cold and gave the ball back.

This time, however, Crowell was unable to get moving, and a poor punt from their own 10 skirted out of bounds at the 30. Seven plays later, Billy Holder headed off-tackle, bounced outside, and went around end for the touchdown. Morrison's kick was good and Archer led 7-0.

After holding Crowell on their ensuing possession and taking over on their own 41, the Wildcats stayed with the run and put together a 14-play drive that ended with Gary Tepfer bulling over from a yard out. Morrison kicked the PAT, and the lead was 14-0 at halftime.

True to Grady's warning at intermission that Crowell wasn't done and would come fighting back, Dan Mike Bird returned the second-half kickoff to the Archer City 45 and on their first play, handed off to Lee Looney, who promptly weaved his way through the Archer defense for a 45-yard touchdown. The two-point conversion attempt was snuffed out as Ray Bussey stopped Bird short of the goal line. One minute into the second half, the score was suddenly 14-6.

Determined to halt Crowell's sudden momentum, the Wildcats promptly answered back by driving to the Crowell three-yard line but once again were stopped on downs and turned the ball over. They then went about the task of preventing a second score by Crowell. They were successful, and after forcing a punt, took over on the Crowell 48. The visitors called timeout.

With a break in the action, the cheerleaders moved on to more important matters and gathered around Jodie.

"Are you serious?"

"As a heart attack."

"You two are breakin' up?"

"No. I said I'm thinkin' about it."

"Why?"

"Cause he's gettin' too big for his britches, that's why. Thinks he's some sorta football hero."

"He *is*."

"Did y'all have another fight?"

"That's all we do."

"Why?"

"Cause he's stubborn as a jacksass, that's why."

"*LOOK OUT!!!*"

Number 74 was suddenly headed their way dragging two tacklers. In the nick of time, the bunch scattered like a covey of quail, Jodie choosing the fence. Just as she reached the top, the three players barreled into it below her almost knocking her off. Once the other two climbed off him, Gary got to his feet and was immediately slapped upside his helmet by the pretty fence rider. Startled, he looked up and spotted her precariously perched above him.

"Gary Tepfer! You did that on purpose!"

The big fullback smiled, handed the ball to the referee, and trotted off.

"You sorry %&#$*@!"

Before she could climb down, a hand grabbed her from behind.

"Watch your mouth, young lady!"

"Mom?"

"Don't mom me. You know better than to use that kind of language here! Now, get down from there and quit making a spectacle of yourself."

Too late for that.

"BUT HE WAS TRYIN' TO KILL ME, MOM!"

"If you girls had been watching the game and doing what you're supposed to be doing, this wouldn't have happened."

"Yes ma'am."

"You hear me?"

"Yes ma'am." She looked for help from her cohorts and found it.

Who are the Wildcats?

We are the Wildcats!

What kind of Wildcats?

"Gotta go, Mom!"

Fighting Wildcats!

Well . . . Yell You Wildcats. Yell!

Following an assortment of kick jumps, the girls regrouped.

"Thanks y'all. I owe you."

Trecie, head cheerleader, was still embarrassed.

"Listen. Your mom's right. We need to get our heads in the game. We could've all been killed."

"*Y'all* don't have to worry. It was *me* he was aimin' for."

Meanwhile, out on the field, Buddy Knox, Billy Pitts, Robert Tepfer, Steve Parsley, and Butch Hannah began tearing huge holes in the Crowell defense for Stewart, Holder, and Gary Tepfer. Stewart eventually scored standing up from the two, Morrison made it 21-6 with his kick, and Crowell never threatened again

When it was done, safeties Bussey and Graham and cornerbacks Parsley and Holder had prevented the talented Crowell quarterback from completing a single pass. Crowell did manage to run for 131 yards, but Archer City amassed 314 on the ground. The Wildcats' stingy defense and punishing running game were just the ticket for winning games. And with only two district contests remaining, thoughts of a district were once again on everyone's minds.

CHAPTER 36

He Ain't Dead, Is He?

Next up was a non-district game against the Throckmorton Greyhounds. The Wildcats would eventually win 27-14, but midway through the third quarter Grady wasn't happy with his team's effort and let them know.

"Looks like Knox is comin' in for you, Pitts."

Billy looked up from the huddle and stepped aside. "What's the matter?"

Buddy shook his head. "Beats me. Coach just told me to get in here for you."

"He mad?"

"I don't know. Maybe a little."

Billy sprinted over to the sideline expecting the worst. One play later he was back in. The others looked at him.

"What happened?"

"Coach said you better quit grabbin' and start hittin' or you're all walkin' home."

"From *here*?"

"I suppose."

"What about *you*?"

"He hasn't decided about me yet. Oh, and somethin' else. Robert, he said if you don't quit loafin' on offense, you're gonna have to *run* home."

The news was bad for the defense, but even worse for the Throckmorton offense. Especially halfback Johnny Allen. On the next snap, he took a pitchout and looked up to see the bulk of the newly inspired Wildcat team converging on him. When they unpiled, Allen was spread-eagled facedown on the ground. Unmoving.

Back in the defensive huddle, the referee's whistle caught the team's attention. They watched as the Greyhound trainers came to the halfback's aid. Then the head coach. Finally, a doctor made his way down from the stands.

The halfback had yet to move.

Mike turned toward his teammates. "Dadgum, guys, which one of you hit him?"

Seven raised their hands.

The stadium was ghostly quiet. Barry voiced everyone's concern.

"You don't reckon he's dead, do you?"

Jimmy Reeves spit, looked up, and grinned. "Naw. He ain't dead."

"How do *you* know, Reeves?" Butch asked.

"Cause I stepped on his hand on my way back to the huddle . . . and he flinched."

The laughs in the Wildcat huddle were drowned out by the crowd's applause. Johnny Allen was on his feet and being helped back to the bench.

Jimmy wasn't done.

"Reckon Coach'll let us ride the bus home now?"

The Wildcats were determined to continue their good play the next week against Knox City. On paper, the Greyhounds were a hard team to figure. They had allowed only 32 points to be scored against them all season, only 18 of them by district foes. Still, their district record was only 3-1-1 having lost to Munday 12-6, and being tied by Henrietta 6-6. With one game to go, they planned on playing the role of spoiler *and* keeping their play-off hopes alive, and they had the weapons to do it.

Greyhound junior running back Phil Williams was coming off a four-touchdown effort against Crowell the week before, and quarterback Brack Shaver was a threat every time he touched the ball. And, as evidenced by the few points they'd given up, they could also play defense.

But so could the Wildcats. And midway through the second period, Archer got the only score it would need. Knox

City's Williams had the ball knocked loose at the Greyhound 26-yard line, and an alert Steve Parsley pounced on it. On the next play, Gary Tepfer exploded through a huge hole and went untouched for the score. Carl Brock blocked Morrison's kick, and the score was 6-0.

Late in the third period, behind the running of Williams, Knox City managed to drive to the Archer City seven-yard line where the tenacious Wildcat defense shut them down and took over on downs. Tepfer began a series of relentless runs, plowing over and dragging people, eventually reaching the Knox City 40. A fake to the tough fullback on the next play froze the Greyhound defense, and Morrison, who attempted only five passes in the game, found a wide-open Barney Oliver at the Greyhound nine where, off balance, he managed to stumble into the end zone. Morrison then swept right end for two and iced the game at 14-0.

Once the smoke cleared after Friday's games, the district standings said it all.

Archer City: 5 wins, no losses, no ties.

Munday: 5 wins, no losses, no ties.

The final game of the regular season would decide the district champion.

Deja Vu.

A year ago, the other team came out on top.

Could lightning strike twice?

Grady Graves had arrived in Archer City promising to build a winner. Now, four years later, the Wildcats had a second chance to finish the regular season with a record of 8-2 and win the district . While another 7-3 record would solidly establish them as winners, his idea of winning was having something real to show for it. Like a trophy. The thought of losing to Munday and letting this opportunity slip by again was not acceptable. Period.

PART SIX

BRINGING HOME THE BACON

CHAPTER 37

Now or Never

Heading home following another relentless practice on Monday, Ray Bussey sat spent in the passenger seat across from Grady Graves. He was almost asleep when Grady spoke up.

"Ray, you know what your problem is?"

The senior end bolted upright and answered, "No sir."

Grady looked over at him. "You think too much."

"Sir?"

"You think too dang much. You'd be a whole lot better player if you didn't spend so much time trying to figure out how to get around stuff. You're lazy as dog doo, and you know it. Always have been. How you come to two-a-days in shape I'll never know."

"It's either that or get run over," Ray replied.

Grady turned and looked at him.

"My dad makes me run. We started out on the oilfield road behind our house. It's about seven-tenths of a mile up a hill then down to well number seven. I used to have to run there and back in fifteen minutes—eighteen if it was real hot. But this year we switched to Hilbers Road. Dad follows me in the pickup, and if I slow down too much, he grazes me with the bumper."

Grady smiled. "You don't say?"

"Yes sir. I asked him once how fast I was goin', and he said seventeen miles-an-hour. 'Don't you think that's a little too fast?' I asked. I only had to do twelve goin' back."

"Well, if everybody did that in the off season, we'd get a whole lot more done early on." He paused and then looked over one last time. "You remember what I told you. We've still got some ball left to play."

"Yes sir."

As Grady turned back and concentrated on the road, Ray slipped back into a half-sleep. In his dream, he was catching a touchdown pass in the title game. With the ball on its way—*without* thinking about it—he instinctively reached out, grabbed it, evaded a tackler, and sprinted into the end zone to the delight of the cheering fans.

The dream was real.

That Friday, on a cool November night in front of an overflowing crowd at the Wildcats' stadium, the home team took the field for pre-game warmups to a tremendous ovation. After some loosening up, agility drills, and running through some plays, they retreated to the dressing room to the same ovation. Once situated, Grady kept it short and simple. After all, everyone in the room was aware what was at stake.

"Well, men, here we are. I know I don't have to remind you how it felt to let this thing slip away last year. And for seven of you, there won't be another one. *This* is it." He paused. "Coach Ray, any words of wisdom?"

"Naw. Just get out there, get after 'em, and stay after 'em. Till that final horn."

"Coach Williams?"

Suddenly, Roy was caught and knew it. There was no hiding the emotion on his face. Too late for that. Plucked from the hot, nasty oilfields of west Texas to coach a small group of likable boys to play football, he could never repay Grady. He knew that. Nor could he ever repay these boys, and that made him even sadder. But right now it was joy that clouded his vision. And love that spilled from his eyes. With a smile the size of Texas, he told them as best he knew how.

"Bring home the bacon."

CHAPTER 38

Triumphant!

Two bits. Four bits. Six bits. A dollar.
All for Archer stand up and holler!

For the first time all year, the Wildcat players appeared to be nervous. After receiving the opening kickoff, they were unable to move the ball and punted away to Munday who took over on their own 41. The Moguls proceeded to methodically march 59 yards down the field with left halfback Terry Leflar carrying eight times for 39 yards before eventually punching it over from the five. The kick after made the score 7-0.

Archer City was unable to move on its second possession as well, punted again, but this time held the Moguls, forcing their first punt of the game from their own 44-yard line. A bobbled snap sent the punter scurrying, and the Wildcats dropped him for a 12-yard loss. Following the blocks of Tepfer and Stewart, fellow running back Billy Holder immediately ripped off 28 yards down to the four as the first quarter ended. On the ensuing play, Gary Tepfer plowed in for the TD, Morrison's kick was good, the score was knotted at seven, and any nervousness the Wildcats had been feeling was gone.

Forcing another Mogul punt, the Wildcats then took over at their own 26, and on the first play, Stewart skirted the left side behind Bussey and Parsley and scooted 54 yards, his knee brace squeaking the whole way, before being dragged down from behind at the Munday 20-yard stripe.

On his way back to the huddle, Ray was waiting for him.

"Squeaky, you really need to oil that thing. Or get a lube job."

Following two hard runs by Tepfer and one each by Holder and Morrison, the Wildcats had the ball on Munday's one-yard line. There was, of course, no keeping number 74 out of the end zone from there, and the score was suddenly 14-7.

The Wildcats continued their stellar defensive play, and the Moguls improved theirs so that the score remained until halftime.

The boys sat waiting for Grady, expecting an explosion. Surprisingly, it never came.

"I don't know what you guys were doin' on those first two drives, but it's a darn good thing you got it corrected, whatever it was. Now, you've got a lead, and we own the second half. So go back out there and get that trophy you've been workin' so hard for."

But the Munday Moguls had plans of their own. After receiving the second-half kickoff, they reeled off 56 yards in 12 plays into Wildcat territory at the 29. A 15-yard penalty against the 'Cats moved the ball to the 14. They then stiffened on the next three plays, and the Moguls decided to gamble on fourth down. The Wildcats would make them pay.

Personally seeing to it, a determined Gary Tepfer put a quick stop to an option play to his side by dropping quarterback Skip Lane for a one-yard loss. Archer City took over at its own 15.

Number 74 wasn't done.

On the first play from scrimmage, he shot through an opening just left of center provided by Knox and Pitts and rumbled for 35 yards to midfield, dragging tacklers along the way. However, with tempers flaring, another 15-yard penalty against Archer halted the drive. After the teams traded punts, the Wildcats set up shop on their 35 early in the fourth period. Hoping to catch Munday sleeping, Grady sent in "Texas Throwback."

The misdirection play worked perfectly as Morrison swept left behind Tepfer and Stewart, pulled up at the last instant, and then hit a wide-open Oliver streaking down the opposite sideline for a 40-yard gain down to the Mogul 25. Two plays later, from the 18, Morrison threw to end Ray Bussey who, like in his dream, snared the ball, dodged a defender, and raced untouched into the end zone. The kick failed, and the Wildcats held a 13-point lead, 20-7.

Late in the game, the Moguls managed one last-ditch effort drive that was snuffed out at the Archer City 25, and the celebration began on the sidelines and in the stands.

We're the champs
We're the champs
We're the CH-AM-PS!
We're the best
We're the best
We're the BE-ST Best!
Wildcats are the best
YES!

The Wildcats ran out the remaining four minutes, and only after the final buzzer sounded did they celebrate on their own. In the locker room, Grady congratulated each and every player. When he'd finished, he said, "You know what this means, don't you? We've got another game to play."

The locker room exploded.

The Archer City Wildcats were district champions.

As exciting as that was, the players knew it meant something else, too.

Another week of workouts. And knowing Coach Graves, they knew practices weren't likely to ease up any. They were right.

PART SEVEN

BATTLE ON THE FROZEN TUNDRA

CHAPTER 39

Laughter, the Best Medicine

PROCLAMATION
WHEREAS, the residents of Archer City are proud of the 1964 Wildcat football team in winning the District 11-A Championship, and,
WHEREAS, this is the first time Archer City has been represented in the state play-offs, and,
WHEREAS, every man, woman and child of Archer City should be at Decatur Friday night to cheer the Wildcats to victory in the bi-district match with Keller.
NOW, THEREFORE, I, L. D. Bailey, mayor of Archer City, do hereby proclaim Friday afternoon, November 20, a legal holiday in Archer City.
(signed) L. D. Bailey, Mayor

An odd thing happened following the Munday game. There was none of the usual "Why'd he call that play?" Or, "Why the heck did they do that?" Rather it was "Way to go!" And "We're behind you!" And they were. The town was in a frenzy. The Wildcats were in the play-offs for the very first time. Or second. Some remembered a team winning district back in 1926, but official records didn't go back that far. Either way, it was the biggest thing to hit Archer in a long, long time. Perhaps ever.

Later that week another odd thing happened—all of the Wildcats lost weight. Except for Mickey. He *gained* several pounds. Overnight, in game programs and newspaper articles, the weights of the players changed.

Before Coach Ray could begin his scouting report on Keller, Buddy Knox raised his hand. "Coach, are the weights of them players accurate?"

"By my best estimation they are."

"Well, how come ours aren't?"

Grady stepped forward. "Well, Buddy, let me put it this way. What if you worked out all week believin' you were going up against a 150-pounder and thinkin' 'man oh man, I'm gonna eat this guy up,' and then on the first play of the game a 170-pounder knocks you plum off the line of scrimmage?"

Buddy looked over at Jimmy Reeves and said, "This is gonna be fun!"

Once the laughter settled, Grady got down to business. "Guys, Keller doesn't give a flip about that little trophy you got for beatin' Munday. They have one of their own and plan on gettin' another. So if you've got any ideas about doin' so yourself, you better get ready to fight for it because they mean business. And somethin' else. Weathermen say there's a good chance a blue norther' will move through sometime Friday evening. Now, I usually don't go in for this kinda stuff, but if you think a pair of long johns or turtleneck will help you play better, then I guess you can wear 'em. Myself, I won't even have on a jacket. But Coach Ray and Coach Williams think this is the route we should go, so if you feel you need 'em, you can wear the darn things."

Butch Hannah raised his hand. "Coach, what about pantyhose? I hear they keep you *real* warm."

Amid the laughs and whistles, even Grady had to smile at his starting right tackle. "Butch, if you think wearin' your mother's pantyhose is what you wanna do, you go right ahead on; but I wouldn't let that guy across the line from you know." More laughs.

"Uh, Coach, I'm not gonna wear my *mom's* pantyhose!"

"Where're you gonna get 'em, Butch?"

The big tackle smiled. "I's thinkin' of borrowin' a pair of Parsley's."

The room roared with laughter.

Steve, his face only slightly red, didn't miss a beat. "You can, but they won't fit you—they'll be way too big in the crotch. But I probably still got an old pair of your girlfriend's in my car somewhere."

The laughter could be heard for blocks. The players couldn't remember ever having fun like this in Grady's presence. It felt really strange. And it felt darn good.

CHAPTER 40

Admiration

Finally, Grady put a halt to it. "Okay, guys, that's enough. Let's get back to the business of beatin' Keller." He looked over at Fuzzy. "Coach. What can you tell us about 'em?"

Coach Ray walked to the front. "Now, fellas, you're gonna see something Friday you haven't seen before and probably won't again. The Indians employ a true two-platoon system. That is, they have entirely different offensive and defensive teams with the exception of one player—Thornton, their fastest back. And the only reason he's playin' defense this week is their startin' safety's hurt. This means they'll always have fresh guys on the field. So you better get ready. As far as their players go, well, they've all got good size and good speed; but right now, I'd have to say their defense is their strong point. They've shut out the last four teams they've played and have given up only 88 points all year. You've definitely got your work cut out for you."

Grady got up from his seat. "There's a bunch of 'em, but they can only play eleven at a time. As for us, we're gonna run the ball right at 'em like we have everybody else. We've got a pretty good defense of our own, and if the weather's as cold as they say it might be, the game will probably be low scorin'. That means it'll come down to who's toughest and who wants it more. Any questions?"

Being none, Grady continued. "Mr. Leach is here from the Wichita paper to get some pictures. Now that you're in the play-offs, a lot of people are gonna be interested in what you have to say. Don't you go around tellin' 'em how you're gonna stomp anybody or any such nonsense. Don't you say anything like that. You just tell 'em to come watch. Don't talk about what you're gonna do; *show* 'em."

A few minutes later, there came a knock on Grady's office door. Ted Leach stuck his head in.

"Come in, Ted. Those boys behavin'?"

Ted laughed. He loved Grady's sense of humor. He suspected he might be the only person in north Texas who thought Grady had one.

"Coach, I've told you on numerous occasions those kids are the best-mannered group of young men I have ever had the pleasure of dealing with. I'm not going to tell you again."

Grady smiled back. "Yeah, but they're in strange waters these days after beatin' Munday."

"That's what I want to talk to you about. I was wondering if I could cover the game from the sideline instead of the press box this week."

"Be happy to have you, Ted. Just keep your eyes open and don't get run over. The boys are liable to be a little spirited come game time. And watch out for Joe as well. He gets pretty excited, too."

Ted couldn't help but smile. Covering the team for their respective newspapers the past three years, he and Joe Stults, editor of the Archer County News, had become friends. Ted considered Grady a friend as well. The Wildcat head coach was one of the most private and hard-to-get-to-know people he'd ever met. He had his own way of doing things, that's for sure, but Ted didn't mind that. And whether his methods were right or wrong, good or bad, he *had* turned these boys into football players. Darn good ones.

"Thanks, Coach. I'll be sure and do that. By the way, have you taken a look at the brackets to see who you might play should you win Friday night?"

"No, Ted, I haven't. Whoever it is, I figure we'll just put our pads on and go out there and find out who really wants to play football."

Ted nodded, turned to leave, paused at the door, and looked back.

"Coach, I don't know what the rest of the season holds for you and those young men out there. But I want you to know it's been my privilege to have witnessed what you've done here and what they've accomplished. I know Joe feels the same. And if anyone deserves to win, it's them. And you."

Grady looked at Ted, rose from his chair, and walked over.

"Thank you, Ted. I appreciate that. I don't know how it'll all play out, but I do know it's fixin' to get real interestin'."

Ted smiled, reached out and shook his hand.

"It doggone sure is."

CHAPTER 41

Into the Cold

The cold front hit Decatur during pre-game warmups, and it was a booger bear. The initial blast from the freezing north wind sent fans scurrying by droves to their vehicles and the restrooms to don added layers of clothing, brought just in case. It was there that a brand new fashion fad was invented by Archer City's Mary Lee Crowley—the skirt and wool long johns combo—which caught on quickly with the gals in the crowd. Minutes later inside the locker room, long johns, turtlenecks, gloves, extra socks, and a pair or two of pantyhose were put to use. A few of the linemen scoffed at the idea of extra attire and chose the "cold is just a state of mind" philosophy exhibited by their head coach.

After going over some last-minute details, a still-shivering Grady, in his white, short-sleeved sport shirt, addressed the troops. "Okay, now we know. It's cold out there. And that's the last I wanna hear about it. When you hit that field, you had darn better have your mind on football and nothin' else. I mean it. Let those other guys fritter about the weather."

As the players left the field house and stepped back out into the night, they were almost knocked back by the frigid air. In fifteen minutes' time, the temperature had dropped forty degrees into the twenties and was still dropping, the wind howling. As they waited for the signal to go, Barry stood next to Mike.

"How's your knee?" he asked, teeth chattering.

"Not too bad right now. And in ten minutes it won't matter. It'll be frozen solid like the rest of my body. Good Lord, it's cold out here!"

"Here comes Coach."

"All right, boys. Let's do this."

Most of Archer City was on hand. Those unable to attend had congregated at the Royal Theater around Sam Yeager's radio or were listening at home. Meanwhile, on the field, a surprising number of fans had left their blankets and hot coffee to form the customary victory line for the team to run through. As the cheerleaders fought to hold a giant "Scalp the Indians!" paper sign up against the wind, the team, anxious to get on with it, busted through it and headed down the sideline.

Once in front of their bench, the Wildcat players' eyes settled on the Keller Indians across the field. There appeared to be a hundred of them.

"Dadgum." Buddy turned and looked at Jimmy. "Their school's the same size as ours, ain't it?"

"Far as I know."

"Then how come they got so many guys on their team?"

"Coach Graves ain't their coach."

The referee's whistle blew, and the players took the field for the opening kickoff. After the first three possessions, it was clear who was going to dominate *this* contest: the cold. Simply holding onto the ball was a difficult task, and passing was out of the question. On the night, the Wildcats would complete only one pass, for five yards. Keller: one pass, for nine yards. Every snap, every kick, every block, and every tackle hurt. A lot.

Their first two times with the ball, Archer City failed to get near midfield and punted. Then, on Keller's second possession, Thornton escaped around end for 33 yards down to the Wildcat 41-yard line. From there, three running plays netted them nine-plus yards, leaving a fourth-and-inches at the 32. Disregarding the pass, the Wildcats lined up in their Gap-8 goal line defense.

The Wildcat cheerleaders and fans chanted, "*Hold that line! Hold that line! Hold that line!*" And they did.

Taking over, they managed only one first down, and then on their own fourth-down try, were unable to move the markers. Keller took over at the 49, and four plays later crossed the 20 down to the 18, gaining the game's first penetration. A fumble recovery by the Wildcats stopped the drive and prevented a score. After moving the ball out to their 29, Larry Graham checked into the huddle and looked at Robert.

"Coach wants to know why you're just standin' around."

"Cause my legs don't work, that's why!"

"Well, you better get 'em working, cause he's pissed." He then turned to Barry. He said to run 30 Dive and keep runnin' it till we get it right."

Barry took a deep breath and exhaled a thick fog. "All right, guys. 30 Dive. On hut."

At the snap, Robert willed his legs into action, Gary shot through the opening, ran over the linebacker, and was finally dragged down from behind at the Keller 36. But a 15-yard penalty and incomplete pass put an end to the drive.

The defenses for both teams took control, and the battle see-sawed back and forth with no real scoring threats. As halftime neared, most players' minds were on the warmth of the locker rooms. Except Steve Parsley's. He was determined to use the last play before the buzzer to get in one more good lick on Keller, and he got in a good one. *Too* good. As he climbed off the Indians' big fullback Danny Wilson, Steve noticed the face mask on his helmet was missing. And something else. His nose was busted. Not that he could feel it, numb as it was, but the direction it was pointed and all the blood coming from it were pretty good indicators.

Many years later, during an examination by an ear, nose, and throat specialist, he was asked, "Do you know what the inside of your nose looks like? You have a deviated septum."

"You don't say."

"It's been badly broken."

"Yeah, I know. I was there when it happened."

CHAPTER 42

The Boys of Winter

With the score tied at zero and Keller leading in penetrations 1-0, the teams sprinted to their respective locker rooms. Once inside, the Wildcat players were shocked to find something they'd not seen before: small, bottled Cokes set out for each. They gulped them down as they examined fingers and toes for frostbite. Grady walked in. He was as white as a sheet.

"B-B-B-Boys. I b-b-b-believe I'm g-gonna have t-t-to p-put on a j-j-jacket."

Banking on the sudden good nature Grady had exhibited in the scouting meeting earlier in the week, Barry couldn't resist.

"How come, Coach?"

"C-C-Cause it's c-c-c-c-c-cold out there."

The players could only remember not getting a butt-chewing a handful of times in all the games they'd played, and on those rare occasions they'd usually gotten the silent treatment, which was even worse. Tonight it appeared they might escape both.

Ten minutes later, having thawed and wearing a jacket, Grady returned.

"The platoon system isn't workin' for 'em. It might be good on a hot day, but tonight, those boys standin' on the sideline waitin' to come back in are sufferin'. And now that Robert's decided to play ball and block, we're startin' to move it. You runnin' backs are doin' a good job. Especially you, Tepfer. If we keep it up, we'll get in the end zone where we belong. We don't wanna win this thing on penetrations or first downs or any of that nonsense. We wanna beat 'em on the scoreboard, where it counts. So let's go do that."

As the players stepped outside, an eerie sight greeted them. A handful of 55-gallon drums had been placed around the perimeter of the field and set afire—the black smoke held low to the ground by the wind giving the appearance of a battlefield. Their return signaled by the blast of the cannon, down the sideline they went, the acrid smoke burning their eyes.

"Wonder whose bright idea this was?"

Mike looked over at Gary. "I guess they're there to keep people warm."

"Well, maybe they'll burn out pretty soon."

"I wouldn't count on it. That smells like diesel."

With red eyes, the two teams lined up for the second-half kickoff—something Wildcat kicker Barry Morrison was not looking forward to. He awaited the referee's whistle, then advanced on the ball, trying to imagine it being a feather rather than the 10-pound chunk of granite it felt like.

Continuing their stout defensive play, the Wildcats quickly forced Keller to punt and took over the ball on their own 46-yard line. Behind the blocking of his brother Robert and Butch Hannah, number 74 stormed through a hole, cut to his right, picked up a block by Barney Oliver downfield, and galloped 40 yards to the Indian 14. Mike then carried for four to the 10 and Gary for eight to the one. With the fans on both sides on their feet, Tepfer crashed in for the score, Barry's PAT into the stiff wind was true, and Archer City led 7-0.

As it had on Steve Parsley's earlier in the game, the extreme cold began taking a toll on the players' fiberglass face masks, and by the third quarter trainer David Wright had become adept at changing them quickly. He looked up to see Mike Stewart headed his way, his broken for the second time. Number 35 handed his helmet to David who just shook his head and smiled.

"What's so funny?"

"I guess you don't know you've got a piece of this thing stickin' out the side of your face."

Mike reached up, felt it, and pulled it out. "Is it bleed-in'?"

"Yeah, but don't worry. It'll stop soon as it freezes."

They both laughed, David handed him back his helmet complete with a new face mask, and off he went.

Archer was forced to punt, and on the first play from scrimmage, the Indians came ever-so-close to changing the entire complexion of the ball game.

Hoping to catch the Wildcats off guard, Keller went with a fake reverse. As soon as Billy Holder recognized the fake, he came flying up from his cornerback position to stop the ball carrier. Committed, he then watched in horror as the runner pulled up suddenly and lofted a pass over his head down the field where Billy *should* have been. He turned and ran, knowing he had no chance. Time slowed to a crawl for the Archer players and fans as they spotted the wide-open player in full stride. Helpless, all watched the ball softly drop out of the night sky directly into the Indian receiver's hands.

And through them.

Incomplete.

A jubilant and grateful Billy Holder stopped and raised both hands high above his head with one thought in mind. "Thank you, Lord. Thank you."

While it's unlikely the Lord was concerned with the score or the game's outcome, it *is* possible He might have heard Billy's silent pleas and thought of his welfare. For had the ball been caught, facing Grady might have carried life and death implications.

From that point forward, a tenacious Wildcat defense put the clamps on Danny Wilson, Charles Thornton, and the rest of the Keller offense, and coach Paul Allen's Indians never threatened again in the second half. Archer City controlled the ball and the clock on its way to a hard-fought 7-0 victory. In addition to scoring the game's only touchdown, Wildcat full-back Gary Tepfer carried the ball 32 times for 157 yards and blocked a punt. The final rushing tally was Archer City - 255 and Keller - 183. Seven fumbles were lost in the contest, four by the Wildcats and three by the Indians. It wasn't a pretty win, but it was Archer's.

PART EIGHT

STRANGERS IN A STRANGE LAND

CHAPTER 43

Larger Than Life

The next morning, Barry and Mike reported to Haigood and Campbell Butane Co. for work as they normally did on Saturdays. However, in recent weeks their job duties had changed, and now they spent their first two hours recounting every play in detail from the previous night's game. When they finished some two hours later, Cecil "Butter" Haigood and A. O. "Bully" Campbell quickly headed for the diner to share their knowledge with a host of anxious listeners—a Saturday morning ritual. The boys enjoyed reliving the games but weren't too interested in spending their entire weekends doing so. Therefore, some locations about town had to be avoided. Among those was the Walsh Brothers' Mobile Station on the courthouse square. The Walsh brothers—Jay, Tom, Fred, and Frank—were football connoisseurs of the highest order, and not satisfied with covering every play from the previous night's game, but every play of every game that year. And if the player wasn't strong-willed, the season before and the season before that. It was an affair that continued for decades.

All twenty-one players on the Wildcat squad were finding themselves in a strange, new world. Adrift in uncharted waters, the boys had crossed to a whole, other level. They were no longer simply heroes.

Now, they walked the earth like gods.

The town worshiped them, and Grady was dangerously close to losing his grip on them and knew it. Everywhere they went, they were approached. Told how great they were. How much they were appreciated. Asked to stand and be recognized at church. Honked at on the streets. Each receiving enough handshakes and pats on the back to last a lifetime.

Some were even asked for autographs.

Grady had warned them, but these were just kids, and the pitfall he feared most was at hand: They were losing their focus. And that just wouldn't do.

As the players laughed and joked getting ready for Monday's workout, the door to the dressing room flew open and against the wall with a loud BANG.

"You boys think you're special now? Big shot bi-district champs. Everybody loves you. That what you think?"

"No sir."

"Well, gentlemen, get your butts dressed and out on that field, because you're fixin' to come back to the real world." Then he left, slamming the door on his way out.

After a nervous moment or two, Steve broke the silence.

"Okay, which one of you sorry good-for-nothins broke his favorite coffee cup?"

The anticipated doom that lay outside the locker room door materialized as expected.

The workout was ferocious. The players had been through worse but couldn't remember when. Afterwards, they sat on the benches in front of their lockers too exhausted to remove their uniforms to shower. Or even speak. Shortly, all three coaches walked in, led by Grady.

"Okay, now that we got that straight, and your attention back on football, let's talk about the Goldthwaite Eagles. Beginning with their record which happens to be 5-4-0. That's right, four losses. Now, I can stand here and tell you those were their first four games of the season and most were against bigger schools, but that doesn't matter. What matters is that they have won five games in a row and are playin' for the same regional title as you. And as much as I hate it, some people are even pickin' us to beat 'em. Well, for that to happen several things have to go our way. First, we have to stop their fullback Jim Childress. And their halfback Charles Blackburn. And their quarterback Johnny Hammond. AND, we have to figure out a way to move the ball ourselves. Coach?"

Coach Ray stepped forward. "The thing that impresses me most about this team is their defense. They're well-coached, they're quick, and these boys hit. All night long. So have your jocks on straight when you take the field cause they *will* lay a lick on you. Oh, and Parsley, the kid across from you outweighs you a hundred pounds. Name's Duren. And before you go thinkin' he's big and slow, think again. He can move, and you'd better have your head screwed on straight or he'll straighten it for you. You hear?"

"Coach, have you *ever* known me not to have my head on straight?"

The team was too tired to laugh, which was probably a good thing.

The fun and games were over.

CHAPTER 44

Hard Knocks

With their jocks and heads on straight, in perfect fall weather on the Friday following Thanksgiving at Public School Stadium in Abilene, the Archer City Wildcats took the field in the nicest facility they'd ever played in.

Broadcasting the play-off game on the radio, Jack Britton—sportscaster for the local CBS television affiliate in Wichita Falls—was unfamiliar with Big Champ. The cannon's blast shook the windows and everything that wasn't nailed down in the press box.

"Holy Moses!" he yelled into his microphone. "On the far side of the field somebody shot off a cannon, and if I'm not mistaken, that is the Archer City cannon that I've heard so much about! And here come the Wildcats!"

In person, the Eagles were bigger than first thought, and following the Wildcats' first possession, one thing was clear: When push came to shove, Goldthwaite didn't mess around. They hit. And hit *hard*. Many of the hits could be heard throughout the stands—but none louder than Ray Bussey's on the Eagles' Jim Childress and teammate Robert Tepfer midway through the first quarter. Flying up from his safety position, Bussey exploded into both just as Robert was making the tackle. Ray got up. So did Childress. So, finally, did Robert. The stout linebacker, who was usually on the delivering end of such blows, slowly climbed to his feet and meandered back to the defensive huddle.

"You okay?" Ray asked.

Nothing.

His brother Gary grabbed his jersey. "HEY! You all right?!"

Nothing.

"You need to go out?"

Still nothing. Time for the next play.

As they headed for the line of scrimmage, number 61 instinctively followed tackle Butch Hannah to the line, stopping just behind him in his customary linebacker position. And so it went. For the remainder of the game, he relied on vague memories from the far reaches of his mind to get him where he needed to be and do what needed to be done.

Meanwhile, there were other battles taking place, and Steve Parsley didn't like how his was going. Finally, he walked over to the ref.

"That big guy's holdin' me."

"What do you mean? You're on offense."

"I *know* that. He keeps fallin' on me and not gettin' up. I can't get downfield to block."

"Son, I've been watching, and he's not holding you."

Steve Parsley and Jimmy Reeves had been known to pluck a few chickens (pull the hair from opposing players' legs in pileups) on occasion, and when needed, take even more drastic measures. This was one of those times. On the next play, with the big tackle on top of him, Steve grabbed low and let him have it. After climbing off Steve and staggering off the field—stopping to throw up along the way—the big fella returned a few plays later.

"You okay?" Steve asked.

"Yeah, but let's not do that anymore."

"Well, if you don't hold me, we won't."

And they didn't.

With the game still scoreless midway through the second quarter, Archer City dropped back to punt from their own 34-yard line. A good rush by the Eagles hurried punter Morrison whose boot traveled only 10 yards. In business at the Wildcat 44, Childress carried for six, Charles Blackburn for three, and quarterback Johnny Hammond for four and a first down at the 31. From there, Childress managed only two yards before Blackburn was dropped for a loss of one. Following an incomplete pass, the Eagles faced a fourth-and-nine in the first critical test for both teams. Staring down a fierce rush, Hammond calmly tossed a screen pass to halfback Jimmy Ball who raced down to the 11-yard line.

Push 'em back. Push 'em back. Waaaaaaaaay back!

With fire in their eyes, the Eagles hurried to the line of scrimmage. Hammond handed to Childress who bulled ahead for five. Ball then followed with two of his own, and on third down, Childress again got the call and stormed up the middle for the score with 4:05 remaining in the half.

Without hesitation, Goldthwaite lined up to go for two.

Childress took the ball and plowed ahead to the goal line where he was momentarily stacked up until Ray Bussey ended the run with a punishing blow that ended all doubt. The result: Goldthwaite was left with a 6-0 lead, Childress with a broken face mask and a cut to his face, and Bussey with a humdinger of a headache.

CHAPTER 45

A Matter of Pride

A battered and bruised group of players sat quietly in the Wildcat locker room downing their Cokes awaiting the storm. Shortly, the door flew open and the gale blew in.

"So that's how it is? You run into a team that hits back and suddenly the game's not fun anymore?" He glared about the room, his eyes coming to rest on Robert.

"Son, are you hurt? Cause you're just sleepwalkin' out there. You want somebody to take your place?"

Number 61 slowly shook his head.

"What about the rest of you? Anybody wanna sit out the second half? Out of harm's way?"

"No sir!"

"Maybe I shoulda left gold in your uniforms after all."

"No sir!"

"Men, I'll put the subs in if I have to. They get the crap beat out of 'em in practice every day by you big, tough guys, and *they* don't back down. That way, at least we'll leave here with our dignity. That what you want?"

"NO SIR!"

"Well, then, get your butts back out there, and show it!"

As they trotted back onto the field, Steve ran up to Ray.

"I don't know what he's so pissed about. You knocked old Childress's face mask plum off. You know that?"

"I did?"

"Yeah. That oughta slow him down a little."

"Who?"

Number 85 looked into Ray's glassed-over gaze, shook his head, and chuckled.

"Forget it."

The fierce hitting on both sides continued. Following a Wildcat punt late in the third quarter, Jimmy Reeves headed onto the field only to be jerked back by Grady. He turned loose of the nose guard's jersey and grabbed his face mask.

"Son, we need the ball back. *You hear me?* Now, get in there and get it for us!"

His adrenalin at a dangerous level, Jimmy Reeves sprinted onto the field as fast as he could run.

A few of the Wildcats heard what sounded like hoof beats approaching only to discover it was a human bowling ball. Jimmy hit the huddle without slowing, scattering Wildcats like bowling pins.

Barry wasn't amused. "What the heck are you doin'? Are you crazy?"

"Coach told me to get the ball."

Billy Pitts squeezed back into his place. "That's fine, but watch where you're goin' next time!"

Jimmy raised up and looked. "Will do."

At the snap, Jimmy thought it in his best interest to follow Coach's orders, so, like a man possessed, he promptly tore past the center into the backfield. This time it was the opposing players who were knocked every which way. As the whistle blew and the officials scrambled looking for the ball, Jimmy held it up.

"This what you're lookin' for?"

The Wildcats took over on the Eagle 41-yard line and went to work.

On the first play, Morrison found Stewart open in the left flat at the 35 where he shook free and was finally brought down, dragging two defenders, at the 23. Three consecutive tough runs by Tepfer got them to the 17-yard line where they faced fourth-and-four. From there, Barry rolled to his right, and behind the blocking of Barney, Butch, Gary, and Mike, rambled 12 yards to the five-yard line. First-and-goal.

Three straight hand-offs to their bruising fullback took the ball to the one-inch-line where it was fourth down. As the teams lined up with the crowd on its feet, three things were certain. First, the next play would be a running play. Second, the ball carrier would be number 74. And third, no one was going to keep Gary Tepfer out of the end zone.

Right on all accounts.

Morrison's kick was true, and with 2:46 left in the third quarter, the Archer City Wildcats took the lead 7-6.

CHAPTER 46

Direct Hit!

"Jodie, will you *please* take off that god-awful green toboggan?"

"Okay, Trecie, don't have a hissy."

"Well, it just doesn't look good with our outfits. Does it, Judy?"

"Not unless you're color blind."

"All right, all right!"

Just in the nick of time. Having already introduced the Eagle cheerleaders to the Archer crowd, it was now time for them to meet the Goldthwaite faithful. They lined up in pairs, their rivals doing the honors.

"Hey, everybody, this is Pat Holder. And she's a freshman!"

"Hey, everybody, this is Wort Lear. And she's a sophomore!"

"Hey, everybody, this is Sun Ann Brock. And she's a junior!"

"Hey, everybody, this is Jodie Wright. And *she's* a junior!"

"Hey, everybody, this is Judy Crowley. And she's a senior!"

"Hey, everybody, this is Trecie Trigg. And *she's* a senior. *And* head cheerleader!"

The Eagle band hit a few notes, the crowd clapped, and the Wildcat cheerleaders performed a cheer, substituting the word *Eagles* for Wildcats. They then waved goodbye and started back around the perimeter of the field just as Tepfer was crashing over for the touchdown. Realizing what had happened, cheering and waving pom-poms, they sprinted toward the Wildcat stands passing directly in front of the Archer cannon at precisely the wrong moment. *KA-BOOM!*

To the shock of everyone in the stadium, the petite blonde in the green toboggan went tumbling across the field, finally coming to rest on the 30-yard line. Her partners, mesmerized, stood staring and then ran to her aid.

Wort reached her first. "Jodie! Are you all right?!"

"What?"

"Are you *hurt?!*"

"Talk louder."

"Oh my gosh! She's deaf!"

Jodie Wright sat up, shook her head, and asked, "What the heck just happened?"

"The cannon shot you!"

Cannoneers Monroe Williams and L.J. Cathey promptly arrived on the scene.

"Goodness gracious, little lady, are you okay?!"

In a panic, Jodie said, "Yes! I'm fine! Please leave. You're makin' a scene!"

"You're sure you're all right?"

"*Yes!*"

Jodie watched them walk away. In the distance—an even more horrifying sight.

"Oh, Lord. Here comes Mother!"

In a matter of seconds, Lorene Wright was on the scene.

"Mom! For goodness sakes, I'm fine. Will you get outta here?!"

"I thought you were dead!"

"Well, I'm not. But I'll certainly die from humiliation if you don't leave this instant."

"Well . . ."

"NOW!"

"Okay. If you're *sure* . . ."

"GO!"

And she did.

The others helped her to her feet and waved off any other concerned onlookers.

The ringing in her ears subsiding, she asked, "Who scored the touchdown?"

"Gary, who do you think?"

"Oh, Lord, *he'll* be hard to live with this week."

"You can *hear?!*"

"Yeah, come on, let's go. Everybody's starin'."

As they led Jodie away, Trecie ran back to fetch something left behind. She caught up and handed it to Jodie.

"Here. We wouldn't want you to lose *this*."

It was the green toboggan.

"Ain't you sweet?" She started to put it on, but hesitated.

"Aw, go ahead," Trecie instructed. "And next time watch where you're goin', okay?"

"Don't you worry, hon."

CHAPTER 47

The Call

Following the touchdown, Archer City kicked off and Goldthwaite drove into Wildcat territory. On the first play of the fourth quarter, they fumbled the ball away to Archer.

Following a 15-yard penalty—their only penalty of the night—the Wildcats eventually had to punt the ball back. Once again, their defense, which allowed the Eagles just eight first downs all night, put the clamps on and forced another punt.

The kick, a boomer, sailed over the heads of Ray Bussey and freshman Bob Gaines, hit between them, and bounded toward the goal line as they gave chase. Gaines caught up and grabbed it just before it went into the end zone at the three-yard line where he was downed immediately. He climbed up, headed off, and spotted a ballistic Coach Graves waving him over. As soon as he arrived, Grady grabbed his face mask and gave him what for.

"Son, are you crazy? Why'd you pick that ball up?!!!"

"It was a live ball."

"That was a *punt*, not a *kickoff!!!*"

"Well, Bussey kept yellin' at me, "Pick it up! Pick it up!"

With the action on the field halted, Grady motioned Ray over. Anticipating the worst, the tall end sprinted over stopping just out of arm's length. "Yes sir?"

"What'd you tell Gaines to pick that ball up for?"

"I didn't. I was yellin', "Get away from it! Get away from it!"

Back on the field, the referee explained the delay.

"Offside on Goldthwaite. Repeat fourth down."

Bob and Ray looked at each other.

Saved.

Still holding Bob's face mask, he slung him back out onto the field. "Get back in there!" Ray, having been around four years, was already headed back out, just outside the reach of Grady's foot.

Gaines fielded the next kick cleanly and after a short return, the Wildcats had the ball on their 28-yard line. First-and-10.

V - I - C - T - O - R - Y

That's the Wildcat battle cry!

Once again working on the clock, Morrison fed Tepfer the ball five straight times, gaining 20 yards and running precious time off. For the most part, Grady had always let Barry call his own plays—after, of course, much discussion during the week and the establishment of a clear game plan dictating which ones he could choose from. Occasionally, he sent his own in from the sideline, as was the case just now. Horany checked in replacing Stewart.

"Coach said to keep feedin' it to Gary."

Then, to everyone's amazement, in his usual calm, commanding voice, Barry called something different: 27 Belly, a fake to Gary up the middle and a handoff to Holder off tackle. They looked at him like he'd just lost his mind. Changing up the play Grady wanted run was not going to be taken lightly; they might *all* be considered co-conspirators—a scary thought. And Barry wasn't finished.

"Billy, instead of runnin' off tackle, I want you go around end. Ray, Steve, don't even block your guys. Just turn 'em loose, you hear?"

He really had lost his mind. Not knowing what else to do, they nodded.

"On hut. Ready, break."

As outlined, Barry took the snap at the 48, faked to Gary up the middle, and handed to Billy Holder who headed left. Expecting a sixth straight plunge by Tepfer, the Eagles fully bit on the fake, and Billy waltzed around end, dashing untouched to the end zone. The touchdown run covered 52 yards. The PAT kick was wide, but the Wildcats led 13-6 with just over five minutes remaining in the contest.

After a brief celebration on the field, and without ever looking over at Grady, Morrison kicked off. The kick was a good one. Jimmy Ball gathered it in at his 15 and took off. He sidestepped a tackler and broke into the open! In another place and time, the unthinkable might have happened. But not here. After a good return, he was dragged down by several determined Wildcats at the Goldthwaite 38-yard line. There, the Eagles commenced their final drive.

Hammond dropped back and hit Ball for eight quick yards out to the 46. The next pass was incomplete. On third-and-two, Hammond dropped back again but could not escape number 74. The Wildcat workhorse dropped the Eagle QB for a seven-yard loss.

Faced with fourth-and-nine deep in their own territory, Goldthwaite opted to punt with 2:28 left, hoping to stop the Wildcats and get the ball back one last time.

They didn't.

At the final buzzer, the elder Tepfer grabbed his younger brother and asked him for the umpteenth time, "You sure you're okay?"

Robert stared at the familiar voice waiting for the face to come into focus.

"Game over?" he asked.

"You serious? Yeah it's over!"

"Who won?"

Held to just 161 yards total offense and six points, Goldthwaite fell victim to the same forces as Keller had: a devastating Wildcat defense and unstoppable running game. For the record, Holder led all rushers with 87 yards on seven carries with 52 coming on his TD run. Gary had 79 yards on 25 carries, Stewart 56 yards in 15 tries, and Morrison 20 in 4.

Despite the score, Barry was still nervous about having called the audible, but he needn't have been. Grady never mentioned it. Good, bad, or otherwise.

Their victory sparked the interest of sports writers and high school football fans everywhere as the Texas schoolboy play-off brackets were updated. Next up, the surprising, upstart Wildcats from Archer City versus the Clifton Cubs. And Superman.

PART NINE

MEET MR. HAYWOOD

CHAPTER 48

Faster Than a Speeding Bullet

Grady leaned back in his office chair, looked over at Roy, then at Fuzzy.

"Haywood's that good, huh?"

"Coach, this kid is fabulous. He's not big—155—but he's *fast*."

"How fast?"

"*Mucho* fast. He can scoot. We don't have anyone *close* to him. If he gets outside us, he's gone. Doesn't matter if it's ten yards or ninety—it's six points. And he's got all the moves. He's gonna be a handful, I'm tellin' you."

Roy spit into his coffee cup. "What's his stats?"

"In his first ten games alone, he rushed for over 1,700 yards and scored 172 points. And get this—he never played in the second half. Spent the third and fourth quarters in his street clothes!" Fuzzy glanced at his notes. "As a team, they've scored 428 points and given up only 31. All three of their play-off games have been shutouts. So, they can play defense, too. Also, this ain't their first rodeo. It's their ninth trip to the play-offs and third in a row."

"You paint a pretty grim picture."

"Yeah, but they can be had. Haywood's the main wheel. We just need to stop it from turnin'."

"Anything else?"

"Not really. Did I mention he's fast?"

Grady smiled. "Yes, you did"

"I kinda remember hearin' that, too," Roy added with a big grin.

"Did I mention he's black? Not that it matters."

"No, you didn't. And no, it don't." Grady looked over at Roy. "Sounds like Gary and Barney have their work cut out for 'em."

Roy wiped his lip with the back of his hand. "What I wanna know is who we got that can play that kid in practice?"

Coach Ray stood and laughed. "Nobody."

Grady stood as well. "Well, then, we best get to it," he said, heading out the door to the practice field.

As soon as calisthenics were over, Grady gathered everyone together.

"Okay, let's have the first-team defense. Coach Ray's the Clifton quarterback, and Horany, you're gonna be their hot-shot running back, James Haywood."

"Yes sir."

"You defensive players listen up. Now, Mickey's pretty quick, but I want you to imagine him twice as fast as he is. Got that? That means you need to be there to tackle him a full two seconds in advance, and your angle of attack needs to be a whole lot wider. In other words, aim for a spot a good five yards out in front of him."

Mickey was a little embarrassed. He knew he wasn't *that* slow. "Five whole yards, Coach?"

"You're right. Better make it seven."

There were scattered laughs among the players.

"Guys, you better get this right. Or Friday's gonna be your last game. You hear?"

"Yes sir."

"Now, the most important part. Gary, Barney, get over here."

The two hustled over to where Grady was standing.

"Listen very carefully, this is of utmost importance. You can *not*, under *any* circumstance, let this guy get outside you. Is that clear?"

"Yes sir."

"Cause if you *do*, a six is goin' up on the scoreboard, and it won't be under our name."

"Yes sir."

"That about it, Coach?"

Fuzzy smiled and nodded. "That's the whole truth."

"Men, I want someone hittin' Mr. Haywood on every play whether he has the ball or not. If he goes to the bathroom, I want someone tacklin' him when he comes out. Do *not,* I repeat, do *not* let him out of your sight. That clear?"

"YES SIR!"

"Okay, then let's get to work."

CHAPTER 49

The Visitor

The visitors' locker room at Arlington State College Stadium on Friday just prior to the start of the quarter-final championship game night was quiet.

"Okay, guys. You know what you need to do. If each of you do your job on every single play tonight, we stand a chance. But you cannot let up for a moment, or Mr. Haywood and the rest of that bunch will eat you alive. You *have* to go out there and play *our* kind of football, and you have to send these guys a signal early. *Especially* Mr. Haywood. Let him know he's in for a long night." Grady looked around the room. For the first time in a long while, he thought he spotted some doubt on some of their faces. Maybe even fear. He wasn't sure. "All right, let's go!" And he followed them out. Soon enough, he'd know.

Archer City won the toss, elected to receive, and began the game with their bread and butter—Tepfer up the middle and Stewart and Holder going wide. The Cub defense soon stiffened, forcing the Wildcats to punt, and the Archer City fans collectively held their breaths as James Haywood dropped back to receive. Barry's punt was high and long, and just as he fielded the ball along the sideline, the talented runner was creamed by Gary Tepfer, who continued to drive Haywood out of bounds until the two crashed into the cyclone fence surrounding the field. Gary climbed to his feet to find Mike's dad Gene standing right there, leaning against the fence, smiling.

"Can't you hit any harder'n that, Tepfer?" he kidded.

Gary grinned and started away.

"Hey, you hit me out of bounds!"

Gary stopped and turned around.

"Coach told me to hit you on every play, and that's what I'm gonna do. You best get ready." The signal had been sent.

There was no flag on the play, so Clifton began deep in their territory. After huddling, quarterback Jerry Allen brought his team to the line of scrimmage, and just before the ball was snapped, a whistle blew. It was quickly decided the whistle had been inadvertent, and there was no foul on the play. Barney glanced over at Billy Pitts to his right. "If they don't huddle up again, they're comin' this way."

"How do you know?"

"Cause their end picked up his hand and leaned your direction. If he's blocking down on you, Haywood's comin' around this end. You can bet on it."

Both watched as the Clifton players returned to the line without huddling. They took their stances, and as soon as the ball was snapped Barney put a lick on the end so he couldn't get a good block on Billy, then he picked a point to the left of Haywood and shot across the line. As soon as he took the handoff and started to his right, Barney dropped him for a two-yard loss. Hard. And the Archer fans went wild.

A second signal had been sent. After a couple of short gains, Clifton punted and Archer took over on its 40 and began a long, time-consuming, 11-play drive behind the running of Tepfer and Stewart. Four plays into the second quarter, from the two-yard-line, Stewart took the ball off tackle behind the blocks of Butch Hannah and Barney Oliver and scored. The kick was wide, but the Wildcats led 6-0.

Following a good kickoff return, Haywood got it in gear, and the Cubs were quickly at midfield. Then, without a cloud in the night sky, lightning struck. Quarterback Jerry Allen took the snap and pitched back to his talented running back. In the blink of an eye, a blitzing Gary Tepfer lunged between Haywood and Allen, tipped the ball with his fingertips, fished it out of the air, and took off. A quick 48 yards later, the Wildcats led 12-0. The play happened so fast that many in the stadium, including players, weren't for sure what had happened. Archer City elected to try for two, but the pass attempt failed. A shell-shocked Clifton huddled up on the sideline trying to regroup.

Interestingly, just prior to the Wildcat scoring barrage, a Cub fan had wandered over to the Archer City side of the field and joined Claude Morrison and J. D. Pitts leaning against the fence watching the game. He introduced himself as the father of one of the Clifton players.

"Just so you fellas know, we respect your team and this Cinderella thing you've had goin', so we're not gonna run up the score on you tonight like we usually do." As he waited for their response, Mike plowed over for his touchdown.

The stranger shook his head. "Oh gosh, you shouldn't have never done that. Our boys'll run that score sky high on you now."

Three plays later, Gary intercepted the pitchout and scampered to pay dirt. As the Archer fans behind him exploded, the visitor bid his farewell.

"You know what? I'd better get on back over to the other side. Hell, we might not even beat y'all."

Claude and J. D. smiled at each other and went back to watching the game. Neither had spoken a word.

CHAPTER 50

The Myth

On Clifton's next possession, Steve Parsley decided enough was enough. He hadn't managed a solid hit yet on Clifton's much ballyhooed running back and was plenty upset. In fact, since Gary's and Barney's hits at the beginning, no one had. The reason was simple: The guy was good. On some plays, three different players had shots at him and *all* missed. Only hustle and gang tackling had prevented him from running wild. No more. That crap had to stop. And number 85 was gonna see to it.

Undaunted by the catastrophe the last time they pitched to Gary's side, on third down they came again. This time Haywood started to his left, grabbed the toss, cut inside a waiting Gary Tepfer, then outside past a diving Butch Hannah and into the open. From his cornerback position, Steve lined him up and bore down. There wasn't gonna be any of this gettin' faked outta his jock this time. Instead, he gambled. At the last instant Steve went right hoping to heck Haywood didn't go left.

He didn't.

There was a tremendous collision—the kind Parsley longed for and was known for. Haywood turned what amounted to a back flip while Steve bounced backwards and somersaulted to a stop five yards back. Not one to let anyone know any different, he climbed to his feet and headed in the direction where he last remembered the defensive huddle being. Larry Graham saw him drifting and grabbed his arm.

"You okay?"

"He get up?" Steve asked without looking back.

Larry looked over his shoulder. "Yep. He looks kinda woozy, though."

Steve stopped, spit, and looked up at Larry, still trying to clear his head.

"You know that thing Grady's always tellin' us about how the harder you hit somebody the less you feel it?"

"I think what he said was, 'If you hit him harder than he hits you, it hurts less."

"Yeah, well, that's a buncha bull. That hurt like *hell*."

A few plays later, Clifton punted and the Wildcats took over on their own 28-yard line with 6:40 showing on the clock. Pounding away with their running game, they managed to run off nearly six minutes before finally giving the ball back to the Cubs on their own 27. Four plays later the half ended with the Wildcats in the lead 12-0.

As soon as they hit the locker room, Grady exploded.

"Parsley, what kinda tackle was that? For goodness sakes, I thought we taught you better'n that. If you're gonna hit somebody, *HIT* 'em! Don't just run up there and bounce off 'em. It's embarrassing."

The way Steve saw it, there were three things he could do with the Coke bottle in his lap. One, he could throw it. Two, he could eat it. And he could, too, he was that mad. Or three, he could take a deep breath, finish drinking from it, and set it aside knowing Coach was either pickin' on him as he had the past two years or trying to make him mad so he'd play even harder. He decided it was a little of both and set the bottle aside. Madder'n hell.

Jimmy Reeves was next.

"We worked all week on not lettin' Haywood get outside. So far, Gary and Barney are doin' a halfway decent job of it. They quit hittin' him, but at least he's not gettin' outside. So what's he do? He starts goin' up the gut on us. Reeves! You think you might start tryin' to stop that little screen up the middle of theirs? Or is that too much to ask?"

"Yes sir."

"Yes sir, that's too much to ask, or yes sir, you might get around to tryin' to stop it?"

"Yes sir, I might get around to . . ."

"Well, you dad-blasted better stop it if you know what's good for you! *You got that?"*

"Yes sir. Got it. I'll stop that up-the-middle crap. Sir!"

"And that goes for you linebackers, too. Barry! Robert! I want that middle clogged up! *NOW!"*

"Yes sir!"

"Let me tell you somethin', boys. You think you've got 'em? Just cause he hasn't scored, you think Haywood's done? Well, I got news for you. He's not even warmed up yet. He's over there in that locker room right this second wantin' half-time over with so he can get back out there and show you and everybody else what for. You know why? Cause you quit hit-tin' him! You started grabbin' and arm tacklin' him like a bunch of girls. So you best get ready." He paused, glaring around the room.

An official stuck his head in the door and announced, "Five minutes, Coach."

"We don't need five more minutes! We're ready now!" He turned and faced the team. *"What're you waitin' for? GET OUT THERE!"*

CHAPTER 51

Escort Service

On Clifton's first possession of the second half, with Haywood dancing around in the backfield looking for a place to run, Billy Pitts and Barry Morrison each saw an opportunity to finally deliver the kind of blow Grady was demanding; but at the last instant, Haywood spun away and the two collided, Billy's helmet splitting down the middle. Dazed, he reached down, picked up the two halves along with the face mask lying a few feet away, and jogged to the bench, relaxed in knowing that, at least for the moment, he was safe from Grady grabbing his face mask and jerking him over.

"Somebody give me a helmet!"

Jimmy Boone quickly relinquished his to help the cause. Billy grabbed it and returned to the field. He found Barry in the huddle looking equally shaken.

"He okay?" he asked.

Mike grinned. "Yeah, Barry's okay." Then, "Whose helmet you got?"

"Boone's."

"It looks a mite small."

"It is. It's very uncomfortable."

The referee signaled ready for play, and just as Coach had predicted, Haywood got going. The Cubs promptly put together a 13-play drive with their star carrying the ball on eight of them and chewing up big chunks of yardage all the way down to the Wildcat two-yard line where the speedster went airborne for the score. Frank Tyler's kick made it 12-7.

The tide appeared to have turned completely when Billy Holder fumbled the ensuing kickoff in his end zone and managed only to return it to the nine-yard line. Five plays netted them 13 yards out to the 22 and a little breathing room. Grady felt the stage was finally set and sent in *the* play. *Power Sweep.* Designed especially for the Clifton Cubs.

Normally on end-runs, Barry would pitch the ball to Mike who would closely follow Barry and Gary around end, his free hand on Barry's hip directing traffic. Because Coach Ray's scouting revealed the Cubs pursued better than any team they'd played, Grady added "Power Sweep" in which Mike would stop, reverse his field, and take off around the opposite end without blockers, all of whom would be headed the other way hoping the defense followed.

At the snap, every Wildcat went left. Mike then reversed his field, circled the right end position vacated by Barney, and galloped into the open at midfield where he received a key downfield block by Billy Pitts eliminating the lone defender. All alone with 25 yards to go, he suddenly felt his knee going, the pain slowing him against his will. Soon, he heard footsteps behind him and braced for the inevitable. Then came the voice.

"Coast on in, Stewart. I gotcha you covered."

The Rebel.

His knee screaming in protest, Mike knelt down to hold for the extra-point try. Barry's kick was again wide, but the lead had been extended to 18-7.

The touchdown run had covered 78 yards.

The Cubs didn't quit. On the ensuing drive, they marched all thc way to the Wildcat 20 where the ball was jarred loose from Haywood, and Gary Tepfer recovered. From there, the Wildcats put together a picture perfect 13-play, 60-yard, time-consuming drive down to the Cubs' 18-yard line where a fourth-down attempt was unsuccessful, and the ball went over.

As time was running out in the final quarter, Clifton stormed back once more behind Haywood's fantastic running and precise passing by Allen. With 1:16 showing on the clock,

Allen pitched to Haywood who flew around his left end for the score. The PAT was good, and Archer City's lead was cut to 18-14.

The Cubs' onside kick attempt appeared to be successful as Billy Pitts mishandled the ball, but freshman Charlie Goforth recovered it for the Wildcats.

Expecting Archer City to try and run the clock out, Clifton stacked the defensive line determined to stop the run and perhaps get a fumble. As expected, the ball went to the Wildcats' dependable fullback up the middle. In a final display of his talent, determination, and ability to seize the moment, number 74 exploded through the line and sprinted 55 yards for the touchdown and another amazing upset victory for the Wildcats.

Archer City had survived the Clifton Cubs and answered with another fine rushing performance of their own. In the end, tailback Mike Stewart totaled 146 yards on 16 carries and Gary Tepfer 139 yards on 22 totes. For the first time all year, James Haywood was held below 100 yards. The talented back had 90 on 24 carries. And played the whole game.

PART TEN

IN THE VALLEY OF THE GIANTS

CHAPTER 52

Swan Song?

Across the state, Saturday morning sports pages were in agreement. The upcoming Class A semi-final game at Tiger Stadium in Snyder on Saturday was a done deal. "Highly Rated Big Lake Looks Like Finalist." "Powerful Owls Pose Problem for Wildcats." "Big Lake Favored to Stop Cat Climb." "Archer City Set For Big, Big, Big Lake."

The articles went on to point out that after losing the first game of the season to Alpine, a 2-A school, coach Wilburn George's Owls had won twelve in a row, and in doing so, had scored 413 points while holding their opponents to 120. This was their third straight trip to the play-offs, and they were the Associated Press's consensus pick to meet Ingleside, winner of the south zone, next week for the title.

In the papers, Coach George expressed concern about the predictions. "Archer City has a fine-hitting, well-balanced, and well-coached club. They do everything well, including running over you. There are no weaknesses that we can find, and contrary to what most folks think, they've got a pretty big squad, even though the program doesn't show it."

Not according to Grady.

"Shoot, their linemen are as big as mountains. We're so dadgum little they're going to look even bigger. We're mighty mites compared to them. I tell you, we'll have to play better than we ever have to win. Still, we may be just going through the motions. This may be the end of the line."

During Sunday morning services at the First Christian Church in Archer City, Grady Graves stood ready to help serve communion as he did each and every Sunday. In the congregation, Jodie Wright and Gary Tepfer sat in their usual spot. Gary had been attending with Jodie for some time—much to Grady's delight. What didn't thrill him was that Gary occasionally passed on taking communion. To the coach's dismay, on this day, Gary handed him the plate of wafers without taking one. Grady handed it back. Startled, Gary handed it back. Grady shoved it back to his talented fullback. Gary looked up to see Grady smiling. He then took one, chewed it, washed it down with blessed grape juice, and smiled back. With Big Lake waiting down the road, they needed all the help they could get.

At Wednesday's practice, the team was dealt a blow when Barney Oliver fell on and rolled over Billy Pitts during punt return drills. The result: a separated ankle. By week's end, the foot was a mess and looked it. Billy was tough as all get out, but he could hardly walk. On top of that, Ray's foot never had healed properly, and the calcium deposit in Gary's thigh was worsening. And Mike, well, his knee was just about finished, shots or no shots. Darn near everyone on the team had something wrong with them. Grady had never been one for silly extra pads but decided it was finally time to fudge. Tape and foam would be in high demand in Snyder on Saturday. And so would courage.

"Don't believe all you read in the newspapers," Grady told his boys. "In fact, you steer clear of 'em this week and concentrate on the game. That clear?"

"Yes sir."

"It doesn't matter one iota what all the so-called experts think. If it did, we'd be sittin' at home." He turned to Fuzzy.

"Coach, what have you got for us?"

"Now, fellas, I'm not gonna lie. With the exception of their two guards Arms and Massey, who are quick as all get out, these are some big ol' boys. And unlike Clifton, who was basically a one-man show, they've got a lotta weapons. Love's a good runnin' back. He's had some injuries but can still turn the corner on the sweep. With all that's at stake, look for him to be in top form. Horton, the quarterback, can flat throw the ball. So you secondary guys have got to be on your toes. His favorite target is their all-state end Howard. He's a hard blocker as well and also plays a mean linebacker. Gary? Barney? When they're on offense, you're gonna *have* to tag this guy every time he comes off the line of scrimmage or he *will* wreak some havoc. You hear?"

"Yes sir."

"And that brings us to their fullback Mr. Childs. Gentlemen, he is a warhorse. He's big as two barns and runs like a wild deer. Unlike Mr. Haywood, you won't be chasing *him* all over the field. He comes right at you. This young man's got 1,881 yards and 198 points this year and figures on gettin' more. We need five guys hittin' him when he carries the ball. One or two men aren't gonna bring him down."

Grady raised his hand.

"Yes, Coach?"

"Any good news?"

Fuzzy smiled. "Yes, there is. We'll beat these guys. If we play our game, they'll wear down in the second half. We're playin' at two in the afternoon, and the weather folks say it's gonna be 'unseasonably warm, if not downright hot.' By the fourth quarter, they'll be done."

Grady looked across the room. "Any questions?"

He noticed a few smiles. Usually, he discouraged such.

"All right, then. Let's get out on the practice field and see what we can do."

Eventually the excitement around town, which had been at a fever pitch for the past month, finally began to wane and conversations among townspeople became increasingly reflective.

"Heck, look what a great season it's been."

"Right. Nobody ever expected us to get this far."

"One thing about it, win or lose, these boys have put Archer City on the map."

On Friday afternoon, Grady's phone rang. It was Joe Stults, editor of the local paper.

"Well, Coach, what do you think?"

"Joe, I just hope we don't get embarrassed."

There was laughter on the other end of the line.

"Coach, you've been saying that for the past three weeks. Heck, for the past four years."

Grady smiled into the receiver. "Well, they're a good team."

"So is ours."

"We play hard. That's worth somethin'"

"A trip to the championship game?"

Suddenly, there it was. Against his better judgment, for the briefest of moments, Grady thought about what it would mean to his boys. The town. And him. He felt the lump in his throat rising, and his vision cloud. If he hurried, he could get some words out without being discovered.

"See you Saturday, Joe." And he quickly hung up.

"I'll be there," the caller said into an empty receiver.

"I wouldn't miss it for the world."

CHAPTER 53

Five Smooth Stones

An hour before Saturday's game, the Archer City Wildcats lay strung about the cool concrete floor, dressed in game pants and T-shirts, staring at the ceiling. The door to their locker room was partially open, and Larry Graham glanced out just as Don Childs walked past.

He punched Steve Parsley who was lying next to him.

"You see that?"

"See what?"

"That thing that just walked by."

"Nope. What was it?"

"A giant."

"What?"

"I think it was that Childs guy."

Just then Big Lake's all-state end Johnny Howard, walked past. Larry and Steve looked at each other.

"Dadgum! Coach Ray said they were big. Wonder if they're *all* like that?"

Tackle Billy Rankin was next.

Larry got up and closed the door, returned, and closed his eyes. "Oh well, the bigger they are, the harder they fall."

"Yeah, right."

"Hey! Will you two shut up! You're gonna get us all in trouble!"

Later, as the team took the field for warmups, everyone got a good look at the Big Lake Owls. The Archer crowd sat staring, almost silent, at the opponents. Finally, someone proposed, "Size isn't everything. Maybe these Owls aren't all they're cracked up to be. Besides, David killed Goliath with a slingshot, remember? Heck, anything's possible."

Perhaps. After volunteering to face the fearsome Philistine and refusing King Saul's armor and sword, the young Israelite named David went down to the brook, gathered five smooth stones, placed them in his pouch, and headed to the Valley of Elah to do battle. In the end, he needed only one stone to defeat the giant. Archer City, on the other hand, would need all five of theirs.

The Wildcats won the toss, elected to receive, and following a short runback went to work. Behind the solid running of Tepfer and Stewart, they gained four first downs and ate up over seven minutes on the clock en route to the Owls' 13-yard line. Following a penalty back to the 18, a keeper by Morrison lost a yard. Holder then gained eight around the left side to the 11. An incomplete pass left fourth-and-eight. Grady signaled for a field goal, and Morrison lined up the 28-yard attempt.

Mike Stewart, the holder, had noticed Barry had been hooking the ball a little of late in practice and had begun to cheat over to the right a yard or so without telling Barry. In all the excitement he forgot to do so this time. Just prior to the snap, he saw the center Billy Pitts shaking his head at him through his legs but never made the connection. The snap and hold were good, but the ball was wide left. By a yard.

The Owls took over on their own 20, and any notion the Archer City fans had that the Big Lake Owls might be less than they were cracked up to be was quickly dispelled. On their first play from scrimmage, Don Childs took a handoff from Horton and blasted straight up the middle, running over and shedding Wildcats with apparent ease. Finally, Steve Parsley, hanging on for dear life, managed to bring him down by the ankles after a 23-yard gain, saving a touchdown. He climbed to his feet and joined the defensive huddle.

"Any of you tough guys care to help me out next time?"

"What kinda tackle was *that*?"

"Hey! I got him down, didn't I? If it wadn't for me, he'd *still* be runnin'."

Barry looked around the huddle. "Guys, I hit him as hard as I could, and he never even knew it."

Big Lake ambled to the line of scrimmage.

"Now, *come on!*"

Using the same ball-control offense the Wildcats had displayed, behind Childs the Owls proceeded to march down to the Archer 10-yard line. First-and-goal.

Hold that line! Hold that line! Hold that line!

Big Lake lumbered to the line, Horton barked the signals, and just as the center snapped the ball, nose guard Jimmy Reeves tore into him like a man possessed, knocking him backwards into Horton. Suddenly, the ball was loose.

There was a furious battle for it, and when the smoke had cleared, Gary Tepfer lay clutching it as the horn signaled the end to the first quarter with no points on the scoreboard.

One stone gone, four remaining.

CHAPTER 54

The Stop

The Wildcats took over and slowly moved down the field, running the ball and time off the clock. After a 14-yard pass to Barney Oliver, the drive finally stalled with 5:48 remaining in the first half. Every Wildcat supporter was thinking the same thing: If they could pin Big Lake deep and just hang on to the end of the half with no score, they'd have a chance. Morrison's punt, however, traveled only 13 yards, and the Owls took over on their own 25.

The high-powered, high-scoring Owls chose to stick with their running game and methodically marched 13 plays down to the Wildcat 19, the big play a 19-yard scamper on an end-around by Johnny Howard. Following another touchdown-saving tackle by Parsley on Childs at the 13, the big fullback carried again down to the five. With no timeouts left and less than a minute showing on the clock, Horton brought his team to the line of scrimmage and handed to Childs, who dished it to Howard on another end-around. Larry Graham came flying up from his safety position to stop it. This time, however, the big end pulled up at the last moment and passed to a wide-open Richard McReavy all alone in the end zone.

The extra-point kick was good, and the Owls led 7-0.

Wait a minute. A red flag. Offside against Archer City.

On the Wildcat sideline, Fuzzy turned to Grady.

"Coach, we're fixin' to win this game."

Grady looked at him curiously, then back out at the field. The Big Lake players were looking to the sideline for instructions. And got them. *Take the penalty.* Big Lake was going for two. The point was taken off the scoreboard, and the ball was moved to the 1 ½-yard line. Fuzzy smiled and announced once more, "Yes sir. We are gonna win this ball game."

As the players prepared to huddle up, there was some commotion on the field. Shouting. And finger-pointing, the brunt of which seemed to be directed at Robert Tepfer. The message: *This play's comin' your way, big boy. Right over you.*

Though unclear exactly what prompted the provocation, one thing was for certain: the Wildcats didn't take too kindly to such dealings. Particularly number 61.

Big Lake broke their huddle, Archer lined up in its Gap-8 goal line defense, Horton called the signals, and then a curious thing happened. Whether it was a missed assignment on a lineman's part, or explicitly instructed in the offensive huddle by Childs, once the ball was snapped, the left side of the offensive line parted like the Red Sea. The ball was handed to the big fullback, and suddenly there were just three. Don Childs. Robert Tepfer. And the goal line.

At the one-yard line, the unstoppable force and the immovable object collided.

And the immovable object won.

The extra-point attempt had failed, and the score remained 6-0. As the Archer City band, cheerleaders, and fans went wild, Fuzzy slapped Grady on the back and shouted, "We've got 'em now."

Stone number two had hit its mark.

With seventeen seconds remaining in the first half and a good portion of the air out of their balloon, Big Lake kicked off to Archer. Ray Bussey fielded the ball at the 11 and, dodging tacklers and showing his speed, raced all the way to the Owl 49-yard line before being tripped up with a touchdown-saving tackle. The clock ran out before the Wildcats could get a play off, and the teams, both exhausted and bruised, headed for the locker rooms. Big Lake had narrowly averted catastrophe on Bussey's return, and by doing so the larger, more potent, and favored team appeared to still have the game under control.

In the Wildcat locker room, Grady unloaded.

"You gonna let those guys just march up and down the field all day?! With the exception of that extra-point try, all I've seen is a bunch of arm tackling. And let me tell you somethin': If you're waitin' on them to get tired and peter out, you can forget that. The way you're suckin' air and carryin' on right now, you've got nothin' on them." He walked over to Barry. "You scared of those guys? They too big for you?"

"No sir."

He turned to Billy Pitts. "What about you? You gonna let a little sore ankle stop you?"

"No sir!"

Then Gary. "You?"

"No sir!"

"Well, you sure act like it. You *all* do. For gosh sakes, *this is the state semi-finals!* What'd you *expect* out there?" He paused. "You gonna be satisfied to lose six to nothin' just cause nobody gave you a chance? That it?"

"No sir."

"That how you wanna be remembered?"

"No sir!"

"That you tried hard and *almost* did somethin' worthwhile?"

"NO SIR!"

"Then do this! Whip those finger-pointers! Show 'em they might can get by with that someplace else, but not here. And not with us! Dadgumit! Us coaches know. And I think down deep, *you* know: We didn't come here to make a game of it. You didn't do all that hittin' and runnin' to be 'nearly as good as Big Lake.' Least I hope not. No, you did it so you could win the tough games." He paused, looking around. "Men, they can't carry your jocks. There's not a group of boys anywhere that can. They don't have the heart. Now here's your chance to let 'em know. Right now. So go back out there and show them and everybody else what the Archer City Wildcats are all about. Let the whole dang world know."

Later, as the team was leaving the locker room, Grady pulled Mike aside.

"How's the knee?"

"It's good, sir."

"They re-wrap it? Give you a shot?"

"Yes sir."

"Billy get his shot?"

"Yes sir."

He pulled Mike even closer. "Son, have you got two more quarters left in you? I have to know."

Mike smiled. "Coach, I've got six." Then he turned and trotted away trying to hide both his limp and his tears.

CHAPTER 55

A Moment to Remember

Big Lake received the second-half kickoff, and after another big gain by Childs over their right side, Barry Morrision picked himself up and motioned Robert over.

"Robert, we gotta do somethin'. He's eatin' me up. I just can't stop him. And he runs to this side more than not. We need to switch places."

"You serious?"

"Dead serious."

"What'll Coach say?"

"I'll worry about that later. What do you say?"

"Okay. I'm game."

On the next play, Horton faked the run and dropped back to pass. In the secondary, Larry Graham suddenly found himself with two receivers to cover near the sideline. At the last instant he picked one, the right one. Except he'd waited too long. The ball was going to beat him there! He dove, outstretched, and managed to deflect the pass with his fingertips at the last instant just in front of the Wildcat bench. Behind the intended receiver was nothing but open field. He rolled over and looked up at Grady who just looked at him and shook his head.

When asked later what he'd have done if the pass had been complete and gone for a touchdown, he replied, "I'd have gotten up, jumped the fence, and kept on running. Coach Graves had already broken one clipboard over my helmet. It was my man, remember, who caught their touchdown pass in the first half on the razzle-dazzle play. When I went off, Coach grabbed me by the face mask and let me have it. Clipboard and all. I wouldn't have gotten off that easy if the other guy had scored too."

After a 15-yard penalty and a sack by Oliver, the Owls had to punt, and Archer City took over at its own 34. A three-yard dive by Tepfer got them to the 37 where the Wildcats flung their third precious stone—a herculean effort etched forever into the minds of those present that day and a piece of Archer City football history and Texas high school football lore forever. The play: 127 Pass.

Barry took the snap, faked to Gary, pulled up, and lobbed the ball into the left flat just over a hobbling Mike Stewart's head which he gathered in at the 45-yard line. From there, he dodged one defender, shook off another, and broke into the open. The crowd on their feet, he had one man to beat. At the 30, along the sideline directly in front of the Wildcat band, his knee pleading for him to stop, he threw his lower body one way and the rest of him another. The hapless defender lunged, grabbing nothing but air. Steve Parsley dispensed of a latecomer, and Mike limped into the end zone. The play covered 63 yards.

Hardly able to stand, the boy known as Swivel Hips was helped to the sideline where he was embraced by the remainder of the team and Coaches Ray and Williams. Behind the bench, the cheerleaders hugged Judy as the fans continued to stand and cheer—their hearts afire, many crying openly.

Barry's kick was high and true and Archer City led 7-6.

Amid the celebration, Coach Graves barked instructions to the kickoff squad trying his best to stay focused. It wasn't easy.

Shocked and dazed, Big Lake regrouped. They began their next drive with Love going around end for 10. Then Childs up the middle for another 10. Grady immediately called Robert Tepfer over.

"You gonna tackle anybody or just coast the rest of the way?"

Robert didn't answer.

Grady grabbed his face mask. "You listenin' to me?"

"Yes sir."

He slapped his helmet so hard some thought it was the cannon.

"No you're not!! You're not listenin' to me!!!"

He was now. "Yes sir. I am."

"Then get back in there and get your head in the game! You hear me?"

"Yes sir!"

The Wildcat linebacker ran back onto the field, unaware he was carrying with him stone number four.

On the next play, Horton dropped back to pass, and a hard-charging Gary Tepfer tipped it as he let it go. Robert intercepted.

Unfortunately for the Big Lake defenders, number 61 was still reeling from his talking to and plenty upset. Instead of running to daylight, he immediately began searching for someone to hit. He spotted two big would-be tacklers ahead to his right and headed their way. There was a tremendous collision, and the three of them went down at the 30 where Robert bounced to his feet, having put a halt to the Owls' momentum. Archer took over and following three short gains, the Wildcats were faced with a fourth-and-two inside their own 40. In Grady's mind, leading 7-6 late in the third against a heavily favored team, gut-check time had arrived. They were going for it.

It's possible a handful of people in the stadium didn't know what was coming next, but it's doubtful. As the crowd rose to its feet, twenty-two exhausted, hurting boys lined up knowing who was getting the ball and where he was going: Number 74, up the middle. Gut-check time, indeed.

He got three.

Big Lake called time out. Sprawled about the field, kneeling or bowed with hands on knees, their helmets off, the Owls appeared finished. The Archer City players, on the other hand, stood tall, helmets on. Equally exhausted and hurting. Just not showing it.

When play resumed, the drive continued into the fourth quarter and into Owl territory, running time off the clock. Then suddenly, at the 17, Howard stepped in front of a Morrison pass, intercepted, and returned it all the way to the Archer City 48-yard line. They may have been down and out, but the Owls weren't done. Not by a long shot.

CHAPTER 56

Hanging On

Buddy Knox checked into the defensive huddle. "Pitts, you're out."

"What?"

"Coach sent me in for you."

"He mad?"

"I don't know, he just told me to get my butt in here for you, so here I am."

Nervously, Billy headed to the sideline. He pulled up next to Grady. Together, they watched the Owls begin their comeback drive with Childs and Love again pounding the line down to the AC 35. A holding penalty pushed the ball back to the 50, where the drive stalled, leaving them with fourth-and-23. With just a tad over seven minutes remaining in the game and fearing they might not get the ball back, Coach George gambled and came up big—a 27-yard pass completion from Horton to Kenneth McFarland, resulting in a first down at the Archer City 23-yard line!

The crowd was on their feet again. Was Big Lake simply too much for Archer? Had the Wildcats gallant effort only postponed the inevitable? If the Owls took it in, could the Wildcats possibly manage another score?

Without taking his eyes off the field, Grady said, "Get back in there, Pitts."

In the defensive huddle, Billy nudged Buddy and said, "You're gone."

"What?"

"I'm back. You're out."

Buddy glanced toward the bench. "He mad at *me*?"

"How should I know? Now, get outta here."

Buddy headed off, and as he neared Grady, he saw him nod. All was well. He'd simply given Billy a rare breather.

The referee blew his whistle ready for play, and Big Lake broke the huddle with new life. Horton under center took the snap and handed the ball to their go-to guy, Childs. There were tremendous collisions up and down the line. Hearts being poured out. As the big fullback started right, he was greeted by Barney Oliver, charging in from his defensive end position with every remaining ounce of his energy. Big number 32 attempted to lateral the ball away, but too late. Barney already had him.

Fumble!

Mike Stewart, in on defense with the game on the line, gamely came up from his safety position and alertly pounced on the loose ball.

Smooth stone number five had found its mark.

And Goliath was going down.

Or was he?

The Wildcats went to work on the clock. Behind the fierce running of Tepfer, Stewart, and Holder, they ground out three first downs out to the Big Lake 45-yard line. With just over three minutes remaining and clear of their end of the field, the Archer fans began breathing a little easier. All were thinking the same thing: Run Clock, Run!

Larry Graham checked into the huddle with the play. He looked at Barry. "28 Sweep." He then turned to Mike. "And Coach said, 'Whatever you do, Stewart, don't fumble.'"

Everyone looked at him.

"That's what he said. No kiddin'."

Their attention turned to Mike.

"That's a first," he said. "Wonder why he'd say that?"

"Okay guys. 28 Sweep. On hut. Ready, break."

Barry took the snap, reversed out, and pitched the ball to Stewart who headed around end behind Barry and Gary. After a gain of a yard or two, he was hit hard from behind and went down. Knees first. Elbows. Then chin.

The ball came loose.

Pinned to the ground, Mike watched Big Lake tackle Andy Bowen fall on it. Still, he wasn't too concerned. After all, he was down when it happened. Or thought he was. He got to his knees and noticed the referees huddled together. Surely they don't think . . .

On the sideline, Grady was pitching a fit, pointing to the ground.

"He was down, for cryin' out loud!"

Then came the four most dreaded words on the planet.

Fumble. Big Lake's ball.

CHAPTER 57

A Win For the Ages

Mike's next thought was to look up at the clock and see how much time remained. Or over at his dad against the fence. Or at the concession stand to see if prices on hot dogs had been reduced yet. Anywhere but the sideline. No way was he looking over at Grady. Then it occurred to him he may not have to. Grady might be headed his way this very moment. As hard as he can run. Clipboard in hand.

He waited for the crashing sound of it smashing over his helmet. Or being grabbed and strangled.

Neither happened, so he quickly took his place in the defensive huddle. He was staying put whether Grady wanted him to or not.

All the players looked at him.

None spoke, but their eyes all shouted the same thing.

Coach is gonna kill you.

Big Lake huddled up with renewed hope and one last chance to steal the game and rip the heart out of every person in the stadium who had ever been within a hundred miles of Archer City. Totally spent, with nothing left, the Owls, too, dug deep. Behind Childs's courageous running and Horton's spirited passes, they moved the ball all the way down to the Wildcat 15-yard line. Then, with time running out and no timeouts remaining, they gambled on one more play before attempting a game-winning field goal. Horton dropped back to pass, couldn't find an open man to throw to, and had to scramble. He got to the nine-yard line but was dragged down before he could get out of bounds. With the clock running and not enough time to get set up for a Bren Holland field goal, the Owls hurried to the line of scrimmage and got the snap off with one second showing. As the buzzer sounded, Horton once more dropped back to pass.

The Wildcats reached into their pouch only to find they were out of stones. Under pressure, Horton lofted a pass toward his all-state end Johnny Howard, who had broken free in the end zone. Number 35 got there as the ball sailed just past the big end's outstretched fingers. Mike's jarring hit ended any doubt the pass would be caught. The two went down hard, Mike's knee buckling. But it wasn't the pain he was worried about. He had gotten there early. His hit had come before the ball arrived, he was sure of it. And so he lay there, facedown in the grass, afraid to open his eyes, fearing what he might find.

Suddenly, he heard cheering. Wild, crazy cheering. But whose fans? Archer's or Big Lake's? He wasn't sure.

Then . . . *KA-BOOM!* The Wildcat cannon.

Suddenly, someone was helping him to his feet.

"You okay, Stewart?" Barry asked, smiling.

Mike squinted against the bright afternoon sun, looking with disbelief at the scoreboard, his trademark grin spreading quickly across his face.

"I am now," he answered, watching the frenzy unfold in the Archer City bleachers.

Minutes later, the Wildcat locker room was total chaos as family, friends, fans, and reporters stormed in. In the rush there, someone noticed, "Well, looky there, Claude Morrison finally got excited for once."

"How can you tell?"

"Cause he's halfway to the dressin' room and still tryin' to get his arm through the sleeve of his jacket."

Die-hard fan Ben Buerger hurried into the field house hooping and hollering and found it strangely quiet. It took a moment; then he saw. He was in the Big Lake locker room. Their big fullback Childs lay stretched out on a table just feet away. "Sorry," Ben said, turning to leave. They were too exhausted, bruised, and bloodied to care.

Inside the Wildcat locker room across the way, he found a similar group of black-eyed, scraped, cut, and totally vanquished young men, but these had smiles.

Grady congratulated each player before visiting with out-of-town reporters, school officials, Quarterback Club members, and other well-wishers. Finally, exhausted and drained, he noticed Joe Stults and Ted Leach standing together across the room. Both courteous and patient enough to allow him time with the others first. Grady walked over.

"Men."

Joe was the first to speak. "Coach, if I live to be a hundred, I'll never see another game like that. Ever."

Ted reached out and took Grady's hand and shook it. "That was one of the greatest upsets in Texas schoolboy football history. I guess you know that."

Grady smiled. "Our boys played to the utmost of their ability. All I can say is we just played our best game of football."

Ted returned the smile. "Well, Coach, Cinderella's going to the ball." He paused. "Your boys have one more of these left in 'em?"

"I don't' know, fellas. I guess we'll find out soon enough."

Once the players had showered and had their injuries tended to, they loaded up and headed to a local restaurant for supper where they were greeted by cheers and applause from fans who'd beat them there. Several walked with noticeable limps. Remnants of the battle adorned the faces and hands of all. An hour later, they climbed aboard the bus to more cheers and settled in for the long ride home. Mike sat alone, his leg stretched out across the seat, his knee packed in ice. Grady was the last to climb aboard.

"Men. You're gonna have to play better. If you have any plans of finishin' this thing off right, you're gonna have to play a whole lot better than you did today. Now, I want you to rest up tomorrow and come to practice Monday ready to go. We've got a lot of work to do."

He turned and nodded to Mr. Harville in the driver's seat. As the bus pulled away, he sat down next to Roy. Not a word was spoken as the lights of Snyder began to fade and disappear behind them. With decorated, honking cars leading and trailing, the silent bus continued down the dark highway toward home.

PART ELEVEN

AT GLORY'S DOORSTEP

CHAPTER 58

Reality Check

FOOTBALL TICKETS ON SALE THURSDAY
Tickets for the state championship play-off football game between Archer City and Ingleside will go on sale Thursday, Dec. 17, at 8 A.M. at the Lions Club Building.

The tickets will be on sale from 8 A.M. until 4 P.M. Thursday and again on Friday. Reserved seat tickets will be $2.00 and student tickets will be $1.00. Tickets will be priced the same in Archer City and at the gate.

The game will be played in Nelson Stadium in Austin Saturday, Dec. 19 at 8 P.M. Persons interested in riding a chartered bus to the game can make arrangements by contacting Amos Parsley at Oilfield Service & Equipment Co. The round-trip fare is $5.75 per person. (Archer County News)

The town's jubilation following the team's astonishing victory over the Owls was soon tempered by the realization that, as good as Big Lake was, they were not the best team in the state. That honor belonged to the Ingleside Mustangs who, at 13-1, in successive weeks beat No. 1 Three Rivers and No. 1 Hull-Daisetta before shutting out No. 5 Rosebud last week, ensuring their twelfth trip to the play-offs. While some odds-makers had the Mustangs as two-touchdown favorites, others had them favored by as many as five. Predictions aside, the one thing they did agree on was that the clock was about to strike 12:00 on the Wildcats from Archer City.

Downplaying their role as heavy favorites, Ingleside coach Wayne Wilsher said he was impressed with the team from north Texas. "People I've talked to say they don't impress you, they just beat you. I'd say you have to be impressed with that kind of club. Besides, when you get to this stage, they're all tough."

The Archer City head coach stayed true to form. "We were mighty fortunate to beat Big Lake. And now that we've scouted Ingleside, we've seen enough to know this could be the end of the line for us."

Grady and his staff were treating this as just another game. Absolutely no mention was made of what was riding on its outcome, and the word "championship" was never spoken. His players were getting enough of that elsewhere.

He motioned for the lights to be turned out and started the projector and the film of the Big Lake game. Although the effort had been good, there were still mistakes to be pointed out. Barry and Robert held their breath when the big switcheroo between them at the linebacker position took place on screen. Their eyes on Grady, he leaned forward, studied the incident, then slowly turned and looked at the two of them. Without saying a word, he turned around and continued.

You just never knew. Sometimes he would rant and rave about the smallest miscue and not say a word about a big one. For the most part, it was like the players' good plays had been edited from the films. Oh, they were there, all right. For all to see. Just passed over, that's all. Barry's game-securing audible to Billy Holder in the Goldthwaite game had been no different. Mobbed and congratulated by his teammates and praised by Ray and Williams, Grady never acknowledged it had even happened. But Barry was content in knowing Grady knew. That was enough.

The lights came up.

"All right, Coach, let's have the scoop on Ingleside."

Fuzzy moved front and center and got right to it.

"It all starts with their halfback Bobby Jones. He is, without a doubt, one of the best players I've seen this year including Pinky Palmer from Olney. He's not as big as Palmer or Childs or as fast as Haywood, but boy, can he get the job done. He's averaging about thirty carries per game and is also a terrific receiver and punt and kickoff returner as well.

"Benny Fregia is their number-two runner. He, too, can do everything. He can run, catch, *and* throw. He's also averaging forty yards a punt. Like Jones, he's been doing it for three years. Their fullback John Garcia is another good running back as well. He has really come alive in the play-offs.

"Guard Butch Riley is an exceptional lineman. He plays both offense and defense, hasn't missed a game in three years, and is a definite college prospect. Stewart Wilson, tackle, is another. At 210, he's the biggest player on their roster and, like Riley, is exceptionally quick.

"Keese is a true roving linebacker. He goes where he thinks the ball's going, and he's usually right. That means he gets there fast. He's blocked more than twenty punts in the past three years. He's also the backup quarterback. Their starting QB is David Whitney. He doesn't make mistakes on offense and is an exceptional defensive back. And speakin' of defense, in fourteen games this year, they've allowed just 66 points for an average of just 4.7 points per game.

"These guys are talented, well-coached, disciplined, *and* confident. As well they should be."

Grady looked around the room. On a given night, healthy, his team could play with them. Maybe beat 'em. He was sure of it. But, they *weren't* healthy, and the list of injuries was long. They needed a month to rest up and heal and another to prepare for Ingleside. They had four days.

"All right, guys, let's suit up and get busy."

Pulling out all stops, Grady decided to finally curtail the hitting in practice this last week. As the first team ran through their plays, the subs and trainers held tackling dummies. Suddenly, there was some commotion. Grady looked over to see trainer David Wright, all 120 pounds of him, get up off the ground and take a swing at the guy who'd just leveled him. Gary Tepfer.

"Jerk!"

"What'd you call me?"

"You heard me."

As Roy started in to break it up, Grady stopped him. "Let 'em go."

"You sure?"

Grady nodded. As everyone watched the one-sided fist-fight, he smiled and said, "Yep. Just shows this team's still has spirit. Even the managers."

CHAPTER 59

Cannon Woes

WILDCATS AND MUSTANGS MAKE FINAL PREPARATIONS

Temperatures nosed below the freezing mark in Ingleside Thursday afternoon, creating havoc with the Mustangs' final workout before their championship match with Archer City. The Ponies stayed for about twenty minutes in the elements before coach Wayne Wilsher relented and opened the doors to the gym. The outside temperature had dipped to 26 degrees, rare for their Gulf Coast community this time of year.

Meanwhile, the Archer City Wildcats went through their paces almost oblivious to the 15-degree weather that had gripped north Texas.

"It was pretty nice out there after we got warmed up a little. We had a good workout," head coach Grady Graves reported.

The weatherman is calling for partly cloudy skies with warmer temperatures around 40 degrees at game time in Austin Friday night.

Coach Graves went on to say his team is on schedule in its training efforts but still not quite ready for Ingleside. "They've got a dandy club."

It's been a great season for the Wildcats, the standard-bearer for north Texas as they are the only team in the area still playing. The 'Cats will be carrying a fine 12-2 record into the blue-chip duel in Austin Saturday night against the heavily favored #1-ranked Mustangs from far south Texas. (Wichita Falls Times Record News)

The people of Archer City awoke on game day to find cold still gripping the area. And something else. Ice. Travel was hazardous, but nothing was going to keep the team or its fans from getting to Austin. You could bet on that.

Nor was it going to prohibit the planned send-off pep rally at the courthouse square. The team arrived in a fancy chartered bus to find the band, cheerleaders, and more than half of the town's residents on hand. The 11-degree temperature might have cut the celebration short, but it didn't dampen spirits. After a few cheers, the playing and singing of the school song, and a few token words from Coach Graves (who considered the affair a distraction), Big Champ sent the team on its way with a resounding *KA-BOOM!*

As the players climbed aboard, Monroe Williams left the festivities to sell Obie Deen, a local oilman, a couple of drill bits. After all, he still had to make a living. Anxious to fire again as the bus drove away, the remaining cannoneers hurriedly jammed in more black powder before the barrel had a chance to cool.

KA-BOOM!

The unexpected backfire sent fans scurrying and L.J. Cathey, A.J. Morris, and Buster Boren to the hospital in Wichita Falls with burns. Luckily, no one was seriously hurt, and a short while later, Monroe and L.J. were on their way to Austin in Monroe's pickup with the cannon in tow. Behind it, their wives.

Highway 281 was strewn with cars covered in black and white crepe paper streamers and white shoe polish slogans.

"Go 'Cats. Win State!"

"Archer City Wildcats #1."

"Collar the Mustangs!"

"Wildcats Are Austin Bound!"

Each car they encountered honked, waved, and flashed their lights. Except one—a two-door Rambler driven by Newt Lewis. In it, his wife Lona and their two sons: Jim and his wife Wanda and their two kids, and Bob and his wife Pat and their two. Ten total. They were so tightly packed, Newt couldn't reach the horn or lights, but a few managed to wave. Like many, they would be making the drive back to Archer late that very night. Newt had to be at work at the city lake pump house the next morning.

The icy roads were gone by the time most reached Palo Pinto County, and with time to spare, Monroe and L.J. and their wives stopped at the Painted Horse Inn in Hamilton to eat. It was smooth sailing from there until they reached the front gate at the newly constructed Nelson Stadium where they were stopped by guards.

"Whoa, what's that?"

"What?" Monroe asked, chomping down on his cigar.

"That!"

"That's Big Champ."

"You can't bring that in here."

"What?"

"You'll have to leave it in the parking lot."

"You're kiddin'."

"Nope."

"This is our mascot. It goes to all our games."

"Sorry."

"You tellin' me that we can't bring this to the most important game Archer City's ever had?"

"Not inside the stadium."

He and L.J. looked at each other.

"Mister. We *have* to. Don't you understand? The team and fans are dependin' on it. Whadda you say?"

"Well . . ."

"Come on. What'll it hurt?"

"You can't fire it."

"Okay."

"I'm serious. There's an ordinance prohibiting the discharge of firearms of any kind within the city limits of Austin."

"Fair enough. You're a good man."

"I mean it."

"Gotcha."

And with that, they were let through. As they pulled it into position in the corner of the end zone on the Archer City side, L.J. turned to Monroe and asked, "We're really not gonna fire this thing?"

Monroe smiled big and without removing his cigar replied, "Whadda *you* think?"

CHAPTER 60

Promised Land

The bleachers had begun to fill. Back home, Archer City was a ghost town, its streets completely deserted—those unable to attend, inside, glued to their radios.

As predicted, the temperature was at forty, the wind making it feel even colder. Compared to last week's Big Lake game, it was frigid. Compared to the Keller game, it was downright balmy.

Inside the locker room following warmups, the team sat silently staring into space, their minds reeling. They thought about the path they'd traveled to get here. Meeting Grady for the first time. The wicked workouts. The running. All the running. Goof-Off Squads. Injuries. Wins. And losses. All the losses. Rules. Girlfriends. Families. Dads. Especially dads. And finally, their teammates. More than anything else, they thought about the guy next to them.

It was time for their usual talking-to. Tonight, however, Grady was nowhere to be seen. The only sound was the playing and singing of their school song in the distance.

Archer High we love you.
Love you ever so grand;
We will always be loyal,
And we'll cheer you to a man.
In defeat or victory,
We will always be true;
Dear old Archer we love you
And we'll always fight for you.

Once the cheering had ended, Grady walked in.

"The experts say they're gonna beat us by three or four touchdowns." He looked around the room. "You think that's really gonna happen?"

Seated, head bent, Gary Tepfer watched droplets of perspiration fall from his forehead and dot the floor beneath him. The room had grown so quiet, he thought he could hear each tiny splash. He then looked up and said, "Coach, you remember what we told you after the Olney game? We said we weren't gonna lose another game."

Grady looked into the eyes of his star fullback and saw the emotion and determination that was reflected in the eyes of every boy in the room. *And he knew.* With a brief nod, he turned.

"Either of you have anything to add?"

Fuzzy smiled and shook his head.

Roy, his emotions barely in check, spit into his cup, managed a smile, and shook his head as well.

Grady turned and faced the team.

"All right, then. Let's go beat these guys."

PART TWELVE

MIRACLE ON THE GRIDIRON

CHAPTER 61

Quarter One

Welcome, ladies and gentlemen, to Austin's Nelson Field and the 1964 high school Class A state championship game between the winners of District 11, the Archer City Wildcats coached by Grady Graves with a season record of 12 and 2, and the Ingleside Mustangs, champions of District 31 with a record of 13 wins and 1 loss. They are coached by Wayne Wilsher.

The Wildcats didn't get off to a very good start this year, losing two of their first three games to Nocona and Olney, but since that time they finished the regular season with seven wins and have stormed through the play-offs defying the odds week after week. The "experts," though, still aren't convinced as Archer City has yet to crack the Class A poll's Top Ten despite making it to the championship game. The Mustangs, on the other hand, are currently ranked No. 1 in the state and have lost only one game this year, their lone defeat coming at the hands of the Class AA bi-district finalist, Bishop.

The temperature here at game time is 40 degrees, and the wind is from the south at approximately 15 miles-per-hour as Ingleside makes its way onto the field. Meanwhile, a good many of the Archer City fans have left their warm seats in the bleachers to form what they're hoping will be a victory line for the players to run through in the far end zone. And here they come following the Wildcat cheerleaders onto the field.

The Archer City Wildcats played David to Big Lake's Goliath last Saturday in Snyder, and tonight they face an even more formidable task against these Ingleside Mustangs. The Wildcats from far-north Texas will rely on a tough, hard-nosed defense and the determined running of fullback Gary Tepfer as they have all year. Quarterback Barry Morrison doesn't pass much but is very accurate when he does. The top-ranked Mustangs from the Texas Gulf Coast can do it all. They'll be led by number 12, David Whitney, at quarterback with stand-outs Bobby Jones, number 44, and John Garcia, number 32, behind him in the backfield. The suffocating Mustang defense is led by number 61, Butch Riley.

It looks like we're ready to kickoff this Class A championship game, so fasten your belts and hang on. Ingleside will be kicking to start the game from the south goal to our right. There's the whistle, and with the wind at his back, Tommy Pearson, number 36, advances on the ball and puts his toe into a low, end-over-end kick that rolls down to the Archer City five-yard line where it is picked up there by number 26, Billy Holder. Holder evades a tackle and runs the ball out to the 25-yard line where he is hit hard and upended at that point. So it will be first down and 10 yards to go for the Archer City Wildcats, clad in their black jerseys and light grey pants tonight. Ingleside in blue pants and white jerseys with blue numerals.

Here we go, set to play, moving left to right on your radio dial, as Morrison brings the Wildcats to the line of scrimmage. Straight T-formation in the backfield, and there's a handoff to the fullback Gary Tepfer who bulls ahead for about three with a flag on the play. It appears Archer City was a little too anxious and will be penalized five yards for illegal procedure, bringing up a first down and 15 to go. And now here's Morrison again handing to number 74, Tepfer, who tries the right side and gets about two yards. It's forty degrees here in Austin and the playing field is not in particularly good shape having been played on numerous times this season.

Morrison, the man under, gives again to Tepfer who breaks into the clear over the right side out to the 32-yard line, where he is hit hard by David Whitney, number 12, and a whole host of Mustang tacklers. This brings up a third-and-

four. The Wildcats come to the line of scrimmage, and this time Morrison fakes to Tepfer and hands the ball to number 26, Billy Holder, who plunges ahead out near a first down. We'll wait and see . . . it appears he is a tad short. And he is. So it will be fourth down and half a yard to go, and the Wildcats will punt from just shy of their own 35-yard line. At least it appears they will. No, wait a minute, they've decided to go for it, gambling early in this contest from their own 34! They come to the line of scrimmage, and here's Morrison once again giving to the fullback Tepfer who picks up the first down! The ball is moved out to the 37 where it will now be first-and-10 for the Wildcats in the middle of the field.

On the sideline, Grady Graves never flinched. The gamble was risky, no doubt, but it told him what he needed to know: The play was there should they need it later in the game. Plus, it'd sent a pretty good message to the opposing team.

Following an incomplete pass and two runs, Archer quickly faced another fourth down, this time with five yards to go. Barry punted down to the Ingleside 29 where, following a short run by Bobby Jones and an offside penalty against the Wildcats, the quarterback Whitney handed to ball to his big fullback John Garcia.

And Garcia rambles across the 40 to the 45 and out to the 47-yard line before finally being stopped. Now, first down and 10 to go for the Mustangs. Here's another handoff to Garcia through the same hole across midfield to the Wildcat 47-yard line where it brings up a second-and-four. Whitney brings his team to the line, fakes a handoff to Garcia this time and rolls out. He's being chased by number 74, Gary Tepfer, reverses his field, now being chased by number 84, Barney Oliver, and the two Wildcats finally drag him down for a 17-yard loss! There's a flag on the play. Clipping against Ingleside. That penalty is refused by the Wildcats, bringing up third-and-a mile. A big play for Archer City on that last one.

Now, here's Whitney back to pass on third down, throwing downfield, and it's INTERCEPTED BY NUMBER 10, MORRISON, who returns it to the Mustang 35! And you can hear the Archer City fans across the way going wild.

The Wildcats managed to drive the ball down to the Ingleside 20 where they were stopped on downs. The ball went over, and behind the running of Jones and Garcia, Ingleside quickly moved it out to the 46-yard line where, on first down, Whitney went back to pass and threw downfield to an open John Huerta who was hit hard by Ray Bussey, forcing an incompletion. On the next play, Whitney again handed the ball to number 34, Benny Fregia.

Fregia is hit hard by number 61, Robert Tepfer, and the ball is loose! Let's see who comes up with it. And Barney Oliver has recovered for Archer City! The Wildcats huddle up and quickly come to the line where Morrison hands to Tepfer who pushes ahead for two yards where he is stopped by number 61, Butch Riley, and the rest of the Ingleside defense. Riley has been outstanding on defense for the Mustangs in this first quarter as he has all year for Ingleside. And that's the end of the first quarter with the game scoreless between these two fine teams as they change ends of the field.

CHAPTER 62

Quarter Two

On his way back to the huddle having gone downfield to block, Barney Oliver looked over to the sideline wanting desperately to tell the coaches the defense was paying him no mind. It was an observance that had not gone unnoticed, as Mickey Horany came sprinting in with the next play, 186 Pass, and instructions to watch for Barney.

The Wildcats will now have the wind at their back here in the second quarter as Morrison has them at the line of scrimmage. He barks the signals, rolls out to his right, and throws long downfield to a WIDE-OPEN NUMBER 84 AT THE 10-YARD LINE, WHERE HE TAKES IT IN FOR THE TOUCHDOWN FOR ARCHER CITY! That was Barney Oliver who had gone down, cut in, and was all alone for the score. The scoring play covered 43 yards in all. Here's Stewart to hold and Morrison to attempt the extra point. The ball is back, down, booted; it's up and good, and so our score here at Nelson Field in Austin, Texas, is Archer City 7, Ingleside 0.

The Archer City fans were on their feet and had been since Barney broke into the clear awaiting Barry's pass. As the pandemonium continued, fans Jim and Wanda Lewis suddenly noticed the woman in front of them crumpled at their feet. Frantic, Jim reached down and tried to pull her up. She went back down. He pulled again. Same result. After a third try, she turned and smiled.

"I'm okay! Really. I'm fine! I just got so excited, I lost my false teeth. I'm trying to find them!"

With a timeout on the field, the Mustangs regrouped as the Wildcat fans, band, and cheerleaders continued to celebrate, knowing there was still a long way to go, but if they could just hold on until halftime they might have a chance. After all, throughout the play-offs the Wildcats had not lost a second half.

Awaiting the official's signal, the teams line up for the kickoff. Back deep for Ingleside are Jones, Whitney, and Fregia. Here's the whistle, and Morrison advances on the ball and sends it bouncing all the way down to the two-yard line where it is picked up by Jones who escapes one tackle and manages to return the ball out to the 17 before being hit hard by number 61, Robert Tepfer, and number 81, Ray Bussey, where it will be first-and-10 for the Mustangs. Robert is the younger brother of fullback Gary Tepfer.

Whitney has his team at the line of scrimmage and hands to Garcia who plows ahead for three before being knocked down by junior linebacker Robert Tepfer. That brings up a second-and-seven. Whitney calls the signals, drops back to pass, throws, and it is INTERCEPTED BY NUMBER 35, ARCHER CITY'S MIKE STEWART, who returns it eight yards to the Ingleside 36! Whitney was under tremendous pressure that play by Archer City's Barney Oliver and barely managed to get rid of the ball—the Wildcats coming up with another big play and break in the game. The last time Archer City got the ball on a turnover, you'll remember, they scored quickly on the long pass to Oliver. We'll see what they have up their sleeve this time around.

Grady had nothing fancy for them. Just basic Wildcat football. Tepfer for three yards. Oliver for seven on a jump pass from Morrison. First down. Tepfer for five. Stewart for two. Tepfer for two. Then on fourth down, Morrison on a quarterback sneak for one. First Down. Tepfer dragging tacklers for four. Tepfer for one. Tepfer again for one. And on fourth down and four to go . . .

Another handoff to Tepfer who roars straight ahead down near the first-down marker. They'll have to measure. It appears to be really close. And it's a first down and goal-to-go for Archer City just inside the Ingleside five-yard line with six minutes and seventeen seconds left in the second quarter!

Here's the snap. Morrison fakes to the first man, rolls right, and takes off around end, going for the flag where he is knocked out-of-bounds at the two-yard line by Butch Riley and number 10, Ricky Keese. Quickly to the line of scrimmage, Morrison calls the signals and hands to Tepfer who barrels ahead for a yard with flags on the play. It looks like backfield-in-motion is the charge against the Wildcats, and head coach Grady Graves is visibly upset on the sideline as the five-yard penalty is stepped off against the Wildcats. That brings up a second down and seven to go now. Larry Graham checks in with a play from Graves, and the handoff is to Stewart on a counter play as he pushes ahead back down to the two, getting back the yardage lost on the penalty, where it will now be third-and-goal to go.

Now, in a straight-T backfield, Morrison gives to Tepfer who blasts ahead down near the goal line . . . TOUCHDOWN FOR ARCHER CITY! Gary Tepfer took the handoff and just rammed his way ahead off the left side behind the block of Steve Parsley for the six points. Here comes the try for the extra point. The ball is snapped to Stewart. It's down and on its way, and is wide left this time. So with a little less than six minutes to go in the first half, our score is the Archer City Wildcats 13 and the Ingleside Mustangs 0.

Back in Archer City, the group huddled around Sam Yeager's radio at the Royal and those listening at home danced and cheered wildly as the Wildcat fans in the stadium celebrated while Ingleside's fans tried to shake it off, broadcasters and sportswriters exchanged disbelieving looks, and Wildcat doubters with money invested on the game swallowed hard.

Back to the action now, Morrison's kickoff is another low one, picked up this time at the Ingleside 25 by number 81, Freddy Hudlow, and returned to the 36. So on the near side of the field now, moving from left to right, the Ingleside Mus-

tangs will put the ball in play trailing 13-0 with the fired-up Wildcats from Archer City in the lead.

In a wing-formation to the left, Whitney takes the snap and pitches to Jones, the speedy halfback, who heads left around end and is hit hard and upended at the 45-yard line. It'll be second down and seven when we resume play, but right now an Archer City lad is still down and needs some assistance from his teammates and trainers. Coach Grady Graves is headed onto the field. Graves has done a magnificent job at Archer City this year with a fine 12-2 record, guiding the team not only into the play-offs, but all the way to tonight's game here in Austin.

Gary Tepfer awoke flat on his back staring up into Grady's eyes.

"You okay?"

The best he could tell, he wasn't dead. So he nodded.

"Good."

As he was helped to his feet, he looked around, unsure of his surroundings. This wasn't Archer City's stadium. Or the practice field. He was somewhere else. Where exactly, he wasn't sure.

Number 74, Gary Tepfer, was the lad shaken up on the play but he appears to be all right now and has rejoined his teammates in the defensive huddle.

Mike eyed him closely. "You sure you're okay?"

"You talkin' to *me*?"

"Yeah. You're the one who just got cold-cocked, remember?"

"What?"

"Forget it. You remember where to line up?"

The referee whistled ready for play.

"Come on," Butch said, "I'll show ya."

Looks like we're ready to resume play. Ingleside has it second down and six to go. Here's the handoff going to Jones who goes off the right side for about three on the play out to the 48-yard line near midfield. He was hit hard there by Robert Tepfer and also number 70, Buddy Knox. The entire interior defensive line of Archer City: number 52, Billy Pitts, number 75, Jimmy Reeves, and number 72, Butch Hannah, has had an outstanding game thus far, not only keeping the explosive Ingleside offense from scoring but for the most part, out of Wildcat territory completely.

Whitney now pitches to Jones who heads to his right where he is met by Barney Oliver and Mike Stewart coming up from his cornerback position. He appears to be about half a yard short of a first down. Stewart, who already has one interception, normally doesn't play much on defense. Nor has he even practiced much after severely injuring his right knee on the first day of workouts this year. It was he who took a short pass from Morrison last week against highly-favored Big Lake and ran 63 yards for the winning touchdown sending the Wildcats to this championship game. He's clearly hurting tonight, but he's in there now. Quite a remarkable story.

Ingleside will go for it on fourth down! Wing-right now with Whitney under center, he hands the ball to Jones who shoots straight ahead for the first down at the Wildcat 48. The Mustangs, wasting no time, come to the line of scrimmage, and here's another pitchout to Jones heading right with running room down to the 42-yard line where he is hit very hard by Jimmy Reeves, the Wildcats' talented sophomore nose tackle. Defense is Reeves's specialty and it shows. Garcia takes a handoff this time and plows ahead for yardage to the Wildcat 39-yard line, about a yard short of another first down. Third down and one now for the Mustangs, and it's Garcia again into the middle of the line and another first down for Ingleside. It appears the Ingleside offense is finally getting into gear.

Two minutes and thirteen seconds now remaining in the second quarter. Here's another pitch to Jones who cuts it straight up the middle for a good six yards bringing up second-and-four. And a timeout is called by Grady Graves of Archer City.

Grady sent no one in, leaving the players on the field to stew on their own. Which they did. It was quickly decided that the Mustangs were not about to score right before the half. No friggin' way.

Back to play now, Whitney again pitches to Jones to his left side, and the lightning-quick halfback takes it all the way down to the Wildcat 23-yard line before being stopped. One minute and thirty seconds remaining and another first-and-10 for the Mustangs. Here's Whitney again pitching to Jones who heads right for about four yards before he is clobbered by number 52, Billy Pitts, and driven back several yards while whistles blow, signaling an end to the play. Pitts and the rest of the Wildcat defense appear determined not to let the Mustangs in.

Wing-T to the left this time from just inside the Wildcat 20, with a man going in motion to the left. That's Jones, and Whitney drops back to pass and tosses to Jones in the left flat where he heads left, stops, and starts back to the right on a naked reverse. He's in a world of trouble now as he's chased back, way back, and dropped at the 30-yard line by Barney Oliver! Third down and 16 to go now with 42 seconds showing on the clock.

The Mustangs hurry to the line of scrimmage, and Whitney drops back to pass looking for Jones who can't hold on. The incompletion stops the clock, and that brings up a fourth down and 16 yards to go on the Archer City 30 with 35 seconds left. That play was meant to be a screen pass, but the screen never really set up, and had Jones caught the ball, it's doubtful he could have gone anywhere. The Archer City Wildcats are on the verge of shutting out the powerful Ingleside Mustangs here in the first half, something very few, if any, people expected except maybe those from Archer City. Ingleside set for their fourth-down play now, with the wing to the left, here's Whitney on the reverse play to Jones, now back to Whitney, who now throws back to Jones in the flat, but the pass is too high and over his head at the 25 yard line! And the Archer City fans celebrate now as the Wildcats take over!

As quick as he is, Jones might have picked up considerable yardage on that last play had the pass not been too high. The talented Ingleside passing attack has been completely unable to get anything going tonight, attempting six passes and completing just one, and that one went for an 11-yard loss. They also have had two passes intercepted.

Now, here are the Wildcats at the line of scrimmage. Morrison hands off to Mike Stewart who bulls straight up the middle for little or no gain. The Wildcats are content to let the clock run with nine seconds remaining, and that will be the end of the first half with our score: the Archer City Wildcats 13 and the Ingleside Mustangs 0.

CHAPTER 63

Halftime

An excited group of Wildcats headed to the field house as the Archer fans cheered and waved. Once inside, they enjoyed their Cokes and caught their breath. As Mike was getting his knee worked on and Billy was having his ankle re-taped, number 74 sat looking around the room. Grady walked over.

"How's your head?"

Gary didn't reply.

"You gonna make it?"

"Yes sir," he answered, unsure exactly what *it* was.

Grady smiled and moved on.

"How's the knee?"

"Never better," his halfback said, smiling.

"The ankle?" the coach asked, looking at Billy seated next to Mike.

"Fine, sir."

He walked a ways and stopped.

"Bussey, I'm not gonna ask *you.* With all that garb you've got on, you shouldn't feel a thing."

Number 81 looked like a mummy. He was wrapped nearly head to toe and was wearing extra pads on his shoulders and elbows. He looked up at Grady and smiled.

Grady decided not to complain. After all, he'd given them permission to wear the extra padding. *And,* Ray was having a good game. Had been ever since their talk a few weeks back. Instead, the Archer City head coach moved to the center of room, gazed at the floor a spell, and then looked up.

The room grew quiet.

"Twenty-four minutes," he said softly, looking around the room. Suddenly, it appeared he was getting emotional just as he had on the bus before the Nocona game. He hesitated before continuing.

"Twenty-four short minutes to make all your hard work stand for somethin'." He then swallowed hard, sat down, stared at the floor, and said nothing more.

That room was filled with some of the toughest, hard-nosed young fellas you'd find anywhere in the state. But at that moment, in that dressing room in Austin, Texas, on that cold December night, they were anything but. It wasn't just droplets of sweat dotting the locker room floor anymore. They sat there a full ten minutes gathering themselves and their emotions. Finally, Grady walked to the door, and they quietly filed past him out onto the field, their chance in hand. Once they were gone, he closed the door behind him and looked up to find Coach Williams waiting.

"Coach . . ." was all his assistant could manage before succumbing to his emotions.

Grady smiled and placed his hand on his friend's shoulder.

"Come on, Roy. Let's go watch our boys play ball."

CHAPTER 64

Quarter Three

Well, folks, we're just about ready to begin the second half, and to get it started Ingleside will be receiving the kickoff and will have the wind at their back here in the third quarter with the Wildcats leading 13-0 in this Class A championship contest. Here's Morrison advancing on the ball, and he sends a high floater down to the 20-yard line where it's fielded by Bobby Jones. And with a wave of blockers out in front, he rolls to the right side and is hit hard there by number 73, freshman Charlie Goforth.

Freshmen—for the most part—don't see much playing time on Grady Graves's team we're told, but there was a time when they did. And that was four years ago when the seven seniors on this team started and played every game as freshmen and have ever since. We're talking about Morrison, Stewart, Bussey, Oliver, Pitts, Parsley, and Gary Tepfer.

So it's first-and-10 for the Ingleside Mustangs moving from right to left on your dial. Ends split wide to both sides in an I-formation, Whitney calls the signals, and here's a flag. Offside against the Mustangs backs them up five yards. They re-huddle and line up in the same formation. Whitney takes the snap, rolls to his left, decides to keep it and with blockers out in front takes it out to the 30, across the 35 to the 36-yard line where another flag is thrown. Let's see what this one is about. Grabbing the face mask. Against Archer City. And the referee steps off an additional 15 yards tacked onto the play where he sets it down on the Wildcat 49, first-and-10 for Ingleside.

It has just come to our attention that number 10, Ricky Keese, was at quarterback on that play replacing David Whit-

ney here in the second half, and boy, did he look good on that run. Now, here's Keese again bringing them to the line of scrimmage where he hands off to Jones who plows ahead for two in this, the last game of the season in Class A and for all the marbles. In the backfield with Keese is Jones, Garcia, and number 34, Benny Fregia—pronounced Free-jay. Keese rolls right this time and keeps it across the 45 down to the 39-yard line where it will be third-and-one. After huddling, in a wing T-formation this time Keese rolls left on the option play, keeps it and finds running room all the way to the Wildcat 30 where he is upended by number 61, Robert Tepfer and number 72, Butch Hannah. And the Ingleside Mustangs are moving forward now with new rejuvenation following the second-half kickoff as they march steadily toward the Wildcat goal line.

Now, here's a pitch to Jones trying the right side where he finds room and crosses the 25 down to the 17-yard line and another first down. The Mustang fans, finally with something to cheer about, are on their feet. Keese has definitely put the fire back into his team. Here he is now rolling out to the left again on the option play, but this time he is met hard at the line of scrimmage by Butch Hannah for little or no gain after Gary Tepfer kept him from going wide and turned the play inside. Quickly back to the line, here's a pitch to Jones who shoots across the 15 to just inside the 10 where it will be third-and-two. Archer City's lead less than a quarter ago doesn't look nearly as big now as this is a different Ingleside team here in the second half , and beginning to look like the #1-rated team they are.

Now, here's Keese trying the left side where he is stopped cold by number 74, Gary Tepfer, and suddenly it is fourth down and still two to go, bringing up a pivotal play in the contest. It appears Whitney is coming back in to replace Keese, and Keese gets a very fine hand from the crowd as he goes off. The Mustangs come to the line in a wing-left with Whitney under center and fans on both sides on their feet. Here's a handoff to the fullback John Garcia who forges straight ahead across the 10 near the first down marker where they spot the ball. It's too close to call, and the chains are called in for a measurement.

The ball is short of the needed yardage, and Archer City takes over inside its own 10-yard line! A big stop for the Wildcats. Breaking the huddle, here's Morrison taking the snap and handing to Tepfer, number 74, who you'll remember was injured in the first half but has stayed in the game. He heads left, is hit hard, and FUMBLES! There's a scramble for the loose ball, and the MUSTANGS HAVE IT BACK—number 82, John Huerta, coming up with it on the Wildcat 11-yard line! Wow! What a turn of events!

The Mustangs, who had the starch taken out of them just moments before following an unsuccessful fourth-down try, now have new life. Wasting no time here's Whitney pitching to Jones who carries it to the seven-yard line with six minutes and eighteen seconds remaining in this, the third quarter with Archer City leading 13-0.

Whitney quickly under center hands to Garcia who blasts across the left side down near the goal line where he's stopped at the one by Gary Tepfer and number 81, Ray Bussey. With just a yard to go, here are the Mustangs at the line and Whitney handing again to Garcia who GOES IN STANDING UP FOR THE SCORE! And the score is now 13-6 awaiting the PAT. Fregia normally handles the kicking duties for Ingleside so we'll wait and see. And they're going for two points! Whitney has them at the line, barks signals, and hands to Jones going around the right side where he is DROPPED AT THE TWO by Barry Morrison shooting through the line! A fine defensive play! And so the score remains 13-6 with Archer City in the lead, and we have ourselves a new ball game. And with fans from both sides on their feet—I don't think any have sat down much this entire third quarter—Tommy Pearson kicks off to the Wildcats where

Mickey Horany, Billy Holder, and Mike Stewart await deep. The ball's taken by Holder at the 15, and he brings it back to the 30 where he is stacked up and hit hard by number 61, Butch Riley, and a host of fired-up Mustangs. Five minutes and twenty seconds remaining in the third quarter.

Behind the straight-ahead running of Stewart, Holder, and especially Tepfer, the Wildcats moved the ball out to their own 46 where they faced a fourth-and-two try. Despite going for it on fourth down deeper in their territory earlier in the game, Grady chose to punt. Barry got off a good one in the cold wind, and Ingleside took over on their own 25. Tough defensive play by the Tepfer brothers and others forced an Ingleside punt after just three plays—just as Grady had drawn it up in his head. Now, with any kind of a return and a few good running plays, the Wildcats would be out of harm's way in Ingleside's end of the field.

Fregia boots it and sends a high booming kick with the wind all the way to the Wildcat 24-yard line where it is taken by number 23, Bob Gaines, who is upended immediately by Ingleside's Butch Riley. I tell you number 61 for both teams are playing outstanding tonight, that being Riley and Archer City's Robert Tepfer. And here now are the Wildcats pinned deep in their territory with Morrison handing off to Gary Tepfer who is met at the line and driven back by, who else, but Butch Riley. They give him a gain of one, bringing up second down and nine. And with the quarter drawing to a close, Morrison hands to Stewart who lunges ahead for about three yards to the 28 as the clock shows three, two, one second, and the end of the third quarter here in Austin with the surprising Archer City Wildcats still leading the Ingleside Mustangs 13-6.

As the buzzer sounded, and the teams changed ends, Archer City native Bill Wright walked up the ramp away from the stands to smoke. Along the way, he met two impeccably dressed gentlemen—one tall and thin, the other short and wide. The short one was doing the talking.

"Will you shut up? Now, Archer City's gonna win this game. I know it. And you know it. That means we have lost *all* our money. So let's go get in the damn Cadillac and drive our butts back to Houston. Right now!"

I sure hope he's right, Bill thought to himself. He didn't have any money bet on the game, but like everybody else from Archer he still had a lot riding on it. A whole lot.

CHAPTER 65

Quarter Four

Nothing was said in the Wildcat huddle as the team waited for the whistle signaling the beginning of the last quarter. There was nothing *to* say. They held a seven-point lead with twelve minutes to play against the top-ranked team in the state. They had to find a way to hold it. Somehow.

The final quarter set to begin here in Austin, Texas, with the underdog Archer City Wildcats leading the powerful Ingleside Mustangs 13-6 and facing a third-and-six from their own 28-yard line. Fans on both sides applauding the effort of both teams as Morrison brings the Wildcats to the line. Here's a handoff to Stewart who is stopped short, and the Wildcats will be forced to kick and give the ball back to the Mustangs.

Morrison drops back in punt formation with the wind at his back, receives the snap from Pitts, and lets go an end-over-end boot that is well covered by Gary Tepfer and will roll to a stop at the Mustang 32-yard line—a 43-yard boot.

And number 10, Ricky Keese, has returned at quarterback for Ingleside, taking the place once again of number 12, David Whitney. Taking the snap, Keese runs left, and picks up three yards before being smacked to the ground by number 75, Jimmy Reeves. But credit first must be given to Barney Oliver who grabbed a leg and almost tripped him up in the backfield for a loss. Keese again calling signals fakes to Garcia this time and gives to Jones who ambles across the 40 to the 41-yard line. As they have for most of the evening, the Wildcats line up in a 7-2-2 defense rather than their customary 5-4-2. Here's Keese fumbling the snap, but he manages to get the ball to Garcia who blasts ahead for the first down out across the 45-yard line. Wasting no time, Keese pitches the ball back to Jones who's knocked down in the backfield for a loss of six by Barney Oliver! Several times this half Ingleside has split a man out wide of Oliver and attempted to put a crack back block on him. It worked fine the first time or two, but Oliver is combating that now by simply shooting ahead into the backfield leaving number 52, Billy Pitts, and number 10, Barry Morrison to contend with the off-tackle play which they have done terrifically. Now, Ingleside seems intent to running Jones wide and number 84 is there waiting on him.

Here's Keese rolling to his left and throwing short to Jones in the flat where he is met solidly by Gary Tepfer, and others. Climbing out of the stack is number 61, Robert Tepfer, and number 84, that's Barney Oliver, coming all the way across the field to get in on the tackle. Third-and-fifteen now for Ingleside, and it's Keese pitching to Jones who hands back to Fregia who heads around the right side where he is knocked out-of-bounds by number 35, Mike Stewart, at the 47.

We have eight minutes and twenty seconds showing on the scoreboard clock as Fregia drops back to punt on fourth-and-long. He takes the snap and gets his toe into a low kick which goes untouched and hits and rolls dead at the 17-yard line of the Wildcats where they'll take over hoping to keep the clock running. Ingleside expecting to see a big dose of Gary Tepfer, the fullback, and just as expected, Morrison hands to Tepfer who bulls ahead for five tough yards to the 22. Now, on second down, here's Morrison dropping back to pass! He's throwing long down the field intended for Barney Oliver, but he's well covered and the pass is broken up by David Whitney and number 81, Freddy Hudlow. A rare gamble by Grady Graves, but the Mustangs weren't going to be surprised twice on that play, the first one going for a touchdown in the second quarter. That leaves third down and five to go.

Morrison takes the snap and rolls right deciding to keep the ball this time and is racked up for a one-yard loss by a bevy of Mustang tacklers. Archer City will again have to punt and here's Morrison's kick, a wobbly one, which comes down at the 45-yard line where it's taken by Fregia—across the 50, the 45, and brought down at the Wildcat 40-yard line where he is hit and hit hard by number 61, Robert Tepfer.

And on first down now, already in Archer City territory trailing by a touchdown, Keese gives to Garcia who gets only a yard before being swarmed by a host of Wildcats. And Ingleside calls a timeout.

While both teams stood exhausted, breathing in the wintry air, Mike Stewart limped over next to where Gary Tepfer was standing and asked, "How're you holdin' up?"

Number 74 nodded.

"You ever figure out where you're at?"

He nodded again. "Playin' football."

"You know where?"

Battered and bruised, hands on hips, his uniform grass-stained and blood-stained, his shirttail hanging partially out, Gary looked at his friend and answered.

"Does it matter?"

Mike smiled and shook his head. "Nope. It don't."

And it didn't. Grady's boys only knew one way to play.

The timeout over, and the Mustangs, having talked things over, open back up with a handoff to Jones off the right side, and the speedy running back tears across the line and gains down to the 33-yard line before being stopped by Stewart. And the #1 Ingleside Mustangs, not out of this contest by any means with five minutes and fifty-one seconds showing on the clock, come to the line. Keese is under center, and pitches to Jones around the left side this time, where he is dropped for a loss by number 85, Steve Parsley, and Barney Oliver, again coming all the way across from his end position on the other side. That brings up a fourth down and needing 10 for a first.

Fregia drops back to punt hoping to pin Archer City deep in their territory and get the ball back. The Wildcats send no one back to receive expecting perhaps a fake, and HERE

IT COMES! Fregia tucks the ball and heads around the right side, but the Wildcats are waiting for him, and he will be stopped well short of the first-down marker! And Archer City takes over at the 32-yard line, that play fooling no one.

Taking their time now, Morrison has the Wildcats at the line of scrimmage and hands to his big fullback Gary Tepfer up the middle as he plows for two, maybe three yards. And the gain was four, making it second-and-six with four minutes remaining in the contest. Morrison under center again, gives again to Tepfer who will not be denied, bulling his way up the middle, dragging tacklers out to the 40-yard line. Timeout for measurement. It's very close, but just short by about two inches. A critical play here for both teams on third down coming up.

Here's Morrison on the quarterback sneak needing just inches. And he has them! A first down for the Wildcats! And the clock continues to run. The ball is spotted and the Wildcats come to the line. Morrison gives again to Tepfer who dives ahead for about one.

Throughout the stadium, fans began to realize Archer City might actually do the unthinkable. Winning their district championship had been something of a miracle itself. But then came surprising play-off wins over Keller and Goldthwaite, followed by improbable upset victories over Clifton and Big Lake. And now this: leading powerful Ingleside with just under three minutes to play. *With* the ball. It was possible all right. But how? How in the world had they gotten to this point?

To understand, one only had to look out on the field at number 52. Senior guard Billy Pitts had entered the game hardly able to walk, his severely injured ankle not responding to treatment and needing time to heal—time they didn't have. Now, on the preceding play, running downfield to block should Tepfer have broken free, he tripped over an exposed sprinkler head tearing his good ankle. On his hands and knees, in excruciating pain, unnoticed by the Wildcat sideline—his view blocked by the Mustang players—he began to crawl back toward the line. A referee bent over him.

"Son, are you all right?"

"Yes sir."

Barney Oliver happened to look up and see his friend. Not surprisingly, given the moment, his only thought was, "Billy, get over here! You're gonna be offside!"

Arriving, tears in his eyes, on hands and knees as the team broke the huddle and lined up, Billy Pitts struggled into his stance and continued.

Archer City had a man shaken up on the previous play, but he's back in position now although it appears he's hurting. Freshman Bob Gaines, number 23, has checked into the game now for Billy Holder, and the pitchout is going to Gaines who starts right but has no place to go and loses two yards. That indeed was a surprise call by Graves seeing as how Gaines has seen little action tonight and might possibly not be warmed up like the other players. Remember, it's cold out there, making holding onto the ball even harder.

And on third down and long now with two minutes and twenty seconds remaining, Stewart takes the handoff on the counter play and meets a solid wall at the line for no gain, led there by number 55, James Vaden. And against their wishes, the Wildcats will have to punt the ball back with a minute and forty-five seconds and counting.

Morrison's kick is another high, wobbly one coming down at the Ingleside 22-yard line and fielded there by the speedy Bobby Jones who cuts in and is hit sharply at the 30. Ingleside quickly calls a timeout.

In the huddle, Barney grabbed a handful of Pitts's jersey.

"You gonna make it, Billy?"

Staring at the ground, Billy nodded.

Barney knew better than to suggest he go out. Billy Pitts wasn't going anywhere. None of them were. The whistle blew.

Keese, still the quarterback, has them at the line, splits Fregia out to the right, drops back to pass and lofts one to Fregia in the left flat. He rolls to his right and is met head-on there by Barney Oliver for a loss of about three yards! Forty-nine seconds remaining and it will be second down needing 14 yards when we resume play after another Ingleside time-out. The Wildcats of coach Grady Graves and the Mustangs of coach Wayne Wilsher fighting right down to the wire for this Class A state championship.

The Mustangs have talked it over, and here they come to the line of scrimmage. Here's a pitchout going to Fregia who then passes long down the right side to number 81, Freddy Hudlow, but the pass is broken up by Archer City's number 81, Ray Bussey, who wasn't fooled on the play. Forty-one seconds now with the clock stopped on the incompletion. Bussey has had a good game for the Wildcats as have a lot of his team-mates on defense, most notably Barney Oliver and Robert Tepfer.

Hudlow splits left, I-formation as Keese takes the ball and rolls to the right, cutting upfield with running room across midfield down to the 47-yard line where he steps out-of-bounds to kill the clock with 33 seconds remaining. He needed about 14 yards on the play and picked up 13, so it will be a fourth-and-one now for the Mustangs in a do-or-die sit-uation. And the Ingleside captain has requested a measure-ment even though it appears from here to be about a yard short. And it is.

And a huge play coming up now with fourth down and a yard to go for the Ingleside Mustangs hoping to keep their drive alive. Archer City, meanwhile, trying to hang on and fin-ish off their remarkable Cinderella season. Keese with his strong side to the left this time, has Fregia flanked out far left with 33 seconds showing on the scoreboard clock. Here's the pitchout going to Jones; he cuts in at the 45, across the 40, finds running room down to the 36-yard line. He just would not be stopped as he picked up the first down. The crowd is on their feet, and the clock continues to run with 20, now 19, 18, 17 seconds remaining as the official spots the ball. Keese gathers his team together and quickly under center takes the snap, and here's another pitch going back to Jones who starts right, now looking to throw, HAS A MAN OPEN AND THROWS LONG DOWN THE FIELD!

AND IT'S INTERCEPTED BY ARCHER CITY! PICKED OFF BY THE WILDCATS' NUMBER 35, MIKE STEWART, who goes immediately to the ground! There's a flag on the play with the clock showing one second left. We'll have to wait and see just what the infraction is. The Archer City fans are going crazy as they sense victory here, leading 13-6. The passer, Jones, was hit just as he threw the ball, by none other than the Wildcats' Barney Oliver causing it to fall just short of its target. And the penalty is against Ingleside for an ineligible receiver downfield! Archer City says no thanks, takes the ball with one second left, and I bet you anybody in the whole stadium can call this next play.

In the huddle, there was no celebration. No yelling. No laughter. It was quiet as Barry calmly called the final play. Quarterback sneak. On hut. The Wildcats took their positions at the line of scrimmage, Barry barked the snap count, took the ball and lunged forward. The stadium buzzer was drowned out by the fans, but the Wildcat cannon wasn't. The distinctive *KA-BOOM!* sounded, marking the end of the game, and the season. And everything changed.

PART THIRTEEN

CHAMPIONS!

CHAPTER 66

Field of Dreams

At the bottom of the pileup, quarterback Barry Morrison felt someone grabbing the collar of his shoulder pads and pulling him free. Once on his feet, he saw. It was Claude. The two looked into each other's eyes without speaking, and his dad then did something he'd never done before. He kissed his son.

Families, friends, and fans stormed the field. Years later, players would describe the scene as surreal. Everything moving in slow motion. All noise distant and faint: the public address announcer, the band, people yelling and screaming, and somewhere, a single continuous car horn. In the melee, other players and dads sought out each other. Many, too, embracing as never before.

As Claude moved aside for Trecie, Mike sought out Judy, and as was their custom, an exhausted, and still somewhat dazed Gary Tepfer swooped up Jodie with one arm, blood streaming from the bridge of his nose as it did following every game.

"Oh my God! Can you believe it?" she asked, throwing her arms around his neck.

Gary looked up to see Robert walking over. With his free arm he pulled his younger brother close, and the three of them embraced. In the stands, the Wildcat band struck up "Mr. Touchdown." With the familiar music pouring over them, they laughed. And cried. And laughed some more.

The celebration continued in the stands and along the fence where Wildcat fan Warren Robertson stood cheering. A few minutes later he was busy at work on his knees in the end zone when two policemen approached.

"What do you think you're doing?"

Warren looked up and smiled. "Borrowing some grass."

"I don't think so. Put that back and get outta there."

"You don't understand. This is hallowed ground. This grass is sacred."

Warren's brother, Bill Ed, wandered up, joining the group.

"I'm not telling you again, Mister. Now, get up and get going, or you're gonna be in big trouble."

Warren thought it over, replaced the grass, patted it down with his hand, and stood.

"Thank you," the officer said.

Warren smiled, brushed his hands on his pants, and headed back to the celebration, his brother in tow.

"What were you thinkin'?

Warren stopped and looked at him. "You know how big of a deal this is? This game?"

"Yeah. Huge."

"No. It's bigger than that."

"I know."

Warren looked over his brother's shoulder and saw the officers walking away.

Bill Ed noticed, too. "Forget it, will ya? Come on, let's go,"

"Okay, okay."

"What the heck were you gonna do with that grass anyway? Sell it?"

"No! Well, maybe, if the price was right. But mostly I just wanted a little bit to have as a keepsake. And . . ."

"And what?"

"I thought it'd look good in that trophy case on the second floor of the high school."

CHAPTER 67

A Man Of His Word

The Archer City fans continue to mob their team—the Archer City Wildcats, surprise champions of Class A in the state of Texas in 1964. All the points coming in the first half for the Wildcats in a fine-played ball game by both teams. I don't know if we have a horn stuck in the parking lot or just a happy Archer City fan, but if it is a fan, he has reason to be happy.

Recapping tonight's game, all of Archer City's scoring came in the second stanza including a 43-yard touchdown pass from Barry Morrison to Barney Oliver and a 2-yard blast up the middle by Gary Tepfer. The PAT following the second touchdown failed giving the Wildcats their 13 points. Ingleside's only score came on a 2-yard dive by John Garcia following an Archer City fumble at their own 11-yard line. The try for two extra points was unsuccessful, making the final score 13-6.

We saw some tremendous defensive play tonight especially on the Wildcat side of the ledger. Junior linebacker Robert Tepfer and senior defensive end Barney Oliver were the key figures—but by no means the entire show. Tepfer had 16 tackles, half of them unassisted, and Oliver had eight in all, five of which resulted in losses behind the line of scrimmage and came at critical times in the game. Jimmy Reeves was in on 13 tackles, Barry Morrison in on 11, Ray Bussey nine, and Mike Stewart six. Morrison intercepted one pass and Stewart picked off two, including the big one at the end of the game ending Ingleside's comeback hopes.

On the offensive side, Gary Tepfer led all Wildcat rushers and was once again the workhorse for the Wildcats with 75 hard-earned yards on 25 carries and one touchdown despite having been knocked unconscious early in the contest. Stewart, bad knee and all, contributed 19 yards on 12 carries, Holder had 6 yards on 3 carries, and Morrison just 2 yards on 6 carries. But it was Morrison's long pass to Oliver for the game's first score that set the tone for this game. On the night, the talented quarterback felt the need to pass only two other times, completing one for eight yards, giving him a total of 51 for the game.

Ingleside actually out rushed Archer City 189 yards to 102 with Jones leading their way with 98 and Garcia adding 52. The Mustangs' passing game was completely shut down, however, completing only one pass in 12 attempts for just two yards, hampered by a fierce Wildcat rush and excellent play by safeties Ray Bussey and Larry Graham.

Archer City was penalized four times for a total of 30 yards, while Ingleside was flagged just once for five. But in perhaps the most important category of all, Ingleside turned the ball over a total of four times tonight and Archer City just once.

And now let's thank the sponsors of tonight's broadcast beginning with Haigood & Campbell, Coe Ellis Gift & Appliances, the First State Bank of Archer City, McWhorter's Food Store, Heard's Department Store, Perry Pittman Ford Company, Hickman & Jansen Oilfield Service, Y&Y Service and Supply, Berend Brothers, and the Archer City Plumbing and Heating Company.

That's it for tonight's broadcast, reminding you once again of our final score here at Nelson Field in Austin, Texas: the 1964 Class A State Champion Archer City Wildcats 13, and the Ingleside Mustangs 6.

Following congratulatory handshakes and hugs from his assistant coaches, Grady Graves stood alone on the sideline watching the scene on the field unfold before him. Four years earlier, he had promised Archer City a winning football team. Now they had one. And a big ol' trophy to boot.

CHAPTER 68

The Celebration

"Enjoy it."

Those two words comprised Grady's entire locker room speech following the dramatic game and history-making season. There was no lengthy inspirational foray, but none had been expected. Following their coach's instruction, pandemonium broke loose again. Soon, the place was full of people. Grady slowly worked his way through the madhouse to congratulate each individual player.

When he got to the younger Tepfer, he smiled and said, "You know when I knew we were gonna win this game?"

Robert shook his head.

"When you made the tackle on our first kickoff. You haven't done that all year."

And they laughed.

Suddenly, the crowd quieted. Standing in the doorway were Mustang captains, Bobby Jones, John Garcia, and James Vaden. Jones congratulated the team and coaches, and the three then made their way around the room to shake the winners' hands.

Engulfed by reporters, Grady acknowledged, "Ingleside has a fine outfit. It took an outstanding effort on the part of everyone to beat them."

"What did Coach Wilsher have to say to you about the game?"

"He said we just whipped 'em. I told him we were fortunate, but he didn't agree. He was real nice about it. He certainly took it better than I would have." The Wildcat coach paused briefly, thinking. "We've come a long way since the beginning. I'm real proud of these kids. They've worked hard to get where they are tonight." He spotted his tall safety nearby. "Ray! Was it worth four years?"

"Every bit of it," Ray Bussey answered, smiling.

"How'd all this happen, Coach? What turned it around?"

"Our third game this year. We just got whupped real good by Olney. We didn't need the loss, but learned plenty from it. About ourselves."

An hour or so later after they'd showered and changed, the team climbed into the chartered bus. In the parking lot Grady hugged and kissed his wife Gay and climbed in.

"Guys, we're goin' to eat and then to the motel. After that, you're on your own. Now, this bus leaves at ten in the morning. Sharp. If you get into trouble tonight, call me."

Amid the bedlam, Barney Oliver sat staring out the window thinking about the father he'd lost two years earlier during a basketball game against Holliday his sophomore year. He and his older brother Roddy were both in action on the floor when the game was halted due to a disturbance in the stands. Unknown to them, Staton had suffered a heart attack. One moment he was cheering his sons. The next, he was dead. Just like that.

Barney never noticed as Mike gingerly eased in beside him, his knee on fire.

"Hey, you okay? You're bein' awful quiet."

His buddy nodded.

"You sure?"

Barney continued to gaze out the window. "I sure wish my dad had seen that game."

Mike grinned. "Don't you worry 'bout that, pardner. He didn't miss a play."

The big engine roared and the bus groaned and lumbered away, the lights of Nelson Stadium reflecting in the boys' eyes, growing smaller with each passing minute, until finally, they were gone.

CHAPTER 69

Hero's Welcome

Following supper, the cannoneers and a contingent of delirious fans beat the team to the Villa Capri motel where they were staying. As Monroe and L.J. pulled the cannon through the parking lot encircling the building, several joined the caravan honking their horns and yelling. After a few minutes, a disgruntled guest strode into the office demanding to see the manager.

"What's the problem?"

"All that noise! And all those crazy damn people!"

The manager smiled. "Hell, mister, those folks just won themselves a Class A football state championship! They deserve to celebrate!"

Shortly, the bus arrived, the players threw their stuff in their rooms, and were soon scattered about the big city. Except for a few. As Ted Leach was leaving his own room on his way to meet Grady, he spotted four Wildcats standing just outside the lobby—Ray Bussey, Billy Pitts, Mickey Horany, and trainer Donald Dorris—and walked over.

"How are your ankles holding up, Billy?"

"Fine, sir."

Ted knew better but left it at that. He noticed Mickey standing next to Ray and was reminded just how small the youngster really was. But Mickey didn't play small. None of them did. He wondered if they fully understood just what they had accomplished. If not, someday they would.

"What are you guys up to tonight?"

"We're stuck on foot. There any cabs around here?"

"I don't know. Where are you headed?"

"The Capitol."

"'Excuse me?"

"The State Capitol. We always wanted to see it."

Ted fought back a grin. "Well, heck, take *my* car. I won't be needing it."

"You serious?"

"Sure. He fished for his keys and placed them in the outstretched hands of Donald Dorris. "Here you go."

"Thanks, Ted."

"Yeah, thanks! We owe you!"

"Don't you worry. I owe *you* guys. Your season was every sportswriter's dream."

Ted watched them head to the parking lot. Loaning them his car was the least he could do.

After more than a few wrong turns, the group eventually arrived at the majestic building around midnight. They bounded up the steps to find the large doors locked and were soon greeted by an armed guard.

"Gentlemen? What can we do for you?"

"We came to see the Capitol."

The guard smiled. "It's a bit late. Visiting hours were over quite a while ago."

"Dang!

"Shoot!"

"I told you we were too late!"

"Where are you boys from?"

"Archer City. You probably never head of it. It's up near Wichita Falls."

"What are you doing in Austin? At midnight?"

"We just finished playing football over at Nelson Field."

"Beat Ingleside."

"Beat everybody."

"We're state champs!"

"And now you want to see the Capitol?"

"Did."

"Where's the rest of the team?"

"Probably out drinkin' beer and chasin' Austin girls."

The guard laughed and looked out over the grounds. "Well, I tell you what. You look like a good bunch of fellas. How about I give you a short tour?"

"Really?"

"Yep. You guys have earned it. Come on in."

At 10:00 sharp the next morning, with freshmen Mike Atchley and Bob Gaines tucked into overhead luggage compartments to make more room for the seniors (freshman Charlie Goforth was too big to squeeze into one), the bus full of exhausted, sore, but happy young men left Austin and headed north for home.

A crowd began to assemble at the courthouse square at 1:00 P.M. in anticipation of the team's scheduled 3:00 P.M. arrival. The street on the north side of the square was roped off and kept clear for the bus. Shortly before three, a caravan headed east on Highway 25 to intercept the team. By the time Sheriff Claude Morrison's patrol car and the county ambulance—sirens wailing—led the bus followed by numerous honking cars and screaming fans into town, the crowd had grown to over two thousand people.

As the bus slowed to a stop, the Wildcat cannon sounded its final blast before being permanently retired and installed on a ten by twenty concrete slab (originally built in the 1930s for a World War I cannon) on the west side of the courthouse lawn. When scrap iron became scarce during World War II, the cannon was sacrificed and the slab eventually covered over with dirt and grass, only to be unearthed on Sunday to become the final resting place for Big Champ.

The players, trainers, and coaches departed the bus and were greeted by the largest turnout for any person or group since Archer County had been organized in the 1890s. In the distance, the school song blared from outdoor speakers at the Methodist Church a block over, courtesy of the church organist.

Once the music and singing finished and the boisterous crowd finally quieted, Grady stepped to a makeshift podium.

"The boys have fought a hard battle, and it has all been a team effort. Each and every boy on the team has worked hard, and each boy deserves as much praise as another."

He then introduced them by name, position, and classification. As he did so, each humbly stepped forward, clearly embarrassed and overwhelmed by the reception which ended after some forty-five minutes, but memories of which would last a lifetime.

CHAPTER 70

The Votes Are In

Mike Stewart celebrated New Year's Day, 1965, in the Archer County Hospital following surgery to repair what remained of his right knee. He was the only patient and, needless to say, was well cared for by nurses Aunt Edith and Aunt Violet plus Judy and a constant parade of teammates, family, friends, and other well-wishers. The next morning he looked up from breakfast to find Barry, Barney, and Gary coming through the door. Barry pitched him a newspaper. Mike opened it and read:

FINAL HARRIS RATINGS FINDS AC IN TOP TEN
In the final Harris ratings for high school football for 1964, the Ingleside Mustangs sit atop the Class A rankings as the No. 1 team. The state champion Archer City Wildcats finished the season at No. 7. (Wichita Falls Times Record News)

Mike looked up. "Seventh?"

"Yeah. You believe that? It goes on to say they're based on mathematical evaluations of each team's strength, and that you can't calculate desire. Or somethin' like that."

"In other words, they screwed up."

"Sounds like it. Seein' as how we have the trophy."

The following week's paper held better news.

FIVE WILDCATS PACE ALL-DISTRICT TEAM
The Archer City Wildcats landed five members on the all-district squad as selected by the coaches of District 11-A. Three made honorable mention. Making the all-

district team were Barry Morrison - quarterback, Barney Oliver - offensive end, Robert Tepfer - offensive guard, Gary Tepfer - fullback, and Billy Pitts - defensive tackle. Those receiving honorable mention were Ray Bussey - offensive end, Butch Hannah - offensive tackle, and Jimmy Reeves - defensive middle guard. (Wichita Falls Times Record News)

And a few days later:

TEPFER NAMED ALL-STATE
Archer City's Gary Tepfer has been picked by the Associated Press as the best fullback in Class A in the state of Texas. He is the first and only player in the history of football at Archer City to be named to the all-state team.

Tepfer toted the pigskin for almost a mile this season and would have had more if not for a nagging thigh injury. He played in all 15 games and carried the ball 300 times for a total of 1,536 yards. His average per carry was just over five yards.

Tepfer's brilliant offensive play was matched by his play at right defensive end. His knack for knowing where the ball was going and his fierce tackling were a concern of every team the Wildcats played.

In the state of Texas there are approximately 225 Class A high school teams. Being named number one at one of the most important positions on the team is indeed an honor. (Wichita Falls Times Record News)

The article went on to list the second team all-state players and the third team. Despite having won the championship, the Wildcats did not have a single player picked for either. Many saw this as yet another slap to the face of Archer City. Others, though, saw it in another light: that the Wildcats were not a team loaded with stars but rather a roster full of average boys who, under the direction of a very special coach, accomplished the impossible.

The Texas Sports Writers Association, however, selected Luke Thornton of Class AAA Palestine as the Coach of the Year. Charles Shreve of Class AA Palacios finished second in the voting. Paul Smith of Class AAAA Galena Park was third. Grady Graves finished fourth.

CHAPTER 71

Accolades

CONGRESS OF THE UNITED STATES
HOUSE OF REPRESENTATIVES
WASHINGTON, D.C.

January 5, 1965

Mr. Grady Graves
Archer City High School
Archer City, Texas

Dear Coach Graves:

Congratulations! As a native of Archer City, I am indeed proud of the accomplishments of the 1964 Wildcats football team. All of us who call Archer City home are overwhelmed and most happy with the Class A Championship which the Wildcats won under your most capable guidance.

I am particularly gratified with your statements that this was a "team victory," and your desire to give all the players equal credit. Team effort is vitally necessary in every phase of life in today's complex world. And this evidence of the type of guidance you and your assistant coaches are giving to those young men who play for you is a real credit to your ability to educate young people.

If there is any way at all I can participate in giving the team the recognition they so richly deserve, I hope you will feel free to call on me. Please extend my hearty congratulations to the team.

Again, congratulations, and best wishes for your future success.

With warmest regards,
GRAHAM PURCELL
13th District of Texas

TEXAS STATE JOURNAL
MONDAY, JANUARY 18, 1965

Senator Hightower offered the following resolution:

S. C. R. No. 4, Extending congratulations to the Archer City High School football team.

Whereas, The Archer City High School football team, the Wildcats, won the 1964 State Class A football championship; and

Whereas, The team was guided brilliantly by Head Coach Grady Graves; and

Whereas, The following team members, which includes many individual stars, and their managers, are:

David Wright, Donald Dorris, Jim Harney, Jimmy Boone, Mickey Horany, Mike Stewart, Bob Gaines, Mike Atchley, Danny Hall, John O'Donohue, Buddy Knox, Billy Pitts, Barry Morrison, Larry Graham, Barney Oliver, Billy Holder, Gary Tepfer, Andy Rogers, Robert Tepfer, Steve Parsley, Butch Hannah, Ray Bussey, Jimmy Reeves, Charlie Goforth, and Gary Johnston; and

Whereas, The Wildcats rated ninth in the Play-offs, entered the contest for the crown as 13-Point underdogs, the team, quoting The Archer City News, finished the season as "Top Cats"; and

Whereas, This team effort is an example for all Texans of high ideals and principles of sportsmanship and accomplishment; now therefor be it

Resolved By the State of Texas, the House of Representatives concurring, that the Legislature extend its heartiest congratulations to the Archer City High School football team, its coach, managers, and supporting student body and faculty for winning the State Crown and best wishes for successful seasons throughout the future, and be it further

Resolved That official copies of this Resolution be forwarded to the coach, managers, and members of the football team.

The resolution was read.

On motion by Senator Hightower and by unanimous consent the resolution was considered immediately and adopted.

On February 4, 1965, a capacity crowd at the 11th Annual Archer County Chamber of Commerce Banquet stood and applauded as Grady Graves was presented the first-ever "Citizen of the Year" award by high school superintendent Tim McPherson. Coaches Roy Williams and Bobby Ray and the twenty-one players and four trainers were honored guests. Senator Jack Hightower was guest speaker.

"Graves," he said, "has done more in promoting Archer City than anyone else ever. The team, directed by Graves, has put Archer City on the map. He is a man whose indomitable will has made him overcome and conquer many obstacles that would have defeated other men of less courage. He, the assistant coaches, and the team remind one of the sign in the Sykorsky Air Plant which reads, 'According to recognized aero-technical tests, the bumble bee cannot fly because of the shape and weight of his body in relation to the total wing area. The bumble bee, however, doesn't know this—so he goes ahead and flies anyway.'"

Then, on February 15, the team and coaches were honored at the biggest football banquet in school history. Guest speaker for the affair was University of Texas offensive line coach Jim Pittman. Numerous former All-America college players were on hand, including John Kimbrough of the Texas A&M Aggies and former University of Texas Longhorns greats Jack Crain and Dick Harris. They were introduced by

U.S. Congressman Graham Purcell of the 13th congressional district.

All were there to recognize the accomplishments of the Wildcat ball club which resulted in a 13-2 record and the first state championship in school history. Coaches Graves, Williams, and Ray were presented plaques by the players and honored by the citizens of the community with Bulova watches inscribed, "State Champions 1964."

Coach Graves was then recognized as the Wichita Falls Times Record News "Area Football Coach of the Year" and presented the award by sports writer Ted Leach.

Pittman entertained the large crowd that packed the school gymnasium with his wit and humorous football tales along with some well-placed jabs at Aggies Kimbrough and Purcell. He followed with a serious message for the team.

"Football parallels the game of life," he told the group. "To be champions you must prepare physically and mentally in football, just as you must to be outstanding professionally. Hard work, dedication, a goal, and leadership are the qualities desired both on the field and off." He stressed, "Education is the most important thing, but athletics plays an important part in building the character of young men."

When he finished, six of the Wildcat seniors were inducted into the Archer City Wildcat Hall of Fame. To gain this recognition, a player must have acquired 120 points in his high school career. Points were given for participation in various athletic events, scholastic achievements and extra accomplishments. Gary Tepfer led the newest members with 230 points—the most ever by an inductee. He was followed by Billy Pitts, Barry Morrison, Barney Oliver, Ray Bussey, and Mike Stewart. The group joined members Tommy Eustace, James Walsh, Donnie Linscott, and Bobby Stone from previous years.

If senior Steve Parsley was disappointed, he didn't show it. He knew his hiatus his sophomore year had cost him his spot. And so be it.

Gary Tepfer was named the team's outstanding back and most valuable player as voted by the squad. Billy Pitts was selected top lineman and Barry Morrison as team leader.

Tepfer was recognized as the leading ground gainer with 1,564 yards and Mike Stewart as leading pass receiver with 281 yards. Junior Robert Tepfer led all tacklers with 72 unassisted take-downs. The cheerleaders were presented gifts by the team as was football sweetheart Judy McMurtry.

A few days later, Grady gave the seven seniors each a game ball with the name of the teams and score painted on it. He put one from each of the five play-off games in a box along with balls from the Munday and Crowell games and had the boys blindly pick numbers to determine which ball they got. There was no speech, and the private affair lasted only a few minutes. Mike Stewart drew the state championship ball. Some years later, after moving to Throckmorton, he returned home from work one day to find it stolen from his house and being used by the neighborhood kids in a pickup game. It appeared one of them had tried to scratch off the writing but had given up. Today it sits in a special spot in the Stewart household.

Despite basketball season being in full swing, everyone in town was still talking football. It was the only topic of discussion at the local diner, filling stations, barbershop, and every other place of business in Archer. Adding to the excitement was the news that three Wildcats had been selected to play in all-star games. Mike Stewart was chosen for the Greenbelt Bowl in Childress. Barney Oliver would play in the Oil Bowl in Wichita Falls. And Gary Tepfer had the honor of being selected for the Texas Coaches' North-South All-Star game played in the Cotton Bowl in Dallas. And if that wasn't exciting enough, Barney Oliver and Gary Tepfer had been awarded scholarships to play at Texas Tech University.

"There are some real good football fans in this town," Grady noted, "and some of them were about to give up because they'd gone so long without a winner. No more. Not only is there renewed hope among the townspeople, the whole school's a lot better off now with renewed school spirit."

Openly, he hoped the winning season would encourage more boys to participate in football. "Out of about eighty boys in high school, we had only twenty-one on our squad, and we sure could use some more depth. Maybe more will come out for football now."

While there was certain to be a handful of new glory-seekers at two-a-days the following summer, he knew his reputation would likely precede him and keep many away. He also knew that a great many of those who did show up would not stick because the sad truth was most either didn't have the desire or weren't willing to pay the price to be successful. He knew something else, too.

If he coached another thirty or forty years, he would have bigger teams. Faster. And more talented. But he might never find another group of boys like these. Ever.

And he didn't.

1964 ARCHER CITY WILDCATS

DISTRICT RECORD 6 - 0 SEASON RECORD 13 - 2

Wildcats	0	Nocona	14	Wildcats	27	*Paducah	6
Wildcats	19	Electra	0	Wildcats	21	*Crowell	6
Wildcats	0	Olney	41	Wildcats	27	Throckmorton	14
Wildcats	19	*Henrietta	12	Wildcats	14	*Knox City	0
Wildcats	35	*Holliday	6	Wildcats	20	*Munday	7

* District 11-A Game

PLAY-OFFS

BI-DISTRICT AT DECATUR

Wildcats 7 Keller 0

REGIONAL AT ABILENE

Wildcats 13 Goldthwaite 6

QUARTER-FINALS AT ARLINGTON

Wildcats 26 Clifton 14

SEMI-FINALS AT SNYDER

Wildcats 7 Big Lake 6

STATE FINALS AT AUSTIN

Wildcats 13 Ingleside 6

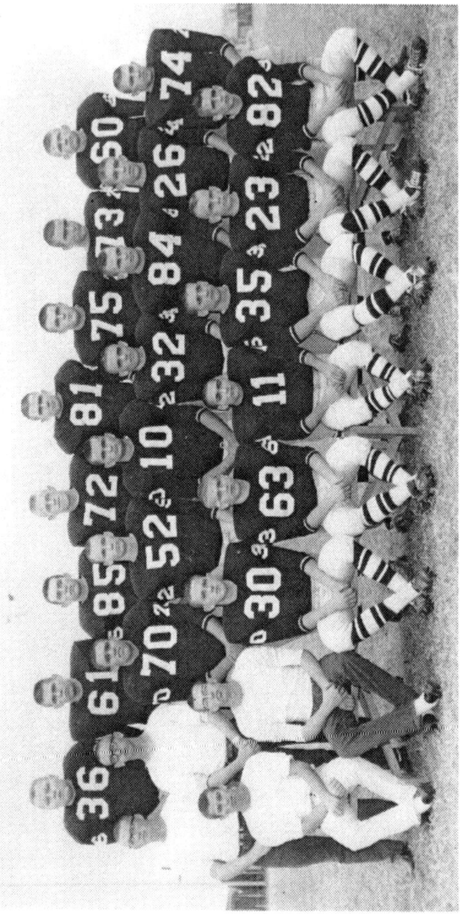

(*Courtesy of Archer City High School*)

Back Row: Andy Rogers, Robert Tepfer, Steve Parsley, Butch Hannah, Ray Bussey, Jimmy Reeves, Charlie Goforth, Gary Johnston.

Middle: Danny Hall, John O'Donohue, Buddy Knox, Billy Pitts, Barry Morrison, Larry Graham, Barney Oliver, Billy Holder, Gary Tepfer.

Front: David Wright, Donald Dorris, Jim Harney, Jimmy Boone, Mickey Horany, Mike Stewart, Bob Gaines, Mike Atchley.

(Archer County News)

From Left: Bobby Ray, Grady Graves, Roy Williams

(Courtesy of Archer City High School)

From Left: Judy Crowley, Jodie Wright, Glenda Lear, Pat Holder, Sue Ann Brock, Trecie Trigg (Kneeling)

(Courtesy of Archer City High School)
Mike Stewart on the move

(Courtesy of Archer City High School)
Fullback Gary Tepfer rumbles

WILDCAT VICTORY HUDDLE—The Archer City Wildcats are shown here huddled around Coach Grady Graves following the 26-14 win over the Clifton Cubs and the State Quarter-Final championship. The Wildcats will play the Big Lake Owls Saturday at 2 p.m. at Snyder.

(Archer County News Photo)

TOUCHDOWN SCAMPER—Archer City's fleet halfback, Mike Stewart, is pictured here on his touchdown run that produced tha counter that gave the Wildcats a 7-6 semi-final victory over Big Lake Owls Saturday at Snyder. The last Big Lake defender is shown here being faked out of his tracks as Stewart gave a good exhibition of the "twist".

(Photo by Jimmy Pitts)

(Archer County News)

WELCOME FOR RETURNING HEROES — Archer City — Archer City turned out en masse Sunday afternoon to welcome home the Wildcat football team, reigning state champion of class A. The Wildcats won the title Saturday night by upsetting heavily favored Ingleside. It was the biggest turnout ever in Archer County history. (Special Photo)

(Times Record News)

MISSION ACCOMPLISHED—Archer City, Tex. (Special)—Big Champ rests on the west side of the Archer County court house after booming the Wildcats to the Class A state football championship. Construction and use of the cannon was a project of the Quarterback Club.

(Times Record News)

HALL OF FAME AWARDS—Six members of the Archer City Wildcats have been named to the ACHS Hall of Fame. The awards are given to students that have excelled in sports, scholastics and leadership. To receive the award a student must compile at least 120 points. This is the largest group to receive the award. Students receiving the awards at the football banquet Saturday night were (l. to r.) Gary Tepfer, Barney Oliver, Mike Stewart, Barry Morrison, Ray Bussey and Billy Pitts.

(Archer County News Photo)

GETS NEWSPAPER AWARD — Archer City — Archer City football coach Grady Graves, left, receives the Record News-Times Area Football Coach of the Year Award from sportswriter Ted Leach during Archer City football banquet held Saturday night. (Staff Photo)

(Times Record News)

STATE CHAMPS SIGN — Archer City—End Barney Oliver, left, and fullback Gary Tepfer, members of Archer City's first state championship football team, signed pre-enrollment applications with Texas Tech here Wednesday. Tech assistant coach Bart Bartlett secured their names. The Wildcats are the fifth and sixth players in the area to sign with Tech since recruiting season began Feb. 3.

(Times Record News)

MARKER FOR THE CHAMPIONS—Workmen were busy last week erecting a huge oval sign on the courthouse lawn so that motorists traveling north and south may know that Archer City has won a State Football Championship. The sign has a brown background with white stripes in resemblance of an actual football. The Archer City Quarterback Club was responsible for getting the sign built and placed on the square. (News Photo)

(Archer County News)

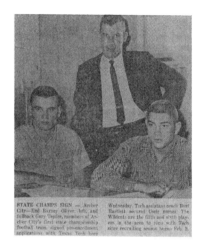

OUTSTANDING CITIZEN — Coach Grady Graves is pictured here receiving the "Citizen of The Year" award from R. A. (Pop) Killian, Chamber of Commerce manager. The award was presented during the annual banquet that was held in the Legion Hall Thursday night. Looking on are Graves' wife, Gay, and Senator Jack Hightower, guest speaker for the banquet. This is the first "citizen" award that has been presented by the Chamber which hereafter will be presented each year at the banquet. (News Photo)

(Archer County News)

A HAPPY DEN OF WILDCATS—The above picture was taken in the Wildcats dressing room just after the locals had won the first district championship in 38 years. Coach Grady Graves immediately went to each individual player, handing out praise and thanks for the overall team effort and spirit that has prevailed thoughout the season. The group then began chanting, "Let's get an Indian." The Wildcats will play Keller Indians in a bi-district match at Decatur Friday night, beginning at 8 p.m. (News Photo)

(Archer County News)

PART FOURTEEN

FINAL THOUGHTS

CHAPTER 72

Pieces of the Puzzle

In forty-five years, the success of the 1964 team has not been duplicated. In 1994, a talented, highly ranked Wildcat team made it to the regional championship game in Arlington against Goldthwaite. Thirty years after the Wildcats had defeated the Eagles in Arlington for that very crown, the losers got their revenge.

Then, in 2008, during the writing of this book, a strange thing happened: The Wildcats began another play-off march. The unbeaten 'Cats, coached by Steve Smith, made it as far as the quarter-finals where the Albany Lions derailed them 14-7. Like their 1964 counterparts, the 2008 version featured a tough, stingy defense and a powerful running game headed by Braden Stovall and Sam Smith, known as Thunder and Lightning. Ol' number 74 and Swivel Hips must've been proud.

In essence, the 1964 Wildcats' climb to the championship was akin to them scaling the tallest of mountains having never even been out of the valley, led not by a mountaineer, but an apprentice of sorts—a guide with a simple plan and an absolute unwillingness to accept failure. It was the right man and the right group of boys crossing paths at just the right point in time. That being the biggest, this puzzle had many pieces.

Assistant Coaches. Having the right assistant coaches was integral. While Bobby Ray and Roy Williams were tough coaches in their own right, each was also approachable and understanding. Visions of Fuzzy tossing ice chips into the grass during a particularly long session of wind sprints and Roy telling Steve to "Hang in there," exemplify this. Many of the players commented on it and on how much they liked the two. Without them, the team might have felt totally isolated, distant, and disconnected.

Leadership. "There are three types of leaders," Billy Pitts told me. "First, there's the natural-born leader. That was Barry. And there's the one who leads by example. That was Gary. Then there's the kind of leader that comes into a tough situation and tells a joke or quick one-liner to relax everyone and clear the air. And that was Mike. We had them all."

Conditioning. There's no way to substantiate it, but the 1964 Wildcat players possibly ran more than any team ever—high school, college, or pros. Luckily, no one died, and their conditioning more than made up for any lack of talent. The second half of ball games really did belong to them—particularly the final quarter. During their five-game play-off run, the Wildcats gave up a total of only seven points in those five final stanzas against the best teams in the state.

Toughness. These guys were tough. Leaving a game with an injury meant not only facing Grady but facing their teammates as well. During a game his sophomore year, Robert Tepfer returned to the huddle complaining his hand had been stepped on. The others told him to quit complaining and suck it up. Following the next play, he returned quietly crying and holding it, but finished the game. Afterwards, he refused to have it looked at and didn't miss a practice the following week. For their next ball game, Grady reluctantly agreed to let him tape a knee pad to the back of it. Then, one year later, after severely breaking a finger in practice, he was taken by Grady to the clinic where, upon examining the X-ray, Doc Schlomach turned to Robert and asked, "Son, what did you do to this hand? Nearly every bone in it has been crushed." Like I said, these guys were tough.

Discipline. The discipline the players exhibited can largely be attributed to the blackboard hanging in the locker room. A single stint on the Goof-Off Squad almost always prevented a recurrence of the violation, be it a missed curfew, poor grade, lack of hustle, or other such behavior deemed inappropriate by Grady. Evidence of their discipline is plentiful. During the play-offs, the team received only 16 penalties for 130 yards—an average of 3 penalties and 26 yards per game, lost only 6 fumbles, and had only 3 passes intercepted. It should be noted that 6 of the 16 penalties, 4 of the 6 fumbles and 2 of the 3 interceptions occurred in the game against Keller in the sub-freezing temperatures that plagued both teams.

Teamwork. The importance of this cannot be overemphasized. Time and again players told me one reason for their success was that each knew exactly what the person next to him was going to do on each play. Without deviation. But more importantly, none could bear the thought of letting his teammates down. Had Grady not stripped "I" and "me" from their way of thinking, it would have happened on its own—the boys having been through so much together they shared a survivors' bond. In the end, they were playing for each other.

Want-to. If there was an intangible, it was this. These guys had a lot of want-to in them. You can call it pride. Or character. Or anything you choose. Andy Rogers knows first-hand. Having coached football for nearly half his life, he spent twenty-five years at Corsicana High School in Texas, during which time the Tigers made the play-offs twenty-three times. Rogers has coached some of Texas's finest athletes. Most went to college and some to the pros. "But there's never been a tougher group of athletes than Archer City's 1964 team," he says. "Nor one as tight-knit. I didn't get to play much, but I was there. We relentlessly ran, blocked, and tackled, and for strength conditioning, lifted steel bars with coffee cans filled with concrete on the ends—none of this state-of-the-art equipment. We worked out for hours on end in the heat of the day with a single, almost non-existent, water break. I tell you, you just don't see guys like that anymore. I know. I've coached top-level high school football for twenty-eight years."

CHAPTER 73

Unsung Heroes

It's been said you'd need a No. 2 washtub to carry the heart of any one of the Wildcat players. That being the case, you'd need an even larger one to carry the heart of any of the subs—seven young men who suited up for practice day after day, week after week, and saw little or no playing time. They must have constantly asked themselves, "What the heck am I doing? Why am I putting myself through this?" And yet they didn't quit.

Freshman Bob Gaines's time would come, but not that year. Beginning in 1965, he would have three stellar years at Archer and eventually go to the University of New Mexico on a full four-year scholarship where he would earn All-Conference honors at cornerback. On this team, he played quarterback and running back and rarely saw time at either position. After all, he was just a freshman, and Grady was in the last year of his four-year plan, when freshmen—for the most part—didn't figure in anymore. But he did get to return punts and kickoffs. He simply was too talented to keep off the field.

Sophomore Jim Harney played fullback behind Gary and occasionally got in for a play or two in each game to give Gary a breather. During practices, Jim served as the "running dummy," emulating the upcoming opposing team's stud running back, a position which carried with it precious little notoriety and a whole lot of punishment handed out by the starting defense. His father Jack, the deputy sheriff, had a slightly more important job. At night, at Grady's request, Jack would pick up the coach and drive him around town looking for prospective Goof-Off Squad members. Jim himself made the mistake of membership just once. That was enough.

Sophomore Andy Rogers, a transplanted Kansan, was just getting the hang of speaking "Texan" in 1964 after moving to Archer City his freshman year. It was a good thing, too. Sounding like a Yankee (Kansas was considered far enough north) got you one of two things on a regular basis—kidding or a butt kicking. A basketball player at heart, football was basically a ticket to the hoops. At Archer City, as it was with many small schools at the time, one played either all sports or none. The totally inexperienced Andy had never even touched a pigskin before his freshman year. As a result, his feet almost never touched the playing field, although he did manage to figure into one play-off game for a single play. In Snyder, against Big Lake, Robert Tepfer broke his helmet, hurried to the sideline, and confiscated Andy's since his was the only one on the team that would fit him. A play later Robert's was repaired, and Andy had his back, complete with a white mark across it courtesy of a hard hit by Robert on an Owl player—a badge of honor Andy proudly displayed and refused to let the trainers clean away.

Freshman Charlie Goforth, a big boy blessed with size and speed, got in most games on special teams and occasionally on offense and defense as a lineman. His fondness for Roy Williams was reciprocated because Roy had great feelings for linemen who tried hard and wanted to learn. Armed with the moves Roy had taught him, he went on to a terrific high school career.

Freshman Mike Atchley's playing was limited almost solely to the practice field. Like all of the subs, his real contribution was via the scout team where he did his best to emulate the opposing team's starting safety on defense and tight end on offense. Doing so afforded him two unique opportunities. At safety, once All-State fullback Gary Tepfer had broken through the line (which was nearly every play), Mike had the privilege of trying to tackle him one-on-one. And he never had to go far because Gary had a knack for running right at him rather than trying to elude Mike's 138 pounds. If that wasn't fun enough, on offense, Mike was shouldered with having to block Texas Tech-bound defensive end Barney Oliver with pretty much the same results. Except for once. With the aid of near hurricane strength winds, he once managed to block number 84 to the ground. Well, Barney got an earful from Grady, and on the next play he knocked Mike almost to Ruby's Grocery a block away, punctuating the deed with a knee to Mike's groin. In later years, Mike would jokingly say the challenges he presented the two of them during practices paid off in the long run, resulting in the championship *and* their scholarships.

The thing is, he's right. The courage these players displayed and the effort they gave directly contributed to the team's success. It did make better players out of the starters. And while it might have seemed so, it did not go unnoticed. Years later, when asked, Grady smiled and said, "We had to have 'em. They might not have been as talented, but they worked as hard, or harder, than anyone on the team, and they suffered for it. No doubt. But they didn't quit. And their effort earned the respect of everyone. As a coach, you just have to have those kinds of guys."

Whether junior Gary Johnston was delivering a hard hit or was the recipient of one at his guard position, he got always back up and smiled. Football was not his greatest talent, but as many would say, "There simply was no backup in Gary Johnston." Sadly, in a way, his courage and character led to his demise.

Just five short years later, while walking point and protecting his men behind him, Army Staff Sgt. Gary Clarence Johnston was shot and killed in the jungles of Viet Nam. Like so many from small towns, he wished to see the world and at the same time, help the people of South Vietnam.

Then, in the cruelest of twists, thirty-seven years later his nephew and namesake, Marine Sgt. Gary Scott Johnston, was killed in the Anbar province during the war in Iraq. Like his uncle, the younger Gary, too, was out front walking point, guarding his own men at the time of his death. Go figure.

That brings us to the last of the Wildcats' unsung heroes, Jimmy Boone. Watching him on his first day of practice as a freshman, Grady surely thought to himself, *That little blonde-haired, snotty-nosed kid won't be here tomorrow.* But he was. And if anyone had reason to quit it was he. The punishment he endured was relentless and came from all sides. He was constantly beaten up on the practice field by larger, quicker players—his nose bleeding at every practice. He was berated by Grady and constantly harassed in the locker room and on bus rides by the older players. In their eyes, he just didn't have what it took. When the ball was snapped, players would go one way, and he'd go another. In drills, he would drop when he was supposed to roll. He lagged behind in wind sprints. In short, his talent just did not match up to his heart. At times, it would just be too much and against his will, he'd break the unwritten rule: He'd cry. This, of course, only escalated his torment.

What he didn't do, though, is quit. This young man who for three years was physically and mentally beat completely down, always got back up. Every single time.

Some twenty years later, Barry Morrison contributed the following poignant piece to the Archer County News about the team's unsung heroes and Jimmy in particular. It is reprinted here with his permission:

THANKS AGAIN, JIMMY BOONE
By Barry Morrison

I have been associated closely with athletes all my life and continue so today. A few such athletes have had influence on my life in some form or another and seldom does a day go by that some remembrance of them does not cross my mind. The remembrances are, for the most part, of the good results from a fair amount of hard work and sacrifice from gifted teammates or competitors. However, the memory of one dedicated not-so-athletic person has helped me over many a stumbling block along life's highway.

I watched his blood flow on the fall grass of the football field. I watched his lunch spill on that same field. I saw his face wince in pain from someone running completely over him at full speed. I felt him pat me on the back when things didn't go well. I saw him lean against his locker dreading, just as we all did, putting on those practice pads. I also saw, after a large majority of the games, his uniform had no grass stains; in other words his game uniform did not resemble his practice uniform at all because he did not play one down.

I look back on all this, and I am sad because I failed to thank him and others at the time for their sacrifice. He knew he wasn't going to get to play on Friday night. It took me a few years of life's little pitfalls to finally see what made him keep coming back for more and more. He was not a quitter. He had no idea anyone was noticing his tenacity, pride and downright gutsy performance, and for years I didn't realize I had noticed either. I did notice, and when the right situation appears, recall immediately his image. He is no longer with us, however I was fortunate enough to tell him many years ago how much he unknowingly influenced my life. The thrill of seeing his chest swell and tears come to his eyes was awesome for me because he didn't realize anyone was noticing his contributions either. A tragic accident took him away from his family and friends but he lives on in our hearts.

Thanks again, Jimmy Boone. I'll always remember and use your influence.

On November 21, 1986, Jimmy Boone died in the oilfield near Bloomfield, New Mexico, after being crushed by a pumping unit. It appeared that a bad knee, injured playing football, suddenly gave way, causing him to fall into harm's way. He left behind a wife, two little girls and a son. He was thirty-eight years old.

You'll find his picture in the Wildcat championship team photo. He's the blonde, unassuming young man on the front row wearing jersey number 63. The one with, perhaps, the biggest heart of all.

CHAPTER 74

The Town

On a breezy spring day in 1965, twelve-year-old Gary Beesinger was sitting in the office of the local Fina station operated by his step-father Benny King, reading a True Detective magazine, eating cheese crackers, and drinking a RC Cola when the pneumatic bell signaled the arrival of a customer. He hurried outside just as Benny appeared from the service bay. Together, they watched a sharply dressed man in western attire climb from his expensive, later-model extended cab pickup.

"This all there is?" the stranger asked, looking around.

Benny wiped his hands on a red rag and replaced it in his rear pocket.

"'Scuse me?"

"Is this all there is here?"

"Well, yes sir. I just have the two pumps."

"No!" he replied, impatiently. "I'm talking about the town." He looked north toward the red light, then south down Center Street. "Is this all there is to Archer City?"

Benny and Gary looked at each other. "Well, yes sir. Pretty much."

"Hmmmph!" Disgusted, the driver climbed back in, started the engine, and sped off. The last thing they saw as he drove away was a large blue and white bumper sticker that read: *BIG LAKE OWLS.*

On the surface, Archer City appeared pretty much the same as it had for quite some years. But looks were deceiving. The people who lived there knew: The town was different. Its transformation had been abrupt and complete, the precise moment marked by a cannon shot signaling the end of a football game at Nelson Field in Austin, Texas, four months earlier.

It was at that exact moment that Archer City, Texas, actually became Archer City.

Although the euphoria over the football championship eventually subsided, the town has never completely relinquished its new persona born of 1964. To this day, the gratifying sense of accomplishment, the new-found optimism of all-things-possible, and above all, the cohesiveness born of sharing something so special and personal still remain—passed down through generations not so much via the written or spoken word, as through the motions of everyday living. It is this kindred spirit that makes Archer City unique among small towns today.

In 1964, the people of Archer City felt connected to the team, and to each other. Many had not and would never accomplish anything as meaningful in their own lives. Whether it was joining the caravan of cars headed to the next play-off game, gathering at the Royal Theater to listen to the radio broadcast, or listening at home, they felt they had contributed. And they certainly had sacrificed. Because Archer was such a poor town, for most, the expense of traveling to and attending the out-of-town games was burdensome if not impossible. As hard as it may be to imagine these days, it was not unusual to find homes that year with small Christmas trees decorated with ticket stubs and other mementoes from that season. Some couples even exchanged envelopes containing these items as their only presents that year.

Robert Adams, owner of the Lucky Dollar Food Store, definitely felt the economic crunch. With the exception of beans, the grocery business was painfully slow that winter. He sold a lot of beans. But you would not hear him complain. Rather, the week of the championship game, he ran the following full-page ad in the Archer County News with individual photos of all the players and sale prices of selected items coinciding with the players' jersey numbers:

ROBERT'S LUCKY DOLLAR FOOD STORE

Mike Stewart - Whole Fryers - 35¢ lb.
Bob Gaines - Baker's Coconut - 23¢ 4-oz. Can
Billy Holder - Mandarin Oranges - 26¢ 11 oz. Can
Barry Morrison - Celery - 10¢ each
Jim Harney - Mince Meat - 30¢ 9-oz. Box
Andy Rogers- Egg Nog - 36¢ qt.
Gary Tepfer - Tide (Giant Size) - 74¢
Gary Johnston - Corn - 60¢ - 4 12 oz. Cans
Jimmy Boone - Light Bulbs - 63¢ for 3
Billy Pitts - Miracle Whip - 52¢ qt.
Buddy Knox - Folger's Coffee - 70¢ lb.
Butch Hannah - Velveeta Cheese - 72¢ - 2 lb. Box
Robert Tepfer - Club Steaks - 61¢ lb.
Charlie Goforth - Crisco - 73¢ - 3 lb. Can
Jimmy Reeves - Carnation Ice Cream - 75¢ Half Gallon
Mickey Horany - Bananas - 11¢ lb.
Ray Bussey - Kimbell Green Beans - 81¢ for 4
Mike Atchley - Kimbell Cherries - 82¢ (4 cans)
Larry Graham - Kimbell Pickles - 32¢ qt.
Barney Oliver - Hunt's Fruit Cocktail - 4 Cans for 84¢
Steve Parsley - Hunt's Peaches - 3 for 85¢

The ad included the following notation: This advertisement was prepared prior to the state championship football game that was held Saturday night and regardless whether the Wildcats are the best in the state or next to best we are proud to pay tribute to a fine group of boys. Congratulations to the boys and coaches for their fine record.

And Santa himself resided in Archer that year. Football, the team, and his hometown meant so much to Benny King he was willing to sacrifice his business and livelihood and very nearly did. Word spread quickly that Benny was willing to let customers charge their gasoline for traveling to the games, and once started, he simply could not find it in himself to turn anyone down. Not surprisingly, his business almost went under and although it survived, he never totally recouped his losses. When he died in 1988, he was still owed money for some of those purchases nearly twenty-five years earlier.

On the other hand, a handful of men with a little money to invest made a killing that year. Starting with the district championship game against Munday, they let it be known that anyone interested in betting against the Wildcats could find them beneath the bleachers ready to accommodate. The further the Wildcats advanced in the play-offs, and the greater underdogs they became, the higher the stakes and their winnings. The story's told of one particular Wildcat skeptic who, down $35,000, walked into the men's restroom at halftime of the Ingleside game and said, "I'll give anyone here Archer City and thirteen points in the second half." Needless to say, he had a lot of takers. And lost a lot of money.

Years later, a new football stadium was constructed in the southeast portion of town relieving the coaching staff of painstakingly plowing and leveling the field and planting grass each July following the Archer County Rodeo. Happily for the players, gone too were the occasional infections inherent with playing on ground strewn with broken beer bottles and horse manure. The old, dimly lit showground was gladly left to the cowpokes, broncin' bucks, and pretty girls in tight, glittery outfits.

Big Champ was eventually moved from its resting place on the courthouse lawn to make room for a new veterans' war memorial. The iconic canon now proudly resides in front of the high school.

In October 2004, a 40-year reunion was held for the team and a granite monument commemorating the 1964 season was unveiled alongside the cannon on the school lawn. Following the dedication ceremony, the team members, their families, and loyal supporters gathered at the Royal Theater to reminisce. However, a pallor hung over the celebration due to the absence of one person—Grady Graves. The night before, he'd suffered a mild heart attack and was recuperating in a Wichita Falls hospital. He eventually recovered fully.

In 2007, the Archer County Courthouse was restored to its original condition of one hundred years ago, and because the grounds were included in the restoration, the commemorative state championship sign which had stood proudly near the curb for over forty years, had to be moved and was relocated to the new stadium.

One night in August 2008, I received a phone call from Ms. Lori Rutledge of Archer City. Her mother had recently passed, and as she was going through her mom's hope chest she came across several ticket stubs, newspaper clippings, and other memorabilia from that year. She'd heard I was working on a book about the '64 Wildcats and wondered if I could use any of the items. As far as I knew, Jeanette and Bobby Stubbs had no direct connection to the team. Lori confirmed this. Her mom and dad had simply been fans.

"That season meant a lot to them, Jim."

"I'm finding out it did to a lot of people," I said.

"Oh yeah. Very much so."

On one level, it was just a handful of small-town high school football games played out one fall and winter many years ago. On another, it was so much more than that. And the town of Archer City is, and will always be, defined by a single date.

1964.

CHAPTER 75

Grady

"**B**oys, coaching football is my job. I have a family to provide for, and the best way I know to do that is to move on to a larger school that pays more. And so I've taken the position of head coach at Burleson next year."

And with that, the four-year reign of Grady Graves in Archer City was over.

Coach Bobby Ray remained at Archer, while Roy Williams left to become line coach at Canadian, Texas.

Grady would not come close to duplicating his success in Archer City throughout the rest of his head-coaching career. Little did he know his opportunity to do so ended when he passed the city limit sign on his way out of town. Burleson, Texas, was not open to his coaching methods. Not the players. The parents. Nor the school board.

Not the Rules. Not the atrocious workouts. Not the, "If you don't do it, there'll be hell to pay" philosophy. And certainly not the total domination of the boys' lives. That's just not the way things were done there.

He lasted two years before moving on to Coleman, another 2-A school, with similar results. Eventually, he bowed to the pressure and frustration there and left for an assistant-coaching job with the Class 2-A Iowa Park Hawks. Under the direction of head coach Tommy Watkins, with Grady handling the quarterbacks and secondary, the Mean Green won two state championships in three years. After Watkin's departure, Grady was offered and accepted the head-coaching position. A month later, his phone rang.

"Grady Graves."

"Coach, it's Barney. Oliver."

"Barney! Good to hear from you, son! How are you?"

"Well, sir, I've grown tired of the construction business and was thinking I'd like to try and get into coaching. And wanted your thoughts."

"How soon can you get here?"

"Sir?"

"Iowa Park. I can always use a good coach."

"Well, uh, I don't have my teaching certificate yet."

"We'll worry about that when you get here."

There was a long silence on the other end. Then softly, "Thanks, Coach. A lot."

"My pleasure, Barney."

Grady's new assistant went to work, studied nights at Midwestern University, earned his teaching certificate, and got busy coaching the junior varsity.

Grady was sitting at his office desk one evening when a man and woman burst through the door.

"Well, Coach Graves, what's it gonna be?"

"'Scuse me?"

"That young coach of yours. Oliver. What're you gonna do about him?"

"What'd he do?"

"He almost killed our boy, that's what! It's a wonder he can still walk."

Grady glanced out the window. Barney was nowhere in sight.

"During practice, that so-called coach of yours grabbed our son's face mask and jerked him around like a rag doll. It's a wonder he didn't break his neck! And then, he proceeded to drag him along the ground. For at least ten yards! By his face mask! And if that wasn't enough, he jerked him to his feet and kicked him! Hard!" The woman paused, out of breath, her face red as a beet. Her husband's, too. Finally, he got his chance.

"Coach, she's not exaggerating. And that type of behavior is not acceptable here. No way. We'll go to the school board if we have to. Or the police!"

Grady stood. "Whoa, no need for that. I'll handle it."

"You better!"

"I will. It won't happen again."

Several minutes later he finally managed to send them on their way. Once they were gone, Barney walked in.

"What was that all about?"

"You."

"Me?"

"Those were the parents of one of your players. They say you were out there jerking him around by his face mask like a maniac. AND, that you drug him across the field for ten whole yards. And then kicked him! That so?"

"Coach, you used to do that all the time."

A smile began to emerge on Grady's face. Barney's too.

"Yeah, but, that was a long time ago. Things are different these days. Times have changed."

"Well, which part you want me to drop? The jerkin', the draggin', or the kickin'?"

"All of it! Or they'll run us both out of town!"

The two laughed, looking into one another's eyes. And hearts.

"Yes sir. Will do. Sorry for the trouble."

Grady nodded. "See you tomorrow."

Barney lcft, only to return a few seconds later. Standing in the open doorway, he knocked. Grady looked up.

"Coach, those two weren't being truthful with you."

"How's that?"

"I didn't drag that boy along the ground for any ten yards."

"You didn't?"

"No sir," he said, his smile returning. "It was more like twenty."

Grady guided Iowa Park to three straight successful 8-2 seasons before the talent pool dried up and the Hawks went 0-10. He then moved on, taking an assistant's job at Hirshi High School in Wichita Falls. From there he went to Class 4-A Wichita Falls High School as an assistant. During his stay there, the position of head coach of the girls basketball team came open and he took it. The five years he spent there were among the most enjoyable in his career.

I had no sooner gotten situated at his kitchen table and turned on my recorder to begin our initial interview for this book when he said to me, "Jim, now this book *is* going to be about those boys, isn't it? I mean, they're the ones who did this."

"Well, uh . . ."

"We just got 'em ready to play. That's about it. They're the ones who got it done. They deserve all the credit."

I looked at him and smiled.

"I knew you were going to say that," I said.

"How's that?"

"I just knew." I opened up the school year book I'd brought with me and turned to the 1964 Class A State Champion team photo. "It's this picture. It just never looked right to me. And it took me a while to figure out why—then I saw. There are no coaches in this photograph. Only players."

I watched him study the picture, feigning surprise.

"Now, this was either the photographer's doings, or yours, and I can't think of a single reason the person taking this photo would ask the coaching staff to stand aside. So that leaves you. What about it?"

He paused, and looked at me. I tried to envision his much-feared infamous glare the players had talked about. I couldn't.

"Well, you know, I don't rightly remember. I could have had something to do with that I guess."

I couldn't help but smile.

"I'm willing to bet this is the only photo of a championship team anywhere without a single coach in it." I was throwing some praise his way, but he was having none of it.

"Jim, it was never about the coaches," he answered, his smile fading. "And contrary to what some folks think, it was never about me. It was about the boys. It was always about those boys."

Over the course of the next several months, I would often hear the players referred to as *Grady's boys*. He had yet to call them *his boys,* and throughout our many conversations, I never once heard him refer to them as such.

"Don't get me wrong. I had some fine assistant coaches. Couldn't have done it without 'em. Roy's as fine a line coach as there ever was. And Fuzzy could scout a team like nobody's business. And, of course, he quarterbacked the scout teams in practice. Even had all the mannerisms of the opposing teams' quarterbacks. You should've seen him." He paused.

"And something else. Joe Stults and Ted Leach had a lot to do with our success. Not only could I always count on their articles being upbeat and positive, but they always kept it one game at a time, and never got the cart before the horse. And anytime I asked 'em to print something specific, they did so. For the good of the team. They were a big part of what we were able to do. Folks don't know that."

"I'll make note of that," I said.

"You do that. They're good men."

"Okay, here wc go," I said, officially beginning the interview. "From everything I've heard, you were one tough coach. And I'm told *tough.* Hey, those guys are *still* dreading practice, after all these years."

I expected a laugh or smile. Instead, he looked away, thinking. When he answered, his tone was pensive.

"I was *so* hard on those boys. *So* hard. But I *had* to be. Especially those first few years. Or else they would have gotten killed by the opposition who was big, strong, mobile, hostile, and experienced. Looking back, I did everything wrong back then. Everything they say not to do these days. I never gave 'em enough water. And gave 'em all those salt pills. It's a wonder I didn't kill one." He paused. "Jim, I *loved* those boys. Every *one* of 'em. But I just couldn't show it at the time and get done what we needed to do to in order to meet our objectives."

In researching the book, it became clear that the window of opportunity for this man and his coaching style was open only briefly. Once closed, it was shut for good. That it would do it so early in his career seemed unfair. In that short time, though, this man was responsible for the transformation of a town. Or, more accurately, it's rebirth. And the mark he left on a certain group of young boys has never faded. Today, forty-five years later, these men, now in their sixties, still bear it.

"It was several years," Barry Morrison says, "before I realized he was teaching us more than just football. The lessons we learned and the discipline and toughness he instilled in us have benefitted me throughout my life."

It was a statement I would hear often in my interviews with other players.

"He can say it was all about us boys, but someone had to keep one hand on the throttle and the other on the wheel," Ray Bussey told me, "and that was the little man with the yellow—I mean blonde—hair. And something else. I still say *yes sir* and *yes ma'am* to this day. You know why? Because he taught us to. And it's ingrained right here," he said, his voice cracking and eyes filling as he proudly tapped his chest above his heart. "That, and a whole lot more."

CHAPTER 76

The Boys

Texas Tech's All-America running back and Green Bay Packer standout, Donnie Anderson, to this day does not know how close he came to getting "taken to the woodshed" by an Archer City Wildcat. Mike Stewart had driven to Lubbock in 1965 to visit Gary and Barney and was in Gary's dorm room one night playing cards when Donnie and another big senior walked in, intent on a little hazing. One thing led to another, and soon the 6'3" 210-pound Anderson was swinging Mike's jacket above his head when Mike's pocket watch flew against the wall, breaking—the watch his dad Gene had swapped a German officer a pack of cigarettes for in World War II. A sentimental piece to say the least. Knowing it would just make it harder on him down the road, Gary persuaded his buddy not to retaliate, and he didn't, or things would have gotten really interesting.

Gary eventually became disenchanted with big-time college football and left Tech. "It's one thing to play high school ball and play your guts out for your teammates and what you believe in. But stepping out of that is hard. Some people can do it. I couldn't."

Barney stayed and started on the freshman team. Redshirted the following year, he played quite a bit his third and was injured in his fourth. "I always felt I was too small to play there," he said. "The only way I was able to was because of the superb techniques I'd learned from Roy Williams, and the discipline I got from Grady. My Red Raider teammates would kid me for always being the first one at team meetings, but I was scared of being late. Afraid Grady would find out," he told me, grinning.

In 1999, author Jim Dent published *The Junction Boys—How Ten Days in Hell with Bear Bryant Forged a Championship Team,* depicting the legendary coach's first year at Texas A&M University in 1954. The popular book and subsequent made-for-TV movie depicted the harsh conditions, oppressive heat, and brutal workouts surviving players endured at a remote camp in the Texas hill country. Most quit due to illness, injury, or exhaustion. Comparisons with the '64 Wildcats were inevitable.

Would they have swapped places with the Aggies if possible?

"In a heartbeat," was the general response. This was usually followed by, "except for the grass burrs," and a smile.

One even kidded I should name this book, *Grady's Boys—How Four Years in Hell Forged a Championship Team.*

Following surgery and rehabilitation on his knee, Mike Stewart honored his selection to the Greenbelt Bowl All-Star game in Childress the following summer. The head coach was Grant Teaff of McMurry College, who would go on to a storied career as the head coach of Baylor University. While others complained, Mike couldn't help but laugh at the notion the practices were hard.

"Dadgum, guys, this is a cakewalk. Really, I thought I died and went to heaven." His teammates from around the state thought he was joking. He wasn't.

The notorious Wildcat workouts and playing hurt have apparently taken their toll.

In addition to being hampered with bad knees, Gary Tepfer has had one hip replacement and needs another. Billy Pitts's knee problems are a result of his ankle injuries which never healed properly. Ray Bussey suffers from shoulder and elbow problems and crooked, hurting fingers. Mike Stewart's knee has never forgiven him, and Barry and Barney pretty much hurt all over. Those who played three or less years under Grady are faring somewhat better but not much. Robert Tepfer has had both hips replaced and battles knee problems as well. The list goes on and on.

In the spring of 2004, Steve Parsley began dropping things. Then stumbling. Then falling. Doctors determined he had not had a stroke and eventually ruled out Multiple Sclerosis. A second MRI uncovered the culprit—an old spinal injury gone untreated. Surgery was performed fusing vertebras three and four and inserting a titanium disk. It was concluded the problem stemmed from an old injury, most likely a blow to the head. When asked if he'd received any, Steve replied, "Yeah, football, the oilfield, gettin' hit on top of the head with beer and whiskey bottles, and the such—just the normal growing up things."

The doctor grimaced and asked, "My God, where did you grow up?"

Steve smiled and answered, "Well, if I ever did, it was in Archer City."

The ensuing surgery likely prevented further deterioration, but he still falls often today, and is unable to walk more than twenty-five feet or so before his legs give out. A devoted beachcomber, he's given up the hobby—not because it hurts to fall on the sand, but because it's embarrassing to him. Then in December 2007, Steve wasn't feeling good and his doctor prescribed an angiogram. During the procedure, he had a heart attack. Emergency surgery was performed, and he awoke hours later feeling the weight of the world on his chest and every other part of his body.

He looked up at his doctor. "Damn, Doc. I felt better than this *before* the surgery."

"Maybe so, but you were *dying.*"

You can imagine my shock and horror when Steve plopped to the floor during our interview to demonstrate the secret move Roy Williams had taught all the linemen.

Still the Rebel.

And still a Wildcat.

These days find the heroes of 1964 scattered to the wind. A few remained in Archer City, others moved away only to return, and some left for good. They became accountants, highway patrolmen, coaches, oilfield workers, sheriffs, farmers and ranchers, salesmen, heavy equipment operators, and Fortune 500 company execs. A great many have stayed in touch with each other and Grady through the years. In addition to Gary Johnston and Jimmy Boone, trainer Danny Hall is gone now, having passed away in Houston in April 2003 from throat cancer. At the time of the writing of this book, the rest remain. All are forever linked—sharing a kinship of sorts—blood brothers for sure. And for seven, a bond that simply cannot be put into words.

Perhaps Grady was right. Maybe it *was* just about the boys. Maybe it always has been. Midway through the very first interview I conducted for this book, Barry Morrison shared the following story with me, and I've never forgotten it.

One day in 2007, his six-year-old grandson's class was visiting the high school when they came across the trophies and large team photo from 1964. That evening during a visit, he corralled Barry and wide-eyed, asked, "Grandad! Were . . . you . . . a . . . *Champion?"*

At this point in the telling of the story, Barry paused and looked away. I waited for him to continue. When he didn't, I looked over at Trecie. She smiled at me, her eyes soft and shining. Then she turned and smiled at Barry.

Another few seconds passed. Finally, I spoke. "Well, what did you tell him?"

A moment later, the Quarterback looked back at me. With a hint of wistfulness in his voice, a gleam in his eye, and the same quiet dignity I would find time and again in interviews with the other players, he answered.

"I told him, 'Well, son, I did play some football back then.'"

Yes, Barry, you certainly did.

You *all* did.

EPILOGUE

The idea for this book was born at Red Lobster in Wichita Falls one fall evening in 2007. My wife Lorrie and I were enjoying dinner with my cousin Mike Stewart and his wife Judy when Mike told the following story.

"The summer after we won the championship, I was driving back to Archer one day from working in the oilfield in west Texas when I stopped to get gas. As I pulled into this filling station, this old man puts down his newspaper, gets up, walks over, and says, 'What'll it be, young-un?' I told him regular, and he leans on my pickup and starts pumping gas. Well, about that time, he notices the sticker on my rear window that says, Archer City Wildcats - 1964 Class A State Champions, and he looks at me and asks, 'You from there?' I said, 'Yes sir.' And he says, 'You play ball there?' And I say, 'Sure did. Yes sir.' And he immediately turns off the pump, screws the gas cap back on, and says, 'We're done here.' I say, ''Scuse me?' And he walks back over, sits down, and picks up his newspaper. Well, I look at the pump, and it says three gallons, so I ask him what I owe, and he ignores me! I finally got in and drove off."

Lorrie and I looked at each other, then back at Mike.

"So now I'm driving down the street looking for another station when all of a sudden I see Goldthwaite Hardware. And it dawns on me: Holy cow! I'm in *Goldthwaite!* The guy probably thought I was driving up and down the street showin' off my sticker! Then it occurs to me, a whole carload of those hard-hittin' Goldthwaite Eagles might spot me and think the same, so I hightail it outta there! And for the next thirty miles, I take turns watching my gas gauge and rear view mirror and finally manage to make it to the next town for gas. I tell you, I was never so glad to finally see the city limit sign of Archer City!"

When Lorrie and I finished laughing, he said, "It gets even better. This summer, Judy and I were in Ruidoso in our travel trailer at our favorite RV park where, in the evenings, everybody gathers 'round a big fire pit and swaps stories. Well, I'd just told that one about Goldthwaite, and a couple nearly fell off their durn chairs laughing so hard. Turns out *they* were from Goldthwaite. Then the lady says, 'We've heard that story a hundred times through the years. That old fella is my uncle James!' Well, we all laugh, and then I ask, 'Say, tell me something. Was he really mad?' And she says, 'Damn right he was mad!'"

Over the next few hours, we relived that magical season in 1964 until sometime after 11:00 P.M. when we were kindly informed the restaurant was closing. On our way out, we discovered we were the only remaining customers and had been for quite a while. In the foyer, as we said our goodbyes, it was suggested someone should write a book about the team. Having published two little-known novels and tossing around ideas for a third book, I told Mike I'd think about it and let him know. It would, after all, be a big undertaking. A week later I phoned and said I'd give it a try.

In putting together a plan, I knew that searching out the "real" story would require some trepidation on my part. After all, this is "hallowed ground" as Warren Robertson would say. And who hasn't chased fireflies on a warm summer night, caught some, and upon closer inspection become disenchanted and dismayed—the wonder and magic gone?

Those things in mind, I then made some notes, borrowed a high school yearbook from that year, and embarked on what I refer to as The Grand Tour—tracking down and interviewing my childhood and hometown heroes. Now, sixteen months later, my life is richer for having done so. I have laughed and cried with them and treasure the time we spent together. They have given me some very special memories.

I'll always remember meeting Grady Graves for the very first time. As he graciously ushered me into his home and introduced me to the love of his life, his wife Gay, I was taken back by his soft voice and gentle nature. This certainly was not the domineering tyrant I was expecting. Later, as I drove away, it occurred to me that Grady had perhaps not changed so much as he had evolved. Adapted. On his own terms.

A few short months following my interview with him, coach Bobby Ray died in Wichita Falls on February 16, 2009, following a stroke. A picture of health at age 72, his death took everyone by surprise. Invaluable in the Wildcats' championship season, Fuzzy's true legacy is the myriad of players he taught and inspired on basketball courts in Hennessey, Oklahoma, and Antelope, Archer City, Mineral Wells, Richland Hills, and Wichita Falls in Texas. I know. I was one of those hundreds of kids fortunate enough to call him Coach.

I found Roy Williams in McKinney, Texas, having recently moved there from his home in Canadian to be closer to his sons following the death of his wife Hazel. He was able to provide me not only great fodder for the book but something else as well: a glimpse into why he was so regarded by the players. His enthusiasm and love for the game of football is like none I've ever seen.

I cherish my memorable afternoon spent with Ted Leach and his wife Maudie in Carthage, Texas. His health wasn't good, but his spirit was. In reading his newspaper articles beforehand, it became clear to me that he had developed strong feelings for the team and at times wrestled with his objectivity. When I proposed this, he smiled and 'fessed up. "In my forty-something years of covering high school sports, I don't think I have ever liked a group more. They were just good boys. Know what I mean? And Grady was, and still is, a good man. That and hard work go a long ways. Still, I don't know how they were able to do what they did." Later, as I was preparing to leave, he spoke with sentiment about how poor health had prevented him from attending any of the team's reunions through the years, and how much he longed to see them all again. So we made plans for him to attend the next one, shook hands, and I drove away. On September 17, 2008, Ted Leach passed away in his home, before any such gathering.

I will always hold dear my time spent with the two remaining dads, Claude Morrison and Harvey Boone. I watched and listened as they spoke with such emotion in their eyes and pride in their voices about their sons—Barry and Jimmy—two boys whose roles and status could not have been more different but were strangely intertwined and fittingly connected years later in one's written tribute to the other.

And, of course, I will never forget the sudden emotion in Barry's voice as he described Claude pulling him from the bottom of the pile at the end of the championship game and kissing him for the first and only time in his life . . .

The tears in Ray Bussey's eyes as he talked about sleeping in a recliner with his foot soaking following his surgery, and his dad Travis setting his alarm and getting up to change his son's water every hour during the night in order to keep it hot . . .

Mike Stewart's ever-present smile and complete lack of self pity or regret as he discussed his devastating knee injury and the letter from University of Texas head coach Darrell Royal that might have changed his life . . .

The site of star fullback Gary Tepfer struggling to get out of his chair and shuffling to meet me at his front door . . .

The quiet dignity and pride in the soft-spoken voices of Barney Oliver and Billy Pitts. Many said they would be my toughest interviews. They are still fiercely private, almost reclusive, but both were gracious and giving—for the good of the book, and, I suspect, for their teammates as well . . .

And my side still hurts from laughing at Steve Parsley telling of the time coach Roy Williams climbed in the ring with him in an off-season boxing match. Steve, it seems, had popped off one too many times about his boxing prowess, Golden Gloves trophies, and lack of worthy opponents when Roy obliged him, and after taking a few good jabs from Steve, promptly cold-cocked the Rebel with a single punch to the nose.

Throughout the process, the unexpected became commonplace; I was constantly surprised, but never more so than at Steve's home late one night early in the tour. As I was leaving, he stopped me.

"Wait here. I'll be right back," he said.

He returned with the game ball from the Big Lake game and handed it to me.

"Here you go."

It was flat on the bottom from sitting in one place for years, proudly displayed and untouched. Painted on the front: SEMI-FINALS - 1964 - WILDCATS - 7 Big Lake - 6.

"Take it for inspiration. Keep it as long as you'd like."

I refused, but he insisted.

"I've never done anything to it. Heck, it's still got 1964 air in it."

I graciously took it home, placed it atop the TV in our office and stared at it. The grass, blood, and sweat stains had mostly faded. In it, 1964 air. *The past had come to me.*

Every time I sat down to work on the book I looked at it. Barry Morrison had passed and kicked this very ball on that sunny afternoon in Snyder. Gary Tepfer had carried it, fighting tooth and nail for each tough yard. Don Childs had rambled up and down the field with it only to be stopped at the one-yard line by Robert Tepfer when it counted most. And in the game's third quarter, a hobbling Mike Stewart had limped onto the field, tucked it under his arm and set off on the greatest touchdown run in Archer City High School history.

Steve was right about the inspiration. On more than one occasion, when stumped, I rose from my chair, picked it up and held it. Squeezed it and closed my eyes. And connected.

I am, in fact, looking at it now as I type this, admiring how good it looks sitting there. *Full of 1964 air.*

Steve might not get it back.

1926 DISTRICT CHAMPION ARCHER CITY WILDCATS

Harvey Black
Dummy Powell
Percy Morrison
Bill Larkin
Ernest Hull
Jess Cross
Rip Larkin
Tommie Hutcheson
Ira Spann
Aut Lewis
Ed Robertson
A. J. "Hefty" Morris
Mervyn Miller
Ben Powell
Morris Soloman
Cecil "Butter" Haigood
George Abercrombie
Millard Threet
Dillard Ray
Dayton "Goat" Gholson
Hosea Love

Bill Wilson, Coach
James Larkin, Coach

ACKNOWLEDGMENTS

My sincere thanks to Gary Tepfer, Barney Oliver, Billy Pitts, Ray Bussey, Steve Parsley, Mike and Judy Stewart, Barry and Trecie Morrison, Robert Tepfer, Larry Graham, Billy Holder, Butch Hannah, Jimmy Reeves, Buddy Knox, Mickey Horany, Jim Harney, Andy Rogers, Mike Atchley, Bob Gaines, Charlie Goforth, Grady and Gay Graves, Bobby and Cora Ann Ray, Roy Williams, Donald Dorris, John O'Donohue, David Wright, Jodie Tepfer, Sue Ann McKennon, Glenda Edwards, Joe and Shirley Stults, Ted and Maudie Leach, Ben Buerger, Claude and Patsy Morrison, Harvey Boone, Linnie Hudson, Monroe Williams, Bill Wright, Gary Beesinger, Charles Luig, Laverne Luig, Sammy Milam, Shelley Lewis, Deanna Watson, Randel Beaver, Steve Smith, Bill Nelson, Arlon Sims, Bob Brown, Paul Hopkins, Glenda Bowen, Warren Robertson, Rusty and Paula Pollock, Clay Reid, Angelia Thomason, Tommye Jane Wright, Archer City High School, Archer County News, and Wichita Falls Times Record News.

A special thanks to Matt Murry, Amber Ortner, and all the wonderful people at Dog Ear Publishing.

And finally, I indebted to my wife Lorrie for her patience and understanding during the long hours spent on this project. And for allowing me to hog the computer. I love you, Sweetie.

CPSIA information can be obtained at www.ICGtesting.com
Printed in the USA
LVOW06s2048200913

353435LV00001B/1/P

9 781608 441693